Concentration of Measure for the Analysis of Randomized Algorithms

Randomized algorithms have become a central part of the algorithms curriculum based on their increasingly widespread use in modern applications.

This book presents a coherent and unified treatment of probabilistic techniques for obtaining high probability estimates on the performance of randomized algorithms. It covers the basic toolkit from the Chernoff–Hoeffding bounds to more sophisticated techniques like martingales and isoperimetric inequalities, as well as some recent developments like Talagrand's inequality, transportation cost inequalities and log-Sobolev inequalities. Along the way, variations on the basic theme are examined, such as Chernoff–Hoeffding bounds in dependent settings. The authors emphasise comparative study of the different methods, highlighting respective strengths and weaknesses in concrete example applications.

The exposition is tailored to discrete settings sufficient for the analysis of algorithms, avoiding unnecessary measure-theoretic details, thus making the book accessible to computer scientists as well as probabilists and discrete mathematicians.

DEVDATT P. DUBHASHI is Professor in the Department of Computer Science and Engineering at Chalmers University, Sweden. He earned a Ph.D. in computer science from Cornell University and held positions at the Max-Planck-Institute for Computer Science in Saarbruecken, BRICS, the University of Aarhus, and IIT Delhi. Dubhashi has published widely at international conferences and in journals, including many special issues dedicated to best contributions. His research interests span the range from combinatorics, to probabilistic analysis of algorithms and, more recently, to computational systems biology and distributed information systems such as the Web.

ALESSANDRO PANCONESI is Professor of Computer Science at Sapienza University of Rome. He earned a Ph.D. in computer science from Cornell University and is the recipient of the 1992 ACM Danny Lewin Award. Panconesi has published more than 50 papers in international journals and selective conference proceedings, and he is the associate editor of the *Journal of Discrete Algorithms* and the director of BiCi, the Bertinoro International Center of Informatics. His research spans areas of algorithmic research as diverse as randomized algorithms, distributed computing, complexity theory, experimental algorithmics, wireless networking and web information retrieval.

Concentration of Measure for the Analysis of Randomized Algorithms

DEVDATT P. DUBHASHI
Chalmers University

ALESSANDRO PANCONESI
Sapienza University of Rome

CAMBRIDGE
UNIVERSITY PRESS

32 Avenue of the Americas, New York NY 10013-2473, USA

Cambridge University Press is part of the University of Cambridge.

It furthers the University's mission by disseminating knowledge in the pursuit of education, learning and research at the highest international levels of excellence.

www.cambridge.org
Information on this title: www.cambridge.org/9780521884273

First published 2009

A catalogue record for this publication is available from the British Library

Library of Congress Cataloguing in Publication data

Dubhashi, Devdatt.
Concentration of measure for the analysis of randomized algorithms / Devdatt Dubhashi.
p.   cm.
Includes bibliographical references and index.
ISBN 978-0-521-88427-3 (hardback : alk. paper)
1. Random variables.   2. Distribution (Probability theory).   3. Limit theorems
(Probability theory).   4. Algorithms.   I. Title.
QA273.D765   2009
518´.1–dc22   2009009014

ISBN 978-0-521-88427-3 Hardback
ISBN 978-1-107-60660-9 Paperback

Dubhashi: To the genes before me (my respected parents) and after me
(Vinus and Minoo)
Panconesi: To the memory of my beloved father

Contents

Preface

The aim of this book is to provide a body of tools for establishing concentration of measure that is accessible to researchers working in the design and analysis of randomized algorithms.

Concentration of measure refers to the phenomenon that a function of a large number of random variables tends to concentrate its values in a relatively narrow range (under certain conditions of smoothness of the function and under certain conditions of the dependence amongst the set of random variables). Such a result is of obvious importance to the analysis of randomized algorithms: for instance, the running time of such an algorithm can then be guaranteed to be concentrated around a pre-computed value. More generally, various other parameters measuring the performance of randomized algorithms can be provided tight guarantees via such an analysis.

In a sense, the subject of concentration of measure lies at the core of modern probability theory as embodied in the laws of large numbers, the central limit theorem and, in particular, the theory of large deviations [26]. However, these results are asymptotic: they refer to the limit as the number of variables n goes to infinity, for example. In the analysis of algorithms, we typically require quantitative estimates that are valid for finite (though large) values of n. The earliest such results can be traced back to the work of Azuma, Chernoff and Hoeffding in the 1950s. Subsequently, there have been steady advances, particularly in the classical setting of martingales. In the last couple of decades, these methods have taken on renewed interest, driven by applications in algorithms and optimisation. Also several new techniques have been developed.

Unfortunately, much of this material is scattered in the literature, and also rather forbidding for someone entering the field from a computer science or algorithms background. Often this is because the methods are couched in the technical language of analysis and/or measure theory. Although this may be strictly necessary to develop results in their full generality, it is not needed when the method is used in computer science applications (where the probability spaces are often finite and discrete), and indeed may serve only as a distraction or barrier.

Our main goal here is to give an exposition of the basic and more advanced methods for measure concentration in a manner that is accessible to the researcher in randomized algorithms and enables him or her to quickly start putting them to work in his or her application.

Book Outline

The book falls naturally into two parts. The first part contains the core bread-and-butter methods that we believe belong as an absolutely essential ingredient in the toolkit of a researcher in randomized algorithms today. Chapters 1 and 2 start with the basic Chernoff–Hoeffding bound on the sum of bounded independent random variables and give several applications. This topic is now covered in other recent books, and we therefore give several examples not covered there and refer the reader to these books, which can be read profitably together with this one (see suggestions given later). In Chapter 3, we give four versions of the Chernoff–Hoeffding bound in situations in which the random variables are not independent – this often is the case in the analysis of algorithms. Chapter 4 is a small interlude on probabilistic recurrences which can often give very quick estimates of tail probabilities based only on expectations.

The next series of chapters, Chapters 5–8, is devoted to a powerful extension of the Chernoff–Hoeffding bound to arbitrary functions of random variables (rather than just the sum) and where the assumption of independence can be relaxed somewhat. This is achieved via the concept of a *martingale*. These methods are by now rightly perceived as being fundamental in algorithmic applications and have begun to appear, albeit very scantily, in introductory books such as [74] and, more thoroughly, in the more recent [72]. Our treatment here is far more comprehensive and nuanced, and at the same time also very accessible to the beginner. We offer a host of relevant examples in which the various methods are seen in action.

Chapter 5 gives an introduction to the basic definition and theory of martingales leading to Azuma's inequality. The concept of martingales, as found in probability textbooks, poses quite a barrier to the computer scientist who is unfamiliar with the language of filters, partitions and measurable sets from measure theory. We are able to dispense with the measure-theoretic baggage entirely and keep to very elementary discrete probability. Chapters 6–8 are devoted to a set of nicely packaged inequalities based on martingales that are deployed with a host of applications. One of the special features of our exposition is our introduction of a very useful concept in probability called *coupling* and our demonstration of how it can be used to great advantage in working with these inequalities.

Chapter 9 is another short interlude containing an introduction to some recent specialised methods that were very successful in analysing certain key problems in random graphs.

We end Part I with Chapter 10, which is an introduction to isoperimetric inequalities that are a common setting for results on the concentration of measure. This lays the groundwork for the methods in Part II.

Part II of the book, Chapters 11–14, contains some more advanced techniques and recent developments. Here we systematise and make accessible some very useful tools that appear scattered in the literature and are couched in terms quite unfamiliar to computer scientists. From this (for a computer scientist) arcane body of work we distill out what is relevant and useful for algorithmic applications, using many non-trivial examples showing how these methods can be put to good use.

Chapter 11 is an introduction to Talagrand's isoperimetric theory, a theory developed in his 1995 epic, which proved a major landmark in the subject and led to the resolution of some outstanding open problems. We give a statement of the inequality that is simpler, at least conceptually, than the ones usually found in the literature. Yet, the simpler statement is sufficient for all the known applications, several of which are given in the book.

In Chapter 12, we give an introduction to an approach from information theory, via the so-called *transportation cost* inequalities, which yields very elegant proofs of the isoperimetric inequalities in Chapter 10. This approach, as shown by Kati Marton, extends in an elegant way to prove Talagrand's isoperimetric inequality, and we give an account of this in Chapter 13. In Chapter 14, we give an introduction to another approach from information theory that leads to concentration inequalities – the so-called *entropy* method or *log-Sobolev* inequalities. This approach too yields short proofs of Talagrand's inequality, and we also revisit the method of bounded differences in a different light.

How to Use the Book

This book is, we hope, a self-contained, comprehensive and quite accessible resource for any person with a typical computer science or mathematics background who is interested in applying concentration of measure methods in the design and analysis of randomized algorithms.

This book can also be used in an advanced course in randomized algorithms (or related courses) to supplement and complement some well-established textbooks. For instance, we recommend using it for a course in the following fields:

Randomized algorithms together with
- R. Motwani and P. Raghavan. *Randomized Algorithms*. Cambridge University Press, Cambridge, 1995.
- M. Mitzenmacher and E. Upfal. *Probability and Computing*. Cambridge University Press, Cambridge, 2005.

Probabilistic combinatorics together with the classic
- N. Alon and J. Spencer. *The Probabilistic Method*, second edition. John Wiley, Hoboken, NJ, 2000.

Graph colouring together with
- M. Molloy and B. Reed. *Graph Coloring and the Probabilistic Method*. Springer, New York, 2002.

Random graphs together with
- S. Janson, T. Luczak, and A. Rucinski. *Random Graphs*. John Wiley, Hoboken, NJ, 2000.

Large-deviation theory together with
- F. den Hollander. *Large Deviations*. Fields Institute Monograph. American Mathematical Society, Providence, RI, 2000.

Acknowledgements

Several people have been helpful by providing much-needed encouragement, suggestions, corrections, comments and even drawings. We thank them all: Luigi Ambrosio, Flavio Chierichetti, Stefan Dziembowski, Alan Frieze, Rafael Frongillo, Bernd Gärtner, Michelangelo Grigni, Johan Hastad, Michal Karonski, Fred Kochman, Silvio Lattanzi, Alberto Marchetti-Spaccamela, Aravind Srinivasan and Sebastiano Vigna. Very special thanks go to Eli Upfal. The responsibility for any mistakes or omissions, alas, rests only upon us.

We thank our parents for their sacrifices to give us the best opportunities in life. Devdatt also thanks his family, Anna, Minoo and Vinus, for all the time that was rightfully theirs. Finally we thank Himanshu Abrol of Aptara and Lauren Cowles of Cambridge University Press for their kindness and effectiveness.

Concentration of Measure for the Analysis of Randomized Algorithms

1

Chernoff–Hoeffding Bounds

1.1 What Is "Concentration of Measure"?

The basic idea of concentration of measure is well illustrated by the simplest of random experiments, and one lying at the fountainhead of probability theory: coin tossing. If we toss a fair coin once, the result is completely unpredictable – it can be "heads" or "tails" with equal probability. Now suppose that we toss the same coin a large number of times, say, a thousand times. The outcome is now *sharply predictable*! Namely, the number of heads is "very likely to be around 500". This apparent paradox, which is nevertheless familiar to everybody, is an instance of the phenomenon of the concentration of measure – although there are potentially a large number of possibilities, those that are likely to be observed are concentrated in a very narrow range, hence sharply predictable.

In more sophisticated forms, the phenomenon of the concentration of measure underlies much of our physical world. As we know now, the world is made up of microscopic particles that are governed by probabilistic laws – those of quantum and statistical physics. The reason why the macroscopic properties determined by these large ensembles of particles nevertheless appear deterministic when viewed on our larger scales is precisely the concentration of measure: the observed possibilities are concentrated into a very narrow range.

Given the obvious importance of the phenomenon, it is no surprise that large parts of treatises on probability theory are devoted to its study. The various "laws of large numbers" and the "central limit theorem" are some of the most central results of modern probability theory.

In this book we use the phenomenon of concentration of measure in the analysis of probabilistic algorithms. In analogy with the physical situation described earlier, we can argue that the observable behaviour of randomized algorithms is "almost deterministic". In this way, we can obtain the satisfaction of deterministic results, and at the same time retain the benefits of randomized algorithms, namely their simplicity and efficiency.

In slightly more technical terms, the basic problem we want to study in this book is this: Given a random variable X with mean $E[X]$, what is the probability that X deviates far from its expectation? Furthermore, we want to understand under what conditions the random variable X stays almost constant or, put in a different way, when large deviations from the mean are highly unlikely. This is the case for the familiar example of repeated coin tosses, but, as we shall see, it is a more general phenomenon.

There are several reasons why classical results from probability theory are somewhat inadequate or inappropriate for studying these questions:

- First and foremost, the results in probability theory are *asymptotic limit laws* applying in the infinite limit case. We are interested in laws that apply in finite cases.
- The probability theory results are often *qualitative*: they ensure convergence in the limit, but do not consider the *rate* of convergence. We are interested in *quantitative* laws that determine the rate of convergence, or at least good bounds on it.
- The laws of probability theory are classically stated under the assumption of *independence*. This is a very natural and reasonable assumption in probability theory, and it greatly simplifies the statement and proofs of the results. However, in the analysis of randomized algorithms, the outcome of which is the result of a complicated interaction of various processes, independence is the exception rather than the rule. Hence, we are interested in laws that are valid even without independence, or when certain known types of dependences are obtained.

We shall now embark on the development of various tools and techniques that meet these criteria.

1.2 The Binomial Distribution

Let us start with an analysis of the simple motivating example of coin tossing. The number of "heads" or successes in repeated tosses of a fair coin is a very important distribution because it models a very basic paradigm of the probabilistic method, namely to repeat experiments to boost confidence.

Let us analyse the slightly more general case of the number of "heads" in n trials with a coin of bias p, with $0 \le p \le 1$, i.e. $\Pr[\text{Heads}] = p$ and $\Pr[\text{Tails}] = 1 - p$. This is a random variable $B(n, p)$ whose distribution is called the *binomial distribution* with parameters n and p:

$$\Pr[B(n, p) = i] = \binom{n}{i} p^i q^{n-i}, \quad 0 \leq i \leq n. \tag{1.1}$$

The general problem defined in the previous section now becomes as follows: In the binomial case the expectation is $\mathrm{E}[B(n, p)] = np$; we want to get a bound on the probability that the variable does not deviate too far from this expected value. Are such large deviations unlikely for $B(n, p)$? A direct computation of the probabilities $\Pr[B(n, p) \geq k] = \sum_{i \geq k} \binom{n}{i} p^i q^{n-i}$ is far too unwieldy. However, see Problem 1.2 for a neat trick that yields a good bound. We shall now introduce a general method that successfully solves our problem and is versatile enough to apply to many other problems we will encounter.

1.3 The Chernoff Bound

The random variable $B(n, p)$ can be written as a sum $X := \sum_{i \in [n]} X_i$, by introducing the indicator random variables $X_i, i \in [n]$ defined by

$$X_i := \begin{cases} 1 & \text{if the } i\text{th trial is a success,} \\ 0 & \text{otherwise.} \end{cases}$$

The basic Chernoff technique that we develop now applies in many situations where such a decomposition as a sum is possible.

The trick is to consider the so-called *moment-generating function* of X, defined as $\mathrm{E}[e^{\lambda X}]$ where $\lambda > 0$ is a parameter. By formal expansion of the Taylor series, we see that

$$\mathrm{E}[e^{\lambda X}] = \mathrm{E}\left[\sum_{i \geq 0} \frac{\lambda^i}{i!} X^i \right]$$

$$= \sum_{i \geq 0} \frac{\lambda^i}{i!} \mathrm{E}[X^i].$$

This explains the name as the function $\mathrm{E}[e^{\lambda X}]$ is the exponential generating function of all the moments of X – it "packs" all the information about the moments of X into one function.

Now, for any $\lambda > 0$, we have

$$\Pr[X > m] = \Pr[e^{\lambda X} > e^{\lambda m}]$$

$$\leq \frac{\mathrm{E}[e^{\lambda X}]}{e^{\lambda m}}. \tag{1.2}$$

The last step follows by *Markov's inequality*: for any non-negative random variable X, $\Pr[X \geq a] \leq E[X]/a$.

Let us compute the moment-generating function for our example:

$$E[e^{\lambda X}] = E[e^{\lambda \sum_i X_i}]$$

$$= E\left[\prod_i e^{\lambda X_i}\right]$$

$$= \prod_i E[e^{\lambda X_i}] \quad \text{by independence}$$

$$= (pe^{\lambda} + q)^n. \tag{1.3}$$

Substituting this back into (1.2), and using the parametrisation $m := (p + t)n$ which leads to a convenient statement of the bound, we get

$$\Pr[X > m] \leq \left(\frac{pe^{\lambda} + q}{e^{\lambda(p+t)}}\right)^n.$$

We can now pick $\lambda > 0$ to minimise the value within the parentheses and by a simple application of calculus, we arrive at the basic Chernoff bound:

$$\Pr[X > (p+t)n] \leq \left(\left(\frac{p}{p+t}\right)^{p+t}\left(\frac{q}{q-t}\right)^{q-t}\right)^n$$

$$= \exp\left(-(p+t)\ln\frac{p+t}{p} - (q-t)\ln\frac{q-t}{q}\right)^n. \tag{1.4}$$

What shall we make of this mess? Certainly, this is not the most convenient form of the bound for use in applications! In Section 1.6 we derive much simpler and more intelligible formulae that can be used in applications. Now, we shall pause for a while and take a short detour to make some remarks on (1.4). This is for several reasons. First, it is the strongest form of the bound. Second, and more importantly, this same bound appears in many other situations. This is no accident for it is a very natural and insightful bound – when properly viewed! For this, we need a certain concept from information theory.

Given two (discrete) probability distributions $p := (p_1, \ldots, p_n)$ and $q := (q_1, \ldots, q_n)$ on a space of cardinality n, the *relative entropy distance* between them, $H(p, q)$, is defined by:[1]

$$H(p, q) := \sum_i -p_i \log \frac{p_i}{q_i}.$$

---

[1] Note that when q is the uniform distribution, this is just the usual *entropy* of the distribution p up to an additive term of $\log n$.

The expression multiplying n in the exponent in (1.4) is exactly the relative entropy distance of the distribution $p + t, q - t$ from the distribution p, q on the two-point space $\{1, 0\}$. So (1.4) seen from the statistician's eye states: the probability of getting the "observed" distribution $\{p + t, q - t\}$ when the *a priori* or *hypothesis* distribution is $\{p, q\}$ falls exponentially in n times the relative entropy distance between the two distributions.

By considering $-X$, we get the same bound symmetrically for $\Pr[X < (p - t)n]$.

1.4 Heterogeneous Variables

As a first example of the versatility of the Chernoff technique, let us consider the situation where the trials are heterogeneous: probabilities of success at different trials need not be the same. In this case, Chvatal's proof in Problem 1.2 is inapplicable, but the Chernoff method works with a simple modification. Let p_i be the probability of success at the ith trial. Then we can repeat the calculation of the moment-generating function $E[e^{\lambda X}]$ exactly as in (1.3) except for the last line to get

$$E[e^{\lambda X}] = \prod_i (p_i e^{\lambda} + q_i). \tag{1.5}$$

Recall that the arithmetic–geometric mean inequality states that

$$\frac{1}{n} \sum_{i=1}^{n} a_i \geq \left(\prod_{i=1}^{n} a_i \right)^{1/n}$$

for all $a_i \leq 0$. Now employing the arithmetic–geometric mean inequality, we get

$$E[e^{\lambda X}] = \prod_i (p_i e^{\lambda} + q_i)$$

$$\leq \left(\frac{\sum_i (p_i e^{\lambda} + q_i)}{n} \right)^n$$

$$= (p e^{\lambda} + q)^n,$$

where $p := \sum_i p_i / n$ and $q := 1 - p$. This is the same as (1.3) with p taken as the arithmetic mean of the p_i's. The rest of the proof is as before, and we conclude that the basic Chernoff bound (1.4) holds.

1.5 The Hoeffding Extension

A further extension by the same basic technique is possible to heterogeneous variables that need not even be discrete. Let $X := \sum_i X_i$, where each $X_i, i \in [n]$, takes values in $[0, 1]$ and has mean p_i. To calculate the moment-generating function $e^{\lambda X}$, we need, as before, to compute each individual $e^{\lambda X_i}$. This is no longer as simple as it was with the case where X_i took only two values.

However, the following convexity argument gives a simple upper bound. The graph of the function $e^{\lambda x}$ is convex and hence, in the interval $[0, 1]$, lies always below the straight line joining the endpoints $(0, 1)$ and $(1, e^{\lambda})$. This line has the equation $y = \alpha x + \beta$ where $\beta = 1$ and $\alpha = e^{\lambda} - 1$. Thus

$$E[e^{\lambda X_i}] \leq E[\alpha X_i + \beta]$$
$$= p_i e^{\lambda} + q_i.$$

Thus we have

$$E[e^{\lambda X}] \leq \prod_i E[e^{\lambda X_i}] \leq \prod_i (p_i e^{\lambda} + q_i),$$

which is the same bound as in (1.5), and the rest of the proof is concluded as before.

1.6 Useful Forms of the Bound

The following forms of the Chernoff–Hoeffding bound are most useful in applications (see also Problem 1.6).

Theorem 1.1. *Let* $X := \sum_{i \in [n]} X_i$ *where* $X_i, i \in [n]$, *are independently distributed in* $[0, 1]$. *Then*

- *For all* $t > 0$,

$$\Pr[X > E[X] + t], \Pr[X < E[X] - t] \leq e^{-2t^2/n}. \tag{1.6}$$

- *For* $\epsilon > 0$,

$$\Pr[X > (1 + \epsilon)E[X]] \leq \exp\left(-\frac{\epsilon^2}{3}E[X]\right),$$

$$\Pr[X < (1 - \epsilon)E[X]] \leq \exp\left(-\frac{\epsilon^2}{2}E[X]\right). \tag{1.7}$$

- *If $t > 2e\mathrm{E}[X]$, then*

$$\Pr[X > t] \le 2^{-t}. \tag{1.8}$$

Proof. We shall manipulate the bound in (1.4). Set

$$f(t) := (p + t) \ln \frac{p + t}{p} + (q - t) \ln \frac{q - t}{q}.$$

We successively compute

$$f'(t) = \ln \frac{p + t}{p} - \ln \frac{q - t}{q}$$

and

$$f''(t) = \frac{1}{(p + t)(q - t)}.$$

Now, $f(0) = 0 = f'(0)$, and furthermore $f''(t) \ge 4$ for all $0 \le t \le q$ because $xy \le 1/4$ for any two non-negative reals summing to 1. Hence by Taylor's theorem with remainder,

$$f(t) = f(0) + f'(0)t + f''(\xi)\frac{t^2}{2!}, \quad 0 < \xi < t$$

$$\ge 2t^2.$$

This gives, after simple manipulations, the bound (1.6).

Now consider $g(x) := f(px)$. Then $g'(x) = pf'(px)$ and $g''(x) = p^2 f''(px)$. Thus, $g(0) = 0 = g'(0)$ and $g''(x) = p^2/(p + px)(q - px) \ge p/(1 + x) \ge 2p/3x$. Now by Taylor's theorem, $g(x) \ge px^2/3$. This gives the upper tail in (1.7).

For the lower tail in (1.7), set $h(x) := g(-x)$. Then $h'(x) = -g'(-x)$ and $h''(x) = g''(-x)$. Thus $h(0) = 0 = h'(0)$ and $h''(x) = p^2/(p - px)(q + px) \ge p$. Thus by Taylor's theorem, $h(x) \ge px^2/2$, and this gives the result.

For (1.8), see Problem 1.6. ∎

Often, we would apply the bounds given earlier to a sum $\sum_i X_i$ where we do not know the exact values of the expectations $\mathrm{E}[X_i]$ but only upper or lower bounds on it. In such situations, one can nevertheless apply the Chernoff–Hoeffding bounds with the known bounds instead, as you should verify in the following exercise.

Exercise 1.1. *In this exercise, we explore a very useful extension of the Chernoff–Hoeffding bounds. Suppose $X := \sum_{i=1}^{n} X_i$ as in Theorem 1.1, and suppose $\mu_L \leq \mu \leq \mu_H$. Show that*

(a) For any $t > 0$,

$$\Pr[X > \mu_H + t], \Pr[X < \mu_L - t] \leq e^{-2t^2/n}. \tag{1.9}$$

(b) For $0 < \epsilon < 1$,

$$\Pr[X > (1+\epsilon)\mu_H] \leq \exp\left(-\frac{\epsilon^2}{3}\mu_H\right),$$

$$\Pr[X < (1-\epsilon)\mu_L] \leq \exp\left(-\frac{\epsilon^2}{2}\mu_L\right).$$

These bounds are useful because often one only has a bound on the expectation. You may need to use the following useful and intuitively obvious fact that we prove in Section 7.4. Let $X_1, \ldots, X_n$ be independent random variables distributed in $[0, 1]$ with $E[X_i] = p_i$ for each $i \in [n]$. Let $Y_1, \ldots, Y_n$ and $Z_1, \ldots, Z_n$ be independent random variables with $E[Y_i] = q_i$ and $E[Z_i] = r_i$ for each $i \in [n]$. Now suppose $q_i \leq p_i \leq r_i$ for each $i \in [n]$. Then, if $X := \sum_i X_i$, $Y := \sum_i Y_i$ and $Z := \sum_i Z_i$, for any t,

$$\Pr[X > t] \leq \Pr[Z > t], \quad and \quad \Pr[X < t] \leq \Pr[Y < t].$$

1.7 A Variance Bound

Finally, we give an application of the basic Chernoff technique to develop a form of the bound in terms of the variances of the individual summands – a form that can be considerably sharper than those derived earlier, and one which will be especially useful for applications we encounter in later chapters.

Let us return to the basic Chernoff technique with $X := X_1 + \cdots + X_n$ and $X_i \in [0, 1]$ for each $i \in [n]$. Set $\mu_i := E[X_i]$ and $\mu := E[X] = \sum_i \mu_i$. Then

$$\Pr[X > \mu + t] = \Pr\left[\sum_i (X_i - \mu_i) > t\right]$$

$$= \Pr[e^{\lambda \sum_i (X_i - \mu_i)} > e^{\lambda t}]$$

$$\leq E[e^{\lambda \sum_i (X_i - \mu_i)}]/e^{\lambda t},$$

for each $\lambda > 0$. The last line follows again from Markov's inequality.

We shall now use the simple inequalities $e^x \leq 1 + x + x^2$, for $0 < |x| < 1$, and $e^x \geq 1 + x$. Now, if $\lambda \max(\mu_i, 1 - \mu_i) < 1$ for each $i \in [n]$, we have

$$
\begin{aligned}
\mathrm{E}[e^{\lambda \sum_i (X_i - \mu_i)}] &= \prod_i \mathrm{E}[e^{\lambda (X_i - \mu_i)}] \\
&\leq \prod_i \mathrm{E}[1 + \lambda(X_i - \mu_i) + \lambda^2 (X_i - \mu_i)^2] \\
&= \prod_i (1 + \lambda^2 \sigma_i^2) \\
&\leq \prod_i e^{\lambda^2 \sigma_i^2} \\
&= e^{\lambda^2 \sigma^2},
\end{aligned}
$$

where σ_i^2 is the variance of X_i for each $i \in [n]$ and σ^2 is the variance of X. Thus,

$$
\Pr[X > \mu + t] \leq e^{\lambda^2 \sigma^2} / e^{\lambda t},
$$

for λ satisfying $\lambda \max(\mu_i, 1 - \mu_i) < 1$ for each $i \in [n]$. By calculus, take $\lambda := t/2\sigma^2$ and we get the bound

$$
\Pr[X > \mu + t] \leq \exp\left(\frac{-t^2}{4\sigma^2}\right),
$$

for $t < 2\sigma^2 / \max_i \max(\mu_i, 1 - \mu_i)$.

Exercise 1.2. *Check that for random variables distributed in $[0, 1]$, this is of the same form as the Chernoff–Hoeffding bound derived in the previous section up to constant factors in the exponent. You may need to use the fact that for a random variable distributed in the interval $[a, b]$, the variance is bounded by $(b - a)^2/4$.*

The following bound is often referred to as Bernstein's inequality:

Theorem 1.2 (Bernstein's inequality). *Let the random variables $X_1, \ldots, X_n$ be independent with $X_i - \mathrm{E}[X_i] \leq b$ for each $i \in [n]$. Let $X := \sum_i X_i$ and let $\sigma^2 := \sum_i \sigma_i^2$ be the variance of X. Then, for any $t > 0$,*

$$
\Pr[X > \mathrm{E}[X] + t] \leq \exp\left(-\frac{t^2}{2\sigma^2(1 + bt/3\sigma^2)}\right).
$$

Exercise 1.3. *Check that for random variables in $[0, 1]$ and $t < 2\sigma^2/b$, this is roughly the same order bound as we derived earlier.*

In typical applications, the 'error' term $bt/3\sigma^2$ will be negligible. Suppose that the random variables $X_1, \ldots, X_n$ have the same bounded distribution with positive variance c^2, so $\sigma^2 = nc^2$. Then for $t = o(n)$, this bound is $\exp\left(-(1 + o(1))t^2/2\sigma^2\right)$, which is consistent with the central limit theorem assertion that in the asymptotic limit, $X - E[X]$ is normal with mean 0 and variance σ^2.

Exercise 1.4. *Let $X := \sum_i X_i$ where the $X_i, i \in [n]$, are i.i.d. with $\Pr[X_i = 1] = p$ for each $i \in [n]$ for some $p \in [0, 1]$. Compute the variance of X and apply and compare the two bounds as well as the basic Chernoff–Hoeffding bound. Check that when $p = 1/2$, all these bounds are roughly the same.*

1.8 Pointers to the Literature

The original technique is from Chernoff [19] although the idea of using the moment-generating function to derive tail bounds is attributed to Bernstein. The extension to continuous variables is due to Hoeffding [43]. Our presentation was much influenced by [65]. The quick derivation in Problems 1.2 and 1.3 is due to Chvátal [22].

1.9 Problems

Problem 1.1. A set of n balls is drawn by sampling with replacement from an urn containing N balls, M of which are red. Give a sharp concentration result for the number of red balls in the sample drawn.   ▽

Problem 1.2. In this problem, we outline a simple proof of the Chernoff bound due to Chvátal.

(a) Argue that for all $x \geq 1$, we have

$$\Pr[B(n, p) \geq k] \leq \sum_{i \geq 0} \binom{n}{i} p^i q^{n-i} x^{i-k}.$$

(b) Now use the binomial theorem and thereafter calculus to optimise the value of x.   ▽

Problem 1.3 (hypergeometric distribution). A set of n balls is drawn by sampling **without** replacement from an urn containing N balls, M of which are red. The random variable $H(N, M, n)$ of the number of red balls drawn is said to have the **hypergeometric distribution**.

(a) What is $E[H(N, M, n)]$?
(b) Can you apply Chernoff–Hoeffding bounds to give a sharp concentration result for $H(N, M, n)$?

Now we outline a direct proof due to Chvátal for the tail of the hypergeometric distribution along the lines of the previous problem.

(c) Show that

$$\Pr[H(N, M, n) = k] = \binom{M}{k}\binom{N-M}{n-k}\binom{N}{n}^{-1}.$$

(d) Show that

$$\binom{N}{n}^{-1} \sum_{i \geq j} \binom{M}{i}\binom{N-M}{n-i}\binom{i}{j} \leq \binom{n}{j}\left(\frac{M}{N}\right)^j.$$

(e) Use the previous part to show that for every $x \geq 1$,

$$\sum_{i \geq 0} \binom{M}{i}\binom{N-M}{n-i}\binom{N}{n}^{-1} x^i \leq (1 + (x-1)M/N)^n.$$

(f) Combine parts (c) through (e) and optimise the value of x to derive the same relative entropy bound (1.4):

$$\Pr[H(N, M, n) \geq (p+t)n] \leq \left(\left(\frac{p}{p+t}\right)^{p+t}\left(\frac{q}{q-t}\right)^{q-t}\right)^n,$$

where $p := M/N$ and $q := 1 - p$.   ▽

Problem 1.4. Show that for $0 < \alpha \leq 1/2$,

$$\sum_{0 \leq k \leq \alpha n} \binom{n}{k} \leq 2^{H(\alpha)n},$$

where $H(\alpha) := -\alpha \log \alpha - (1-\alpha) \log(1-\alpha)$ is the binary entropy function.

▽

Problem 1.5 (Weierstrass approximation theorem). Prove: *For every continuous function $f : [0, 1] \to R$ and every $\epsilon > 0$, there is a polynomial p such that $|f(x) - p(x)| < \epsilon$ for every $x \in [0, 1]$.* (HINT: Consider $p_n(x) := \sum_{0 \leq i \leq n} \binom{n}{i} x^i (1-x)^{n-i} f(i/n)$.)   ▽

Problem 1.6. Repeat the basic proof structure of the Chernoff–Hoeffding bounds to derive the following bound: if $X_1, \ldots, X_n$ are independent

0/1 variables (not necessarily identical), and $X := \sum_i X_i$, then for any $\epsilon > 0$,

$$\Pr\left[X \geq (1+\epsilon)\mathrm{E}[X]\right] \leq \left(\frac{e^\epsilon}{(1+\epsilon)^{(1+\epsilon)}}\right)^{\mathrm{E}[X]}.$$

(a) Compare this bound to the one obtained by setting $t := \epsilon\mathrm{E}[X]/n$ in the relative entropy bound derived in (1.4).

(b) Argue further that the right side is bounded by $(e/1+\epsilon)^{(1+\epsilon)\mathrm{E}[X]}$ and hence infer that if $\epsilon > 2e - 1$, then

$$\Pr\left[X \geq (1+\epsilon)\mathrm{E}[X]\right] \leq 2^{-(1+\epsilon)\mathrm{E}[X]}. \qquad \triangledown$$

Problem 1.7. Let $X_1, \ldots, X_n$ be random variables bounded in $[0, 1]$ such that for each $i \in [n]$,

$$\mathrm{E}[X_i \mid X_1, \ldots, X_{i-1}] \leq p_i.$$

Show that in this case, the upper tail for $\sum_i X_i$ can be upper bounded by the upper-tail Chernoff–Hoeffding estimate for an independent set of variables $X'_1, \ldots, X'_n$ with $\mathrm{E}[X'_i] = p_i$. Formulate and prove a symmetric condition for the lower tail. $\qquad \triangledown$

Problem 1.8. Let $X_1, \ldots, X_n$ be a set of binary random variables satisfying the condition

$$\Pr\left[\bigwedge_{i \in S} X_i = 1\right] \leq \prod_{i \in S} \Pr[X_i = 1]$$

for all subsets S. Prove that under this condition the Chernoff bound holds for $X = \sum_i X_i$. $\qquad \triangledown$

Problem 1.9. In this problem, we explore a further extension of the Chernoff–Hoeffding bounds, namely to variables that are bounded in some arbitrary intervals, not necessarily $[0, 1]$. Let $X_1, \ldots, X_n$ be independent variables such that for each $i \in [n]$, $X_i \in [a_i, b_i]$ for some reals a_i, b_i.

(a) Suppose $a_i = a$ and $b_i = b$ for each $i \in [n]$. Derive a bound by rescaling the Hoeffding bound for $[0, 1]$.

(b) Does the rescaling work for non-identical intervals?

(c) Derive the following general bound for non-identical intervals by repeating the basic proof technique:

$$\Pr[|X - \mathrm{E}[X]| \geq t] \leq 2\exp\left(\frac{-2t^2}{\sum_i (b_i - a_i)^2}\right). \qquad \triangledown$$

Problem 1.10 (sums of exponential variables). Let $Z := Z_1 + \cdots + Z_n$ where $Z_i, i \in [n]$, are independent and identically distributed with the **exponential distribution** with parameter $\alpha \in (0, 1)$. The probability density function for this distribution is

$$f(x) = \alpha e^{-\alpha x},$$

and the corresponding cumulative distribution function is

$$F(x) = \int_0^x f(t)dt = 1 - e^{-\alpha x}.$$

Give a sharp concentration result for the upper tail of Z. ▽

Problem 1.11. Give a sharp concentration bound on the upper tail of $Z_1^2 + \cdots + Z_n^2$ where $Z_i, i \in [n]$, are independent, identically distributed variables with the exponential distribution as in the previous problem. ▽

Problem 1.12. Suppose a fair die is tossed n times and let X be the total sum of all the throws.

(a) Compute $E[X]$.
(b) Give a sharp concentration estimate on X by applying the result of the previous problem.
(c) Can you improve this by deriving the bound from scratch using the basic technique? ▽

Problem 1.13. In this problem, we shall explore the following question: How does the concentration bound on non-identically distributed variables depend on the individual probabilities $p_1, \ldots, p_n$? Abbreviate $(p_1, \ldots, p_n)$ by $\boldsymbol{p}$. Let $B(n, \boldsymbol{p})$ denote the number of successes in n independent trials where the probability of success at the ith trial is p_i. Let

$$L(c, \boldsymbol{p}) := \Pr[B(n, \boldsymbol{p}) \le c], \qquad U(c, \boldsymbol{p}) := \Pr[B(n, \boldsymbol{p}) \ge c].$$

Fix some $\lambda > 0$. We shall explore how L and U are related for different $\boldsymbol{p}$ in the region

$$D(\lambda) := \{\boldsymbol{p} \mid \boldsymbol{0} \le \boldsymbol{p} \le \boldsymbol{1}, \sum_i p_i = \lambda\}.$$

Let

$$\boldsymbol{p}^*(\lambda) := n^{-1}(\lambda, \ldots, \lambda), \qquad \hat{\boldsymbol{p}}(\lambda) := (1, \ldots, 1, \lambda - [\lambda], 0, \ldots, 0).$$

The first corresponds to the identical uniform case and the second (with $\lceil \lambda \rceil$ ones and $n - \lceil \lambda \rceil - 1$ zeros) to the other extreme. Note that both $\boldsymbol{p}^*(\lambda), \hat{\boldsymbol{p}}(\lambda) \in D(\lambda)$.

(a) Show that for any $\boldsymbol{p} \in D(\lambda)$,

$$L(c, \hat{\boldsymbol{p}}) \le L(c, \boldsymbol{p}) \le L(c, \boldsymbol{p}^*) \quad \text{if } 0 \le c \le \lfloor \lambda - 2 \rfloor$$

and

$$U(c, \boldsymbol{p}) \le U(c, \boldsymbol{p}^*) \le U(c, \hat{\boldsymbol{p}}) \quad \text{if } \lfloor \lambda + 2 \rfloor \le c \le n.$$

(b) More generally, let $\boldsymbol{p}, \boldsymbol{p}' \in D_\lambda$ be such that there is a doubly stochastic matrix Π with $\boldsymbol{p}' = \boldsymbol{p}\Pi$. Equivalently, if

$$p_{\sigma(1)} \ge p_{\sigma(2)} \ge \cdots \ge p_{\sigma(n)}, \qquad p'_{\sigma'(1)} \ge p'_{\sigma'(2)} \ge \cdots \ge p'_{\sigma'(n)},$$

then for each $1 \le k \le n$,

$$\sum_{i \le k} p_{\sigma(i)} \ge \sum_{i \le k} p'_{\sigma'(i)}.$$

The vector $\boldsymbol{p}$ is said to **majorise** the vector $\boldsymbol{p}'$. Show that

$$L(c, \boldsymbol{p}) \le L(c, \boldsymbol{p}') \quad \text{if } 0 \le c \le \lfloor \lambda - 2 \rfloor$$

and

$$U(c, \boldsymbol{p}) \le U(c, \boldsymbol{p}') \quad \text{if } \lfloor \lambda + 2 \rfloor \le c \le n.$$

Verify that this generalises part (a). $\triangledown$

Problem 1.14 (Bernstein inequality). In this problem we outline how to derive the tighter bound in Theorem 1.2. There we used the inequality $e^x \le 1 + x + x^2$. Now we shall tighten the analysis. Set $e^x := 1 + x + x^2 g(x)$.

(a) Show that g is a non-decreasing function. Hence deduce that for $x \le b$,

$$e^x \le 1 + x + x^2 g(b).$$

(b) Use (a) to deduce that if X is a random variable with $X \le b$ and $E[X] = 0$, then

$$E[e^X] \le e^{g(b)\mathrm{var}(x)}.$$

(c) Hence deduce that if $X := \sum_i X_i$ with $E[X_i] := \mu_i$ and $\mathrm{var}(X) = \sigma^2$, then

$$E[e^{\lambda \sum_i (X_i - \mu_i)}] \le e^{g(\lambda b)\lambda^2 \sigma^2}.$$

(d) Use Markov's inequality and choose an optimal value of λ to get

$$P[X > \mu + t] \le e^{-(\sigma^2/b^2)((1+\epsilon)\ln(1+\epsilon)-\epsilon)},$$

where $\epsilon := bt/\sigma^2$.

(e) Use the calculus fact that for all $x \ge 0$, $(1+x)\ln(1+x) - x \ge 3x^2/(6+2x)$ to finally deduce that

$$p[X > \mu + t] \le e^{-\frac{t^2}{2\sigma^2(1+bt/3\sigma^2)}}.$$

$\triangledown$

2

Applications of the Chernoff–Hoeffding Bounds

In this chapter we present some non-trivial applications of the Chernoff–Hoeffding bounds arising in the design and analysis of randomized algorithms. The examples are quite different, a fact that illustrates the usefulness of these bounds.

2.1 Probabilistic Amplification

The following situation is quite common. We have a probabilistic algorithm that on input x, computes the correct answer $f(x)$ with probability strictly greater than $1/2$. For concreteness, let us assume that the success probability is $p \geq 3/4$ and that the algorithm has two possible outcomes, 0 and 1. To boost our confidence we run the algorithm n times and select the majority answer. What is the probability that this procedure is correct?

Let X be the number of occurrences of the majority value. Then, $E[X] = pn > 3/4n$. The majority answer is wrong if and only if $X < n/2$. Note that here we do not know the exact value of $E[X]$, but only an upper bound. In our case we have n independent trials X_i, each of which succeeds with probability $p \geq 3/4$. Using the fact noted in Exercise 1.1, one can apply the Chernoff–Hoeffding bound directly. Recalling (1.9) if we set $t := n/4$, we have that

$$\Pr\left[X < \frac{n}{2}\right] \leq e^{-n/8}.$$

The reader can check that (1.7) yields worse estimates. Problem 2.1 asks to generalise this to the case when the algorithm takes values in an infinite set.

2.2 Load Balancing

Suppose we have a system in which m jobs arrive in a stream and need to be processed immediately on one of a collection of n identical processors. We want to assign the jobs to the processors in a manner that *balances* the workload evenly. Furthermore, we are in a typical *distributed* setting where centralised coordination and control are impossible. A natural "lightweight" solution in such a situation is to assign each incoming job to a processor chosen uniformly at random, independently of other jobs. We analyse how well this scheme performs.

Focus on a particular processor. Let $X_i, i \in [m]$, be the indicator variable for whether job number i is assigned to this processor. The total load of the processor is then $X := \sum_i X_i$. Note that $\Pr[X_i = 1] = 1/n$ because each job is assigned to a processor chosen uniformly at random. Also, $X_1, \ldots, X_m$ are independent.

First, let us consider the case when $m = 6n \ln n$. Then $E[X] = \sum_i E[X_i] = m/n = 6 \ln n$. Applying (1.7), we see that the probability of the processor's load exceeding $12 \ln n$ is at most

$$\Pr[X > 12 \ln n] \le e^{-2 \ln n} \le 1/n^2.$$

Applying the union bound, we see that the load of no processor exceeds $12 \ln n$ with probability at least $1 - 1/n$.

Next, let us consider the case when $m = n$. In this case, $E[X] = 1$. Applying (1.8), we see that

$$\Pr[X > 2 \log n] \le 2^{-2 \log n} \le 1/n^2.$$

Applying the union bound, we see that the load of no processor exceeds $2 \log n$ with probability at least $1 - 1/n$.

However, in this case, we can tighten the analysis using the bound in Problem 1.6:

$$\Pr[X \ge (1 + \epsilon)E[X]] \le \left(\frac{e^\epsilon}{(1 + \epsilon)^{(1+\epsilon)}} \right)^{E[X]}.$$

Set $(1 + \epsilon) := c$ and then

$$\Pr[X > c] < \frac{e^{c-1}}{c^c}. \tag{2.1}$$

To pick the appropriate c to use here, we focus on the function x^x. What is the solution to $x^x = n$? Let $\gamma(n)$ denote this number. There is no closed-form expression for $\gamma(n)$ but one can approximate it well. If $x^x = n$, taking logs gives

$x \log x = \log n$, and taking logs once more gives $\log x + \log \log x = \log \log n$. Thus,

$$2 \log x > \log x + \log \log x = \log \log n \geq \log x.$$

Using this to divide throughout the equation $x \log x = \log n$ gives

$$\frac{1}{2} x \leq \frac{\log n}{\log \log n} \leq x = \gamma(n).$$

Thus, $\gamma(n) = \Theta(\frac{\log n}{\log \log n})$.

Setting $c := e\gamma(n)$ in (2.1), we have

$$\Pr[X > c] < \frac{e^{c-1}}{c^c} < \left(\frac{e}{c}\right)^c = \left(\frac{1}{\gamma(n)}\right)^{e\gamma(n)} < \left(\frac{1}{\gamma(n)}\right)^{2\gamma(n)} = 1/n^2.$$

Thus the load of any one processor does not exceed $e\gamma(n) = \Theta(\log n / \log \log n)$ with probability at least $1 - 1/n^2$. Applying the union bound, we conclude that the load of no processor exceeds this value with probability at least $1 - 1/n$. It can be shown that this analysis is tight; with high probability some processor does receive $\Theta(\log n / \log \log n)$ jobs.

2.3 Skip Lists

We shall discuss a useful and elegant data structure known as the skip list. We want to devise a data structure that efficiently supports the operations of insertion, deletion and search of an element. Elements are drawn from a totally ordered universe X of size n, which can be assumed to be a finite set of natural numbers. The basic idea is as follows: Order the elements and arrange them in a linked list. We call this the 0th level and denote it by L_0. It is convenient to assume that the list starts with the element $-\infty$. With this convention,

$$L_0 = -\infty \to x_1 \to x_2 \to \cdots \to x_n.$$

We now form a new linked list L_1 by selecting every second element from L_0 and putting $-\infty$ in front.

$$L_1 = -\infty \to x_2 \to x_4 \to \cdots \to x_m.$$

Identical elements in the two lists are joined by double pointers, including $-\infty$'s. Continuing in this fashion we obtain a structure with $O(\log n)$ levels like the one in Figure 2.1. This structure resembles a binary tree and likewise allows for efficient searches. To search for an element y we start from the top list L_t and determine the largest element of L_t that is smaller than or equal to y.

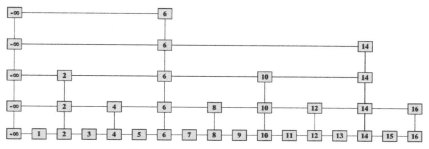

Figure 2.1. A skip list of 16 elements.

Denote such element by e_t. Then we go one level down, position ourselves on the copy of e_t and look for the largest element of L_{t-1} smaller than or equal to y. To do so we only need to scan L_{t-1} to the right of e_t. Continuing in this fashion we generate a sequence $e_t, e_{t-1}, \ldots, e_0$, where e_0 is the largest element in X smaller than or equal to y. Clearly, y is present in the data structure if and only if $e_0 = y$. Although an element could be encountered before reaching L_0, we assume that the search continues all the way down. This makes sense in applications for which the elements are keys pointing to records. In such cases one might not want to copy a whole record at higher levels. This convention also simplifies the probabilistic analysis to follow.

When performing a search we traverse the data structure in a zigzag fashion, making only downturns and right turns (see Figure 2.2). The cost of the traversal is proportional to the sum of the height and the width of this path, both of which are $O(\log n)$. The width is $O(\log n)$ because each time we go one level down we roughly halve the search space. Searches are inexpensive as long as the data structure stays balanced. The problem is that insertions and removals can destroy the symmetry, making maintenance both cumbersome and expensive. By using randomisation we can retain the advantages of the data structure while keeping the cost of reorganisations low.

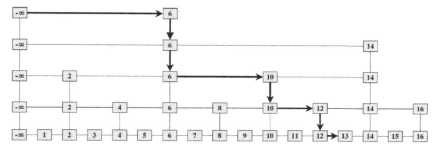

Figure 2.2. A zigzag path through the skip list generated by a search for element 13.

2.3.1 Randomisation Makes It Easy

As before, L_0 is an ordered list of all the elements. Subsequent levels are built according to the following probabilistic rule: Given that an element x appears in level i, it is chosen to appear in level $i + 1$ with probability p, independently of the other elements. Thus, the highest level of an element follows a geometric distribution with parameter p. If we denote by H_i the highest level to which x_i belongs, then

$$\Pr[H_i = k] = p^k(1 - p). \tag{2.2}$$

H_i is called the *height* of x_i. The *height* of the skip list is defined as

$$H := \max_i H_i. \tag{2.3}$$

The data structure is organised as before, with each level being an ordered list of elements starting with $-\infty$ and with copies of the same element at different levels arranged in a doubly linked list. Such a data structure is called a *skip list*.

A search is implemented as before. To insert an element x we do as follows: First, we search for x. This generates the sequence $e_t, e_{t-1}, \ldots, e_0$. Second, we insert x in L_0 between e_0 and its successor. Then we flip a coin; if the outcome is "tail", we stop; otherwise we insert x in L_1 between e_{t-1} and its successor; and so on until the first "tail" occurs. Although we could stop when the last level is reached, we do not do so because this would slightly complicate the probabilistic analysis.

To remove an element x, we first locate it by means of a search and then remove all occurrences of x from all levels, modifying the pointers of the various lists in the obvious way.

How expensive are these operations? Deletion and insertion have a cost that is proportional to that of a search plus the height of the element. In what follows we will show that with high probability, the cost of a search and the height of the skip list have the same order of magnitude $\Theta(\log n)$. First, we bound the probability that H is large.

Proposition 2.1. $\Pr[H \geq k] \leq np^k$, *for any $k > 0$.*

Proof. Each H_i is geometrically distributed with the parameter p. Therefore, for $k \geq 1$,

$$\Pr[H_i \geq k] = \sum_{t \geq k} \Pr[H_i = t] = \sum_{t \geq k} p^t(1 - p) = (1 - p)p^k \sum_{t \geq 0} p^t = p^k. \tag{2.4}$$

Hence, by the union bound

$$\Pr[H \geq k] = \Pr[\exists i, \ H_i \geq k] \leq \sum_i \Pr[H_i \geq k] = np^k. \qquad (2.5)$$

∎

We now bound the cost of a search, showing it to be $O(\log n)$ with high probability. Refer to Figure 2.2. The cost of a search traversal is equal to the number of $\downarrow$'s plus the number of $\rightarrow$'s. If an $\downarrow$-edge is traversed then the element x must be stored in the two consecutive levels L_k and L_{k+1} of the data structure. This means that when x flipped its coin to determine whether to percolate up from L_k to L_{k+1}, the outcome was "head". Similarly, if an element y is entered at level L_k from the left with an arrow $x \rightarrow y$, it means that when y flipped its coin at level L_k the outcome was "tail". We label each $\downarrow$ with p – denoting success – and each $\rightarrow$ with q – denoting *failure*. The crucial observation is the following: The number of arrows in the path is equal to the number of times needed to toss a coin with bias p in order to obtain H successes.

Exercise 2.1. *Down arrows between $-\infty$'s do not correspond to coin flips. Convince yourself that the aforementioned approach to estimate the cost of a search is nevertheless correct.*

The argument proceeds as follows: To fix our ideas let

$$p := \frac{1}{2}$$

from now on. Let $Z := H + W$ denote the number of arrows in a search traversal, where W (as in width) denotes the number of $\rightarrow$s. We want to show that $Z = O(H)$ with high probability. Recalling Proposition 2.1,

$$\Pr(Z > m) = \Pr(Z > m \mid H < k)\Pr(H < k) + \Pr(Z > m \mid H \geq k)\Pr(H \geq k)$$
$$\leq \Pr(Z > m \mid H < k) + \Pr(H \geq k)$$
$$\leq \Pr(Z > m \mid H < k) + np^k$$
$$= \Pr(W > m - k) + np^k.$$

Therefore we need to estimate $\Pr(W > m - k)$. We have $\mu := \mathrm{E}[W] = pm = m/2$.

If we let $m := 14 \log_2 n$ and $k := 3 \log_2 n$, recalling (1.6), we obtain

$$\Pr(W > m - k) = \Pr(W > \mu + 4 \log_2 n) \leq \exp\left\{-\frac{2(4 \log_2 n)^2}{m}\right\} \leq \frac{1}{n^2}.$$

$$(2.6)$$

Summing up,

$$\Pr(Z > m) \leq \Pr(W > m - k) + np^k \leq \frac{2}{n^2}$$

for our choice $k = 3 \log_2 n$. There are n distinct elements to search for. Therefore the probability that any search exceeds $m = 14 \log_2 n$ many steps is at most $2/n$.

2.4 Quicksort

The randomized version of the well-known algorithm quicksort is one of the, if not "the", most effective sorting algorithms. The input of the algorithm is an array

$$X := [x_1, \ldots, x_n]$$

of n numbers. The algorithm selects an element at random, the so-called *pivot*, denoted here as p, and partitions the array as follows:

$$[y_1, \ldots, y_i, p, z_1, \ldots, z_j],$$

where the y's are less than or equal to p and the z's are strictly greater. (One of these two regions could be empty.) The algorithm continues with two recursive calls, one on the y-region and the other on the z-region. The end of the recursion is when the input array has less than two elements.

We want to show that the running time of the algorithm is $O(n \log n)$ with probability at least $1 - 1/n$. The overall running time is given by the tree of recursive calls. The tree is binary, with each node having at most two children corresponding to the y- and z-region obtained by partitioning. Since partitioning requires linear time, if we start with an array of n elements, the total work done at every level of the tree is $O(n)$. Therefore to bound the running time it suffices to compute the height of the tree. In this section the logarithms are to the base 2.

Let P be a path from a leaf to the root and let $|P|$ denote its length. We will show that

$$\Pr(|P| > 21 \log n) \leq \frac{1}{n^2}.$$

Assuming this, the claim will follow from the union bound since in the tree there are at most n leaves:

$$\Pr[\exists P, |P| > 21 \log n] \leq n \Pr[|P| > 21 \log n] \leq \frac{1}{n}.$$

To bound the probability that $|P| > 21 \log n$, call a node of P *good* if the corresponding pivot partitions the array into two regions, each of size at least one-third of the array. The node is *bad* otherwise. After a good pivot the size of the array decreases at least as

$$s_t \leq \frac{2}{3} s_{t-1} \leq \left(\frac{2}{3}\right)^t n.$$

It follows that there can be at most

$$t = \frac{\log n}{\log \frac{3}{2}} < 2 \log n$$

good nodes in any path. If $|P| > 21 \log n$ and X denotes the number of bad nodes along P, we must have $X > 19 \log n$. X can be written as the sum of $|P|$ Bernoulli trials $X_1, \ldots, X_{|P|}$, where $X_i = 1$ if node i is bad and $X_i = 0$ if it is good. The X_i's are independent and such that $\Pr[X_i = 1] = 2/3$. Thus $\mu := E[X] = 2/3|P| > 14 \log n$. Recalling (1.6),

$$\Pr[X > 19 \log n] = \Pr[X > \mu + 5 \log n] \leq \exp\left\{-2 \frac{(5 \log n)^2}{21 \log n}\right\} \leq \frac{1}{n^2}.$$

Exercise 2.2. *Let a pivot be good if it partitions the array into two regions, each of size at least one-fourth of the array. Find a constant c, as small as possible, such that* $\Pr[|P| > c \log n] \leq 1/n^2$.

In Chapter 7 we will derive a stronger bound by using martingale methods.

2.5 Low-Distortion Embeddings

In this section, rather than applying the bounds themselves, we show how a Chernoff-like bound can be obtained by applying the basic Chernoff technique. The problem we consider is as follows: We have a set of n points in a high-dimensional Euclidean space R^d. We want to project the points onto a space of lower dimension R^k in such a way that pairwise distances are distorted as little as possible. More precisely, we want to show the following result, known as the Johnson–Lindenstrauss theorem.

Theorem 2.1. *For any $0 < \epsilon < 1$ and any positive integer n, let k be a positive integer such that*

$$k \geq 4(\epsilon^2/2 - \epsilon^3/3)^{-1} \ln n.$$

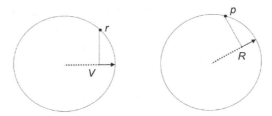

Figure 2.3. On the left, a random point r on the circle is projected onto a fixed axis V. On the right, a fixed point p on the circle is projected onto a random axis R. The distributions of the lengths of the two projections coincide.

Then, for any set V of n points in R^d, there is a map $f : R^d \to R^k$ such that for all points $u, v \in V$,

$$(1 - \epsilon)\|u - v\|^2 \le \|f(u) - f(v)\|^2 \le (1 + \epsilon)\|u - v\|^2.$$

Moreover, this map can be found in randomized polynomial time.

We will follow the treatment in [24]. The basic idea is that if we project the set of points V onto a random k-dimensional subspace of R^d, there is a reasonably good chance that this random projection will exhibit low distortion. To analyse how this effectively works out, the proof uses two main ideas. For the first, refer to Figure 2.3. Consider a unit circle in R^2 and a random point on it. Let X be the length of the projection of this point on the x-axis. Consider now a fixed point on the circle and draw a random unit vector. Let Y be the length of the projection of this point onto the random vector. Then, X and Y have the same distribution. In general, the same holds if X is the length of the projection of a point lying on the surface of the unit sphere onto a k-dimensional random subspace and Y is the length of the projection of a random unit point onto a fixed k-dimensional subspace. X is, up to normalisation, the random variable describing our original random projection. The aforementioned equivalence says that we can work with Y, which is easier to deal with, instead of X. The second main ingredient of the proof is that the norm of Y is sharply concentrated around its expectation. We will prove this by applying the basic Chernoff technique.

We begin by showing how to draw points uniformly at random from the surface of the unit sphere.

Lemma 2.1. *Let $X_1, \ldots, X_d$ be independent random variables, each drawn from the normal (Gaussian) distribution $N(0, 1)$. Let $X := (X_1, \ldots, X_d)$. Then*

$$Y := \frac{1}{\|X\|} X$$

is a random point drawn uniformly from the surface of the d-dimensional unit sphere.

Proof. The distribution function for X has density

$$f(x_1, \ldots, x_d) = \prod_{i=1}^{n} \frac{1}{\sqrt{2\pi}} e^{-y_i^2/2} = \frac{1}{(2\pi)^{n/2}} e^{-\frac{1}{2} \sum_i y_i^2}.$$

Note now that the density function depends only on the distance of X from the origin. Therefore, the distribution of X is spherically symmetric, and by dividing by $\|X\|$ we obtain a random point on the surface of the d-dimensional unit sphere. ∎

For the rest of this section we denote with $Y = (Y_1, \ldots, Y_d)$ the random unit vector of the statement of the previous lemma and with $Z := (Y_1, \ldots, Y_k)$ the projection of Y onto its first k coordinates, and we define $L := \|Z\|^2$. Our aim now is to show that L is sharply concentrated around its mean.

Lemma 2.2. $\mathrm{E}[L] = k/d$.

Proof.

$$\mathrm{E}[L] = \mathrm{E}[\|Z\|^2] = \frac{1}{\|X\|^2} \mathrm{E}[X_1^2 + \cdots + X_k^2] = \frac{1}{\|X\|^2} \sum_{i=1}^{k} \mathrm{E}[X_i^2] = k \frac{\mathrm{E}[X_1^2]}{\|X\|^2}.$$

$$(2.7)$$

The last equality follows from the fact that the X_i are identically distributed. Now, since Y is a unit vector,

$$1 = \|Y\|^2 = \frac{1}{\|X\|^2} \sum_{i=1}^{d} X_i^2.$$

From this, taking expectations,

$$d \frac{\mathrm{E}[X_1^2]}{\|X\|^2} = 1,$$

and thus

$$\frac{\mathrm{E}[X_1^2]}{\|X\|^2} = \frac{1}{d}.$$

Altogether we get,

$$\mathrm{E}[L] = k \frac{\mathrm{E}[X_1^2]}{\|X\|^2} = \frac{k}{d}. \qquad \blacksquare$$

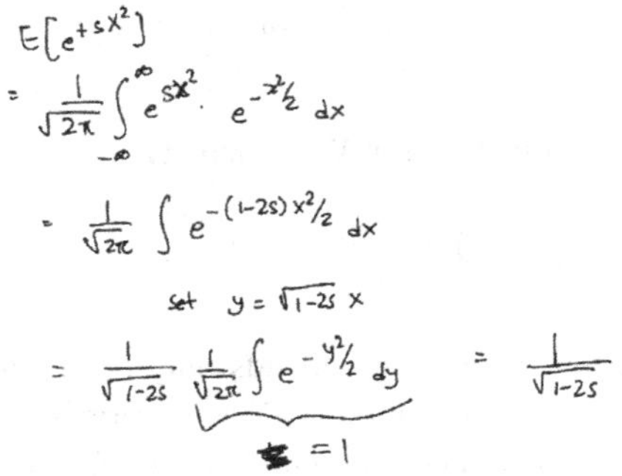

$$E[e^{+sX^2}]$$

$$= \frac{1}{\sqrt{2\pi}} \int_{-\infty}^{\infty} e^{sx^2} \cdot e^{-\frac{x^2}{2}} \, dx$$

$$= \frac{1}{\sqrt{2\pi}} \int e^{-(1-2s)\frac{x^2}{2}} \, dx$$

set $y = \sqrt{1-2s} \, x$

$$= \frac{1}{\sqrt{1-2s}} \underbrace{\frac{1}{\sqrt{2\pi}} \int e^{-\frac{y^2}{2}} \, dy}_{= 1} = \frac{1}{\sqrt{1-2s}}$$

Figure 2.4. Proof of Lemma 2.3. Courtesy of Anupam Gupta.

We show next that L is concentrated around its expectation. Before doing it, we recall a basic fact about the normal distribution.

Lemma 2.3. *If $X \sim N(0, 1)$ then* $E[e^{sX^2}] = 1/\sqrt{1 - 2s}$, *for* $-\infty < s < 1/2$.

Proof. See Figure 2.4. ∎

Lemma 2.4. *Let $k < d$. Then,*

1. *If $\beta < 1$, then*

$$\Pr\left[L \le \frac{\beta k}{d}\right] \le \beta^{k/2} \left(1 + \frac{(1-\beta)k}{(d-k)}\right)^{(d-k)/2} \le \exp\left(\frac{k}{2}(1 - \beta + \ln \beta)\right). \tag{2.8}$$

2. *If $\beta > 1$, then*

$$\Pr\left[L \ge \frac{\beta k}{d}\right] \le \beta^{k/2} \left(1 + \frac{(1-\beta)k}{(d-k)}\right)^{(d-k)/2} \le \exp\left(\frac{k}{2}(1 - \beta + \ln \beta)\right). \tag{2.9}$$

Proof. We will prove Equation (2.8) leaving Equation (2.9), which has a very similar proof, as a problem to the reader (see Problem 2.9). Now, since

$$L = \frac{\|(X_1, \dots, X_k)\|^2}{\|(X_1, \dots, X_d)\|^2},$$

the statement to prove becomes

$$\Pr[d(X_1^2 + \cdots + X_k^2) \le k\beta(X_1^2 + \cdots + X_d^2)] \le \beta^{k/2} \left(1 + \frac{(1-\beta)k}{(d-k)}\right)^{(d-k)/2}.$$

Therefore,

$$
\begin{aligned}
&\Pr[d(X_1^2 + \cdots + X_k^2) \le k\beta(X_1^2 + \cdots + X_d^2)] \\
&\quad = \Pr[k\beta(X_1^2 + \cdots + X_d^2) - d(X_1^2 + \cdots + X_k^2) \ge 0] \\
&\quad = \Pr[\exp\{t(k\beta(X_1^2 + \cdots + X_d^2) - d(X_1^2 + \cdots + X_k^2))\} \ge 1] \quad \text{(for } t > 0) \\
&\quad \le \mathrm{E}[\exp\{t(k\beta(X_1^2 + \cdots + X_d^2) \\
&\qquad - d(X_1^2 + \cdots + X_k^2))\}] \quad \text{(by Markov's inequality)} \\
&\quad = \mathrm{E}[\exp\{tk\beta X_1^2\}]^{d-k} \mathrm{E}[\exp\{t(k\beta - d)X_1^2\}]^k \\
&\quad = (1 - 2tk\beta X_1^2)^{-(d-k)/2}(1 - 2t(k\beta - d))^{-k/2} \quad \text{(by Lemma (2.3)).}
\end{aligned}
$$

We will refer to the last expression as $g(t)$. The last equality gives us the additional constraints $tk\beta < 1/2$ and $t(k\beta - d) < 1/2$. The latter is implied by the former, since $t \ge 0$, and so the constraint on t becomes $0 < t < 1/2k\beta$. Now, to minimise $g(t)$ is equivalent to maximising

$$
f(t) = (1 - 2tk\beta)^{d-k}\,(1 - 2t(k\beta - d))^k
$$

in the required interval $(0, 1/2k\beta)$. Differentiating f, we obtain that the maximum is attained at

$$
t_0 = \frac{1 - \beta}{2\beta(d - k\beta)},
$$

which is in the permitted range. Hence we have

$$
f(t_0) = \left(\frac{d - k}{d - k\beta}\right)^{d-k} \left(\frac{1}{\beta}\right)^k,
$$

and since $g(t_0) = 1/\sqrt{f(t_0)}$, the inequality (2.8) follows. ∎

We can now prove Theorem 2.1. If $d \le k$, the statement holds trivially. Assume then $k < d$. Take a random k-dimensional subspace S of R^d. We will project every point $v \in V$ into S denoting with v' the projection. Let

$$
Y := \frac{v - w}{\|v - w\|}
$$

be a unit vector and

$$
Z := \frac{v' - w'}{\|v - w\|}
$$

be its random projection, and let $L := \|Z\|^2$. As observed, Z is distributed like a random unit vector projected into the space defined by the first k

coordinates. Therefore, by Lemma 2.2, $E[L] = k/d$, and by (2.8), for $0 < \epsilon < 1$, $\beta = 1 - \epsilon$,

$$\Pr(\|v' - w'\|^2 \le (1 - \epsilon)\|v - w\|^2 k/d) = \Pr(L \le (1 - \epsilon)k/d)$$

$$\le \exp\left(\frac{k}{2}(1 - (1 - \epsilon) + \ln(1 - \epsilon))\right)$$

$$\le \exp\left(\frac{k}{2}\left(\epsilon - \left(\epsilon + \frac{\epsilon^2}{2}\right)\right)\right)$$

$$= \exp\left(\frac{-k\epsilon^2}{4}\right)$$

$$\le \exp(-2\ln n) = \frac{1}{n^2},$$

where, in the second line, we used the inequality $\ln(1 - x) \le -x - x^2/2$, holding for $0 \le x < 1$. Likewise, we can apply (2.9) and the inequality $\ln(1 + x) \le x - x^2/2 + x^3/3$, valid when $0 \le x < 1$, to get

$$\Pr(\|v' - w'\|^2 \ge (1 - \epsilon)\|v - w\|^2 k/d) = \Pr(L \ge (1 + \epsilon)k/d)$$

$$\le \exp\left(\frac{k}{2}(1 - (1 + \epsilon) + \ln(1 + \epsilon))\right)$$

$$\le \exp\left(\frac{k}{2}\left(-\epsilon + \left(\epsilon - \frac{\epsilon^2}{2} + \frac{\epsilon^3}{3}\right)\right)\right)$$

$$= \exp\left(-\frac{k(\epsilon^2/2 - \epsilon^3/3)}{2}\right)$$

$$\le \exp(-2\ln n) = \frac{1}{n^2}.$$

Let us define the randomized map

$$f(v) := \sqrt{\frac{d}{k}}\, v'.$$

By the preceding calculations, for any fixed pair of points $u, v \in V$, the probability that

$$(1 - \epsilon)\|u - v\|^2 \le \|f(u) - f(v)\|^2 \le (1 + \epsilon)\|u - v\|^2$$

does not hold is at most $2/n^2$. By the union bound, the chance that there exists a violating pair is at most

$$\binom{n}{2}\frac{2}{n^2} = 1 - \frac{1}{n}.$$

Therefore f has the desired low-distortion property with probability at least $1/n$. Repeating the experiment $O(n)$ times can boost the desired success probability arbitrarily close to 1, in polynomial time.

2.6 Pointers to the Literature

For more applications of the Chernoff–Hoeffding bounds to the analysis of algorithms the reader is referred to the textbooks [52, 72, 74]. Skip lists are an invention of Pugh [80]. The elementary proof of the Johnson–Lindenstrauss lemma [47] is from [24], to which the reader is referred for further discussions and pointers to similar results.

2.7 Problems

Problem 2.1. A randomized algorithm A, on input x, gives an answer $A(x)$ that is correct with probability $p > 3/4$. $A(x)$ takes values in the set of natural numbers. Compute the probability that the majority outcome is correct when the algorithm is run n times. How large n must be to have a 0.99 confidence that the answer is correct?   ▽

Problem 2.2. The following type of set systems is a crucial ingredient in the construction of pseudo-random generators [75]. Given a universe $\mathcal{U}$ of size $|\mathcal{U}| = cn$, a family $\mathcal{F}$ of subsets of $\mathcal{U}$ is a *good family* if (a) all sets in $\mathcal{F}$ have n elements; (b) given any two sets A and B in $\mathcal{F}$, their intersection has size at most $n/2$; and, (c) $|\mathcal{F}| = 2^{\Theta(n)}$.

Show that there is a value of c for which good families exist for every n. (HINT: Partition the universe into n blocks of size c and generate sets of n elements independently at random by choosing elements randomly in each block. Then compute the probability that the family generated in this fashion has the desired properties.)   ▽

Problem 2.3 (Skip lists).

- Show that the height of skip list with n elements is $\Theta(\log n)$ with probability at least $1 - 1/n^4$. (HINT: Do we need the Chernoff bounds here?)
- Prove a sharp concentration result for the space used by a skip list.
- What is the best value of p in order to minimise the expected time of a search operation in a skip list?   ▽

In the next three problems, we shall derive bounds on the sums of independent *geometrically distributed* variables. Let $W(1, p)$ denote the number of tosses required to obtain a "heads" with a coin of bias p (i.e. $\Pr(\text{heads}) = p$, $\Pr(\text{tails}) = 1 - p =: q$). Note that $\Pr[W(1, p) = \ell] = q^{\ell-1}p$, for $\ell \geq 1$. Let $W(n, p)$ denote the number of tosses needed to get n heads. Note that $W(n, p) = \sum_{i \in [n]} W_i(1, p)$, where the W_i, $i \in [n]$, are independent geo-metrically distributed variables with parameter p. The variable $W(n, p)$ is said to have a *negative binomial distribution*.

Problem 2.4. Let $W(k, p)$ denote the number of coin tosses until the kth head occurs, where p is the coin bias. And let $B(m, p)$ denote the number of heads in a sequence of m Bernoulli trials with bias p. Prove that $\Pr(W(k, p) \leq m) = \Pr(B(m, p) \geq k)$. Derive a concentration result for $W(k, p)$.   ▽

Problem 2.5. A second approach to derive concentration results on $W(n, p)$ is to apply the basic Chernoff technique. Consider for simplicity the case $p = 1/2 = q$.

(a) Show that for any integer $r \geq 1$ and for any $0 < \lambda < \ln 2$,

$$\Pr[W(n, p) \geq (2 + r)n] \leq \left(\frac{e^{-\lambda(r+1)}}{2 - e^{\lambda}} \right)^n.$$

(b) Use calculus to find the optimal λ and simplify to derive the bound that for $r \geq 3$,

$$\Pr[W(n, p) \geq (2 + r)n] \leq e^{-rn/4}.$$

You may find it useful to note that $1 - x \leq e^{-x}$ and that $1 + r/2 \leq e^{r/4}$ for $r \geq 3$. Compare this bound with the one from Problem 2.3.   ▽

Problem 2.6. Here is a third approach to the negative binomial distribution.

(a) By explicit computation, show that

$$\Pr[W(n, p) \geq \ell] = \left(\frac{p}{q} \right)^n \sum_{t \geq \ell} q^t \binom{t-1}{n}.$$

(b) Let $S_n := \sum_{t \geq \ell} q^t \binom{t-1}{n}$. Show that

$$S_n = \frac{q}{p} \left(q^{\ell-1} \binom{\ell-1}{n} + S_{n-1} \right).$$

Hence deduce that

$$\Pr[W(n, p) \geq \ell] = q^{\ell-1} \sum_{0 \leq i \leq n} \left(\frac{q}{p} \right)^{n+1-i} \binom{\ell-1}{i}.$$

(c) Consider the case $p = 1/2 = q$ and find a bound for $\Pr[W(n, p) \geq (2 + r)n]$ and compare with the previous problem.   ▽

Problem 2.7. In this exercise we deal with a very elegant data structure called *treap* (see for instance [54, 74]). A treap is a binary tree whose nodes contain two values, a *key x* and a *priority* p_x. Keys are drawn from a totally ordered set and the priorities are given by a random permutation of the keys. Without loss of generality, assume that the set of elements is $X = \{1, 2, \ldots, n\}$. The tree is a heap according to the priorities and it is a search tree according to the keys (i.e. keys are ordered in order). For instance, if $X = \{1, 2, 3, 4, 5, 6, 7, 8\}$ and

$$p = 3\ 1\ 5\ 4\ 8\ 6\ 2\ 7,$$

we have that $p_1 = 2$, $p_2 = 7$, $p_3 = 1$ and so on.

(a) Show that given a totally ordered set X of elements and a function p assigning unique priorities to elements in X, there always exists a unique treap with keys X and priorities p.

Treaps allow for fast insertion, deletion and search of an element. The cost of these operations is proportional to the height of the treap. In what follows we will show that this quantity is $O(\log n)$ with high probability. The analysis boils down to the following problem on random permutations: Given a permutation $p : [n] \to [n]$ of the n elements, an element is *checked* if it is larger than all the elements appearing to its left in p. For instance, if

$$p = 3\ 1\ 5\ 4\ 8\ 6\ 2\ 7,$$

the elements that are checked are in bold. The problem is to show that the number of checks is concentrated around its expectation.

1. Given a key x, let x_- be the set of elements that are smaller than or equal to x. We will use p_-^x to denote the permutation induced by p on x_-. For example, using p from the preceding equation, we have that $p_-^6 = 3, 1, 5, 4, 6, 2$. Show that all elements of x_- that are checked in p_-^x appear along the path from the root to x in the tree.
2. Prove an analogous statement for the set x^+ of all elements $\geq x$ and use this to calculate exactly the number of elements from the root to x in the tree.
3. Denoting with X_n the number of elements that are checked for a random permutation $p : [n] \to [n]$, prove that

$$E[X_n] = 1 + \frac{1}{2} + \cdots + \frac{1}{n}.$$

(It is known that the quantity $H_n := \sum_{i=1}^{n} \frac{1}{i}$, the nth *harmonic number*, is $\Theta(\log n)$.)

4. Let Y_i be a binary random variable denoting whether the ith element of the permutation (starting from the left) is checked. Prove that

$$\Pr[Y_i = 1 \mid Y_{i+1} = y_{i+1}, \ldots, Y_n = y_n] = \frac{1}{i}$$

for any choice of the y's.

(d) Is the following true:

$$\Pr[Y_i = 1 \mid Y_2 = y_2, \ldots, Y_{i-1} = y_{i-1}] = \frac{1}{i}?$$

5. Show that for any index set S,

$$\Pr\left[\bigwedge_{i \in S}\{Y_i = 1\}\right] \leq \prod_{i \in S} \Pr[Y_i = 1]. \tag{2.10}$$

Property (2.10) ensures that the Chernoff–Hoeffding bounds hold for $Y := \sum_{i=1}^{n} Y_i$ (see Problem 1.8). Using this, give a concentration result for X_n.   ▽

Problem 2.8. The following type of geometric random graphs arises in the study of power control for wireless networks. We are given n points distributed uniformly at random within the unit square. Each point connects to the k closest points. Let us denote the resulting (random) graph as G_k^n.

- Show that there exists a constant α such that if $k \geq \alpha \log n$, then G_k^n is connected with probability at least $1 - 1/n$.
- Show that there exists a constant β such that if $k \leq \beta \log n$, then G_k^n is not connected with positive probability.   ▽

Problem 2.9. Prove Equation (2.9).   ▽

Problem 2.10. A random variable X taking on positive integer values is said to be a *Poisson* random variable with parameter $\lambda > 0$ if

$$\Pr[X = i] = e^{-\lambda}\frac{\lambda^i}{i!}$$

for $i = 0, 1, 2, \ldots$.

- Show that $\mathrm{E}[X] = \lambda$.
- Let $X_1, \ldots, X_n$ be identically distributed Poisson random variable with parameter λ, and let $X := \sum_{i=1}^{n} X_i$. X is Poisson with parameter $n\lambda$ and therefore $\mathrm{E}[X] = n\lambda$. Applying the basic Chernoff technique, show that

$$\Pr[X > (1 + \epsilon)n\lambda] \leq e^{-\epsilon^2 n\lambda}.$$

- Prove an analogous statement for the lower tail.   ▽

Problem 2.11 (Concentration of χ_n^2 [21]). Let $X_1, \ldots, X_n$ be independent, identically and normally distributed random variables, with mean 0 and variance 1.

The chi-square distribution with n degrees of freedom, one of the most widely used in statistics, is defined as

$$\chi_n^2 := \sum_{i=1}^{n} X_i^2.$$

It can be shown that $\mathrm{E}[\chi_n^2] = n$.

- Prove that for $0 \le \delta < 1$,

$$\Pr[|\chi_n^2 - n| \ge \delta n] \le 2e^{-\delta^2 n}.$$

- Let $X := (X_1, \ldots, X_n)$. Prove that for $0 \le \delta < 1$,

$$\Pr[|\|X\|^2 - n| \ge \delta n] \le 2e^{-\delta^2 n};$$

that is, X is a random point whose norm is sharply concentrated around its expected value. ▽

3

Chernoff–Hoeffding Bounds in Dependent Settings

In this chapter, we consider the sum

$$X := \sum_{\alpha \in \mathcal{A}} X_\alpha, \tag{3.1}$$

where $\mathcal{A}$ is an index set and the variables $X_\alpha, \alpha \in \mathcal{A}$, may not be independent. In some dependent situations, the Chernoff–Hoeffding bound can be salvaged to be applicable (as is, or with slight modifications) to X.

3.1 Negative Dependence

We consider the sum (3.1) where $\mathcal{A} := [n]$. Random variables $X_1, \dots, X_n$ are said to be *negatively dependent* if, intuitively, conditioned on a subset $X_i, i \in I \subseteq [n]$, taking "high" values, a disjoint subset $X_j, j \in I \subseteq [n]$ with $I \cap J = \emptyset$, takes "low" values. One way to formalise this intuitive notion is as follows.

Definition 3.1 (Negative association). *The random variables $X_i, i \in [n]$, are negatively associated if for all disjoint subsets $I, J \subseteq [n]$ and all non-decreasing functions f and g,*

$$E[f(X_i, i \in I)g(X_j, j \in J)] \leq E[f(X_i, i \in I)]E[g(X_j, j \in J)]. \tag{3.2}$$

Exercise 3.1. *Show that if $X_1, \dots, X_n$ are negatively associated, then*

$$E[X_i X_j] \leq E[X_i]E[X_j], \quad i \neq j.$$

More generally, show that if $f_i, i \in [n]$, are non-decreasing functions, then

$$E\left[\prod_i f_i(X_i)\right] \leq \prod_i E[f_i(X_i)].$$

In particular,

$$E[e^{t(X_1+\cdots+X_n)}] \le \prod_{i \in [n]} e^{tX_i}. \tag{3.3}$$

Theorem 3.1 (Chernoff–Hoeffding bounds with negative dependence). *The Chernoff–Hoeffding bounds can be applied as is to $X := \sum_{i \in [n]} X_i$ if the random variables $X_i, \ldots, X_n$ are negatively associated.*

Proof. Use (3.3) at the relevant step in the proof of the Chernoff–Hoeffding bound. ∎

Thus one needs techniques to establish the negative association condition. Although the definition looks formidable, it is often easy to establish the condition *without any calculations*, using only monotonicity, symmetry and independence. The following two properties of negative association are very useful in these arguments:

Closure under products If $X_1, \ldots, X_n$ and $Y_1, \ldots, Y_m$ are two independent families of random variables that are separately negatively associated, then the family $X_1, \ldots, X_n, Y_1, \ldots, Y_m$ is also negatively associated.

Disjoint monotone aggregation If $X_i, i \in [n]$, are negatively associated and $\mathcal{A}$ is a family of disjoint subsets of $[n]$, then the random variables

$$f_A(X_i, i \in A), \quad A \in \mathcal{A},$$

are also negatively associated, where the f_A's are arbitrary non-decreasing (or non-increasing) functions.

Exercise 3.2. *Show that these two properties follow directly from the definition of negative association.*

Example 3.1 (Balls and bins). Consider the paradigmatic example of negative dependence: m balls are thrown independently into n bins. We do not assume that the balls or bins are identical: ball k has probability $p_{i,k}$ of landing in bin i, for $i \in [n], k \in m$ (with $\sum_i p_{i,k} = 1$ for each $k \in [m]$). The *occupancy numbers* are $B_i := \sum_k B_{i,k}$. (B_{ik} is defined by (3.4) next.) Intuitively, it is clear that $B_1, \ldots, B_n$ are negatively dependent. To prove this, we first show that a simpler set of variables satisfies negative association and then use the properties of disjoint monotone aggregation and closure under product.

Consider the indicator random variables:

$$B_{i,k} := \begin{cases} 1, & \text{ball } k \text{ falls in bin } i, \\ 0, & \text{otherwise.} \end{cases} \tag{3.4}$$

We have the following.

Proposition 3.1. *For each k, the random variables $B_{i,k}$, $i \in [n]$, are negatively associated.*

Proof. Let k denote (the index of) a fixed ball; let I, J be disjoint subsets of $[n]$; and let f, g be non-decreasing functions. Translating by a constant, we may assume f and g are non-negative and $f(0, \ldots, 0) = 0 = g(0, \ldots, 0)$. Then

$$\mathrm{E}[f(B_{ik}, i \in I)g(B_{jk}, j \in J)] = 0 \leq \mathrm{E}[f(B_{ik}, i \in I)]\mathrm{E}[g(B_{jk}, j \in J)]. \qquad \blacksquare$$

Now by closure under products, the full set $B_{i,k}$, $i \in [n], k \in [m]$, is negatively associated. Finally, by disjoint monotone aggregation, the variables $B_i = \sum_k B_{i,k}$, $i \in [n]$, are negatively associated. $\qquad \triangledown$

Example 3.2 (Distributed edge colouring of graphs). Consider the following simple distributed algorithm for edge colouring a bipartite graph $G = (B, T, E)$. The bipartition is made up of the "bottom" vertices B and the "top" vertices T. For simplicity, assume $|B| = n = |T|$ and that the graph is Δ regular. At any stage of the algorithm,

1. In the first step, each "bottom" vertex makes a proposal by a tentative assignment of a random permutation of $[\Delta]$ to its incident edges.
2. In the second step, a "top" vertex chooses from among all incident edges that have the same tentative colour a winner by using an arbitrary rule (lexicographically first or random for instance). The winner gets successfully coloured and the losers are decoloured and go to the next stage of the algorithm.

The basic question to analyse is, how many edges are successfully coloured in one stage of the colouring algorithm. The situation at a "top" vertex is exactly a balls-and-bins experiment: the incident edges are the balls falling into the bins which are the colours. Call an edge that receives a final colour successfully a "winner" and otherwise a "loser". Recalling that there are Δ edges and Δ colours, the number of losing edges is bounded as follows:

$$\# \text{ losers} = \# \text{ balls} - \# \text{ winners}$$
$$\leq \# \text{ bins} - \# \text{ non-empty bins}$$
$$= \# \text{ empty bins}.$$

Thus we need to analyse $Z := \sum_i Z_i$, where Z_i is the indicator random variable for whether bin i is empty, $i \in [\Delta]$. These random variables are manifestly not independent. However, they are negatively associated because

$$Z_i = [B_i \leq 0], \quad i \in [n],$$

are non-increasing functions of disjoint sets of the occupancy variables $B_1, \ldots, B_\Delta$, which are negatively associated by the previous example.

The analysis of the "bottom" vertices is significantly more complicated and will require the use of more sophisticated techniques of Chapter 7. $\qquad \triangledown$

Example 3.3 (Glauber dynamics and graph colouring). *Glauber dynamics* is a stochastic process generating a sequence $f_0, f_1, \ldots, f_t, \ldots$ of random $[k]$-colourings of the vertices of a graph $G := (V, E)$. The colouring f_0 is arbitrary. Given f_{t-1}, the colouring f_t is determined as follows: select a vertex $v = \sigma(t)$ uniformly at random and a colour $c \in [k] \setminus f_{t-1}(\Gamma(v))$ uniformly at random. ($\Gamma(v)$ is the standard notation for the set of neighbours of v.) The colouring f_t is identical to f_{t-1} except that $f_t(v) = c$.

In the analysis of the convergence of the process to stationarity, one needs concentration of the following random variable X: Fix a time t_0 and a vertex $v \in V$. Then, $X := \sum_{w \in \Gamma(v)} X_w$, where the indicator random variable X_w is 1 if w was selected by the colouring schedule σ in the time window $[t_0 - Cn, t_0 + Cn]$ for some constant $C > 0$. The random variables $X_w, w \in \Gamma(v)$, are not independent. However, they are negatively associated. To see this, consider the indicator random variables $[\sigma(t) = v], v \in V, t \geq 1$. These are exactly like the balls-and-bins indicator variables: the "balls" are the time instants and the "bins" are the vertices. Hence, $([\sigma(t) = v], v \in V, t \geq 1)$ are negatively associated. Now note that $X_w := \sum_{t_0 - Cn \leq t \leq t_0 + Cn} [\sigma(t) = w]$ are non-decreasing functions of disjoint index sets, and hence by the disjoint monotone aggregation property, the variables $X_w, w \in \Gamma(v)$, are also negatively associated. $\qquad \triangledown$

Example 3.4 (Geometric load balancing). Let n points be thrown uniformly at random on the unit circle. This splits the unit circle into n arcs, which we can number $1 \cdots n$ in counterclockwise order starting from an arbitrary point. Let $Z_i = 1$ if the i arc has length at least c/n and 0 otherwise. The variables $Z_i, i \in [n]$, are manifestly not independent. However they are negatively associated. To see this, let $L_i, i \in [n]$, denote the lengths of the arcs. Intuitively, it is clear that $(L_i, i \in [n])$ are negatively dependent, and indeed by Problem 3.1, $(L_i, i \in [n])$ are negatively associated. Then $Z_i = [L_i \geq c/n], i \in [n]$, are non-decreasing functions of disjoint sets of negatively associated variables, and hence, by the disjoint monotone aggregation property, are themselves negatively associated. $\qquad \triangledown$

3.2 Local Dependence

The results of this section are from [88]. We state them without proof and illustrate them with examples. Consider the sum (3.1) where there may be only *local dependence* in the following well-known sense. Call a graph Γ on vertex set $\mathcal{A}$ a *dependency graph* for $(X_\alpha, \alpha \in \mathcal{A})$ if whenever there is no edge between $\alpha \in \mathcal{A}$ and any other $\alpha' \in \mathcal{A}'$, then X_α is independent of $(X_{\alpha'}, \alpha' \in \mathcal{A}')$. Let $\chi^*(\Gamma)$ denote the *fractional chromatic number* of Γ.

The chromatic and fractional chromatic numbers $\chi^*(G)$ of a graph $G = (V, E)$ are defined as follows: Let B be the $|V| \times m$ matrix whose columns are characteristic vectors of independent sets in G. The chromatic number of G is the minimum number of colours needed in a proper colouring of G. Equivalently,

$$\chi(G) := \min \left(1^T x \mid Bx \geq 1, x \in \{0, 1\}^m \right).$$

The fractional chromatic number $\chi^*(G)$ is the relaxation of this to non-negative vectors x:

$$\chi^*(G) := \min \left(1^T x \mid Bx \geq 1, x \geq 0 \right).$$

Clearly, $\chi^*(G) \leq \chi(G)$.

Exercise 3.3. *Compute $\chi(C_n)$ and $\chi^*(C_n)$, where C_n is the circle with n points.*

Theorem 3.2. *Suppose X is as in (3.1) with $a_\alpha \leq X_\alpha \leq b_\alpha$ for real numbers $a_\alpha \leq b_\alpha, \alpha \in \mathcal{A}$. Then, for $t > 0$,*

$$P[X \geq E[X] + t], \quad P[X \leq E[X] - t] \quad \leq \quad \exp \left(\frac{-2t^2}{\chi^*(\Gamma) \sum_{\alpha \in \mathcal{A}} (b_\alpha - a_\alpha)^2} \right).$$

Exercise 3.4. *Check that $\chi^*(\Gamma) = 1$ if and only if the variables X_α are independent, so Theorem 3.2 is a proper generalisation of the Hoeffding inequality.*

Example 3.5 (U-statistics). Let $\xi_1, \ldots, \xi_n$ be independent random variables, and let

$$X := \sum_{1 \leq i_1 < \cdots < i_d} f_{i_1, \ldots, i_d}(\xi_{i_1}, \ldots, \xi_{i_d}).$$

This is a special case of (3.1) with $\mathcal{A} := [n]^d_<$ and includes the so-called *U-statistics*. The dependency graph Γ has vertex set $[n]^d_<$ and $(\alpha, \beta) \in E(\Gamma)$ if and only if $\alpha \cap \beta \neq \emptyset$, when the tuples α and β are regarded as sets. One can check (see Problem 3.7) that

$$\chi^*(\Gamma) \leq \frac{\binom{n}{d}}{\lfloor n/d \rfloor}.$$

Hence, if $a \leq f_{i_1,\ldots,i_d}(\xi_{i_1}, \ldots, \xi_{i_d}) \leq b$ for every $i_1, \ldots, i_d$ for some reals $a \leq b$, we have the estimate of Hoeffding:

$$P\left[X \geq E[X] + t\binom{n}{d}\right] \leq \exp\left(\frac{-2\lfloor n/d \rfloor t^2}{(b-a)^2}\right).$$

Since $d \lfloor n/d \rfloor \geq n - d + 1$, we have $\chi^*(\Gamma) \leq \binom{n}{d-1}$ and we have a bound that looks somewhat simpler:

$$P\left[X \geq E[X] + tn^{d-1/2}\right] \leq \exp\left(\frac{-2d!(d-1)!t^2}{(b-a)^2}\right). \qquad \triangledown$$

Example 3.6 (Subgraph counts). Let $G(n, p)$ be the random graph on vertex set $[n]$ with each possible edge (i, j) present independently with probability p. Let X denote the number of triangles in $G(n, p)$. This can be written in form (3.1) with $\mathcal{A} := \binom{[n]}{3}$ and X_α is the indicator that the edges between the three vertices in α are all present. Note that X_α and X_β are independent even if $\alpha \cap \beta = 1$ (but not 2). The dependency graph Γ has vertex set $\binom{[n]}{3}$ and $(\alpha, \beta) \in E(\Gamma)$ if and only if $\alpha \cap \beta = 2$. Note that $\Delta(\Gamma) = 3(n-3)$ and hence

$$\chi^*(\Gamma) \leq \chi(\Gamma) \leq \Delta(\Gamma) + 1 \leq 3n.$$

We compute $E[X] = \binom{n}{3}p^3$ and hence

$$P[X \geq (1+\epsilon)E[X]] \leq \exp\left(\frac{-2\epsilon^2\binom{n}{3}^2 p^6}{3n\binom{n}{2}}\right) = \exp\left(-\Theta(\epsilon^2 n^3 p^6)\right).$$

This estimate can be improved taking into account the variance of the summands. $\qquad \triangledown$

3.3 Janson's Inequality

Let $R = R_{p_1,\ldots,p_n}$ be a random subset of $[n]$ formed by including each $i \in [n]$ in R with probability p_i independently. Let $\mathcal{S}$ be a family of subset of $[n]$, and for each $A \in \mathcal{S}$, introduce the indicators

$$X_A := [A \subseteq R] = \bigwedge_{i \in A} [i \in R].$$

Let $X := \sum_{A \in \mathcal{S}} X_A$. Clearly the summands are not independent. In the terminology of the last section, a natural dependency graph G for $(X_A, A \in \mathcal{S})$ has vertex set $\mathcal{S}$ and an edge $(A, B) \in G$ if and only if $A \cap B \neq \emptyset$: in this case, we write $A \sim B$.

Theorem 3.3. *Let* $X := \sum_A X_A$ *as before, and let* $\mu := E[X] = \sum_A \Pr[X_A = 1]$. *Define*

$$\Delta := \sum_{A \sim B} E[X_A X_B] = \sum_{A \sim B} \Pr[X_A = 1 = X_B], \tag{3.5}$$

where the sum is over **ordered** *pairs. Then, for any* $0 \le t \le E[X]$,

$$\Pr[X \le E[X] - t] \le \exp\left(-\frac{t^2}{2\mu + \Delta}\right).$$

Exercise 3.5. *Check that when the sets* $A \in S$ *are disjoint, this reduces to the Chernoff–Hoeffding bound.*

In particular, taking $t := E[X]$ gives a very useful estimate on the probability that no set in S occurs which is important enough to deserve a separate statement of its own.

Theorem 3.4 (Janson's inequality).

$$\Pr[X = 0] \le e^{-\frac{\mu^2}{\mu + \Delta}}.$$

As verified in Exercise 3.5, when the sets are disjoint, we are in the independent case. More importantly, when the dependence is "small", that is, $\Delta = o(\mu)$, we get nearly the same bound as well.

Example 3.7 (Subgraph counts). Consider again the random graph $G(n, p)$ with vertex set $[n]$ and each (undirected) edge (i, j) present with probability p independently and focus again on the number of triangles in the random graph. An interesting regime of the parameter p is $p := c/n$. The base set Γ here is $\binom{[n]}{2}$, the set of all possible edges, and the random set of edges in G picked as before is the object of study. Let S be a set of three edges forming a triangle, and let X_S be the indicator that this triangle is present in $G(n, p)$. Then $\Pr[X_S = 1] = p^3$. The property that G is triangle free is expressed as $X := \sum_S X_S = 0$, where the sum is over all such $\binom{n}{3}$ subsets of edges S. If the X_S were independent, then we would have

$$\Pr[X = 0] = \Pr\left[\bigwedge_S X_S = 0\right] = \prod_S \Pr[X_S = 0]$$

$$= (1 - p^3)^{\binom{n}{3}} \sim e^{-\binom{n}{3} p^3} \to e^{-c^3/6}.$$

Of course, the X_S are not independent. But if $\mathcal{A}$ and $\mathcal{B}$ are collections of subsets such that each $S \in \mathcal{A}$ is disjoint from each $T \in \mathcal{B}$, then $(X_S, S \in \mathcal{A})$ is mutually independent of $(X_T, T \in \mathcal{B})$.

We can thus apply Janson's inequality (Theorem 3.4). Here $\mu = E[X] = \binom{n}{3} p^3 \sim c^3/6$. To estimate Δ, we note that there are $\binom{n}{3}(n - 3) = O(n^4)$ ordered pairs (S, T) with $S \cap T \neq \emptyset$, and for each such pair, $\Pr[X_S = 1 = X_T] = p^5$. Thus, $\Delta = O(n^4)p^5 = n^{-1+o(1)} = o(1)$. Thus, we get the bound

$$\Pr[X = 0] \leq \exp\left(-\frac{c^6}{36c^3 + o(1)}\right) \sim e^{c^3/36},$$

which is (asymptotically) almost the same (up to constants) as the aforementioned estimate, assuming that the variables were independent. In Problem 3.5, you are asked to generalise this from triangles to arbitrary fixed graphs. ▽

Example 3.8 (Randomized rounding). The following example is taken from an analysis of approximation algorithms for the so-called *group and covering Steiner* problems [35, 53]. We are given a full binary tree T rooted at a special vertex r.

In the group Steiner problem, we are also given groups $A_1, \ldots, A_n$ of subsets of the leaves of T. The objective is to select a subtree of minimum size rooted at r, whose leaves intersect each of the n groups.

The first step in the problem is to formulate a linear programme which provides a lower bound on the size of any such tree. Solving this linear programme gives a set of values $x_e \in [0, 1], e \in T$. These values have the property that $\sum_{e \in E} x_e \geq 1$ for any set of edges that form a cut between r and a group g_i. Thus these values x_e can be used as a guide to constructing the required subtree.

This is done via the following variant of the *randomized rounding* methodology: for each edge $e \in T$, include e independently with probability x_e/x_f, where f is the unique parent edge connecting e to the next vertex up the tree. If e is incident on the root, we include it with probability x_e. (Alternatively, imagine a fictitious parent edge e_{-1} with $x_{e_{-1}} = 1$.) Then pick the unique connected component rooted at r.

The rounding procedure has the property that any edge $e \in T$ is included with probability x_e. To see this, note that an edge is included if and only if all the edges $e = e_1, e_2, \ldots, e_p$ on the path up to the root from e are included, and this happens with probability

$$\frac{x_{e_1}}{x_{e_2}} \frac{x_{e_2}}{x_{e_3}} \cdots \frac{x_{e_{p-1}}}{x_{e_p}} \frac{x_{e_p}}{1} = x_e.$$

Let us focus our attention on a particular group A and estimate the probability that this group is not "hit". We can identify the group A with the corresponding pendant edges. Let $X_e, e \in A$, be the indicator for whether the element $e \in A$ is selected, and let $X := \sum_{e \in A} X_e$. Then

$$E[X] = \sum_{e \in A} E[X_e] = \sum_{e \in A} x_e \geq 1,$$

where the last inequality is because of the cut property of the x_e values.

Note however that the X_e, $e \in A$, are *not* independent: the dependencies arise because of shared edges on the path up the tree. Let us estimate Δ in this situation. To this end, first we note that the event $X_e = 1 = X_f$ for distinct $e, f \in A$ occurs if and only if (a) all edges up to and including the common ancestor g of e and f are picked, and (b) the remaining edges from g to e and f are all picked. Thus, $\Pr[X_e = 1 = X_f] = x_e x_f / x_g$.

Exercise 3.6. *Check this.*

Thus,

$$\Delta = \sum_e \sum_f x_e x_f / x_g.$$

To continue with the estimation, we make some simplifying assumptions (which are justified in the paper [35]): we assume that the group A is contained in a single subtree of height $d := \lceil \log|A| \rceil$, that $\sum_{e \in A} x_e = 1$ finally and that for any vertex v in the tree whose parent edge is e, we have

$$\sum_{f \in T'} x_f \leq x_e, \tag{3.6}$$

where T' is either the left or the right subtree rooted at v.

Now, to return to Δ, consider that an edge e is the first summation. Number the path up from e to the root $r = v_0, v_1, \ldots, v_{i-1}, v_i$, where $e = v_{i-1} v_i$. Let $T_j, 0 \leq j \leq i$, denote the subtree rooted at v_j, which does not include e_i. Then,

$$\Delta = \sum_e \sum_f x_e x_f / x_g$$

$$= \sum_e \sum_{0 \leq j \leq i} \sum_{f \in T_j} x_e x_f / x_g$$

$$= \sum_e x_e \sum_{0 \leq j \leq i} \frac{\left(\sum_{f \in T_j} x_f \right)}{x_{e_{j-1}}}$$

$$\leq \sum_e x_e \sum_{0 \leq j \leq i} 1, \quad \text{by (3.6)}$$

$$= \sum_e (i + 1) x_e$$

$$\leq (d + 2) \sum_e x_e$$

$$= (d + 2).$$

Thus applying Janson's inequality, we get that the probability that the group A fails to be "hit" is at most $e^{-1/(3 + \log|A|)} \approx 1 - 1/(3 \log|A|)$. $\triangledown$

3.4 Limited Independence

One key objective in modern complexity theory has been to seek ways to reduce the amount of randomness used by probabilistic algorithms. The ultimate objective of course would be to remove the randomness altogether, leading to a deterministic algorithm via a complete *derandomisation* of a randomized algorithm. In this quest, a reduction in randomisation leads to some progress in the form of a partial derandomisation.

One approach to reducing randomness comes from the observation that some algorithms do not need full independence of their source of random bits. We say that a set of random variables $X_1, \ldots, X_n$ is *k-wise independent* if for every $I \subseteq [n]$ with $|I| \le k$,

$$\Pr\left[\prod_{i \in I} X_i = x_i\right] = \prod_{i \in I} \Pr[X_i = x_i].$$

Fully independent variables correspond to n-wise independence.

In this section, we outline the approach of [83] to obtaining Chernoff–Hoeffding-like bounds for the case of random variables with limited dependence, that is, when they are only k-wise independent for some $k < n$.

Consider the *elementary symmetric functions*:

$$S_k(x_1, \ldots, x_n) := \sum_{I \subseteq [n], |I| = k} \prod_{i \in I} x_i.$$

Observe that for $0/1$ variables $x_1, \ldots, x_n$ and an integer $m \ge 0$,

$$\sum_i x_i = m \quad \Leftrightarrow \quad S_k(x_1, \ldots, x_n) = \binom{m}{k}.$$

Also, if $X_1, \ldots, X_n$ are k-wise independent, then

$$\mathrm{E}\left[S_k(X_1, \ldots, X_n)\right] = \mathrm{E}\left[\sum_{|I|=k} \prod_{i \in I} X_i\right]$$

$$= \sum_{|I|=k} \mathrm{E}\left[\prod_{i \in I} X_i\right]$$

$$= \sum_{|I|=k} \prod_{i \in I} \mathrm{E}[X_i].$$

In the last line, we use the k-wise independence of the variables.

Hence, if $X := X_1 + \cdots + X_n$ for binary random variables $X_1, \ldots, X_n$ which are k-wise independent and $\mathrm{E}[X_i] = \Pr[X_i = 1] = p$ for each $i \in [n]$, then

$$\Pr[X > t] = \Pr\left[S_k(X_1, \ldots, X_n) > \binom{t}{k} \right]$$

$$\leq \mathrm{E}\,[S_k(X_1, \ldots, X_n)] / \binom{t}{k}$$

$$= \frac{\binom{n}{k} p^k}{\binom{t}{k}}.$$

In Problem 3.4, you are asked to check that this bound holds also when the variable are not identically distributed and when they take values in the interval $[0, 1]$. This yields the following version of the Chernoff–Hoeffding bound for variables with limited independence.

Theorem 3.5. *Let* $X_1, \ldots, X_n$ *be random variables with* $0 \leq X_i \leq 1$ *and* $\mathrm{E}[X_i] = p_i$ *for each* $i \in [n]$. *Let* $X := \sum_i X_i$ *and set* $\mu := \mathrm{E}[X]$ *and* $p := \mu/n$. *Then, for any* $\delta > 0$, *if* $X_1, \ldots, X_n$ *are* k-*wise independent for* $k \geq \hat{k} := \lceil \mu\delta/(1-p) \rceil$,

$$\Pr\,[X \geq \mu(1+\delta)] \leq \binom{n}{\hat{k}} p^{\hat{k}} \Big/ \binom{\mu(1+\delta)}{\hat{k}}.$$

Exercise 3.7. *Check that this bound is better than the Chernoff–Hoeffding bound* $e^{-\delta^2\mu/3}$ *derived in the previous chapter.*

Another approach due to Bellare and Rompel [4] goes via the kth *moment inequality*:

$$\Pr[|X - \mu| > t] = \Pr[(X - \mu)^k > t^k], \quad \text{since } k \text{ is even}$$

$$< \frac{\mathrm{E}[(X - \mu)^k]}{t^k}, \quad \text{by Markov's inequality.} \quad (3.7)$$

To estimate $\mathrm{E}[(X - \mu)^k]$, we observe that by expanding and using linearity of expectation, we only need to compute $\mathrm{E}[\prod_{i \in S}(X_i - \mu_i)]$ for multisets S of size k. By the k-wise independence property, this is the same as $\mathrm{E}[\prod_{i \in S}(\hat{X}_i - \mu_i)]$, where $\hat{X}_i, i \in [n]$, are fully independent random variables with the same marginals as $X_i, i \in [n]$. Turning the manipulation on its head, we now use Chernoff–Hoeffding bounds on $\hat{X} := \sum_i \hat{X}_i$:

$$E[(\hat{X} - \mu)^k] = \int_0^\infty \Pr[(\hat{X} - \mu)^k > t]dt$$

$$= \int_0^\infty \Pr[|\hat{X} - \mu| > t^{1/k}]dt$$

$$< \int_0^\infty e^{-2t^{2/k}/n}dt, \quad \text{using Chernoff–Hoeffding bounds}$$

$$= (n/2)^{k/2}\frac{k}{2}\int_0^\infty e^{-y}y^{k/2-1}dy$$

$$= (n/2)^{k/2}\frac{k}{2}\Gamma(k/2 - 1)$$

$$= (n/2)^{k/2}(k/2)!$$

Now using Stirling's approximation for $n!$ gives the estimate

$$E[(\hat{X} - \mu)^k] \le 2e^{1/6k}\sqrt{\pi t}\left(\frac{nk}{e}\right)^{k/2},$$

which, in turn, plugged into (3.7) gives the following version of a tail estimate valid under limited, that is, k-wise dependence:

$$\Pr[|X - \mu| > t] \le C_k \left(\frac{nk}{t^2}\right)^{k/2},$$

where $C_k := 2\sqrt{\pi k}e^{1/6k} \le 1.0004$.

3.5 Markov Dependence

We begin by recalling a few standard definitions concerning Markov chains.

3.5.1 Definitions

A Markov chain M is defined by a state space U and a stochastic transition matrix P (i.e. $\sum_x P(x, y) = 1$). Starting with an initial distribution q on U, it determines a sequence of random variables $X_i, i \ge 1$, as follows: for $n \ge 1$ and any $x_1, \ldots, x_n, x_{n+1} \in U$,

$$\Pr[X_1 = x_1] = q(x_1)$$

and

$$\Pr[X_{n+1} = x_{n+1} \mid X_1 = x_1, \ldots, X_n = x_n]$$
$$= \Pr[X_{n+1} = x_{n+1} \mid X_n = x_n] = P(x_{n+1}, x_n).$$

A distribution π on S is called *stationary* for M if $\pi P = P$. Under a technical condition called *aperiodicity*, a Markov chain whose state space is connected has a unique stationary distribution. The aperiodicity condition can usually be made to hold in all the applications we consider here. For more details on these conditions and a careful, but friendly, introduction to Markov chains, see for instance [41].

The general theory of Markov chains (see for instance [41]) shows that under these conditions, the Markov chain, started at any point in the state space, eventually converges to the stationary distribution in the limit. The rate of convergence is determined by the so-called *eigenvalue* gap of the transition matrix P of the Markov chain. Since the matrix is stochastic, the largest eigenvalue is $\lambda_1 = 1$ and the general theory of non-negative matrices implies that the second eigenvalue λ_2 is strictly less than 1. The eigenvalue gap is $\epsilon := \lambda_1 - \lambda_2 = 1 - \lambda_2$.

3.5.2 Statement of the Bound

Let $X_1, X_2, \ldots, X_n$ be a sequence generated by a Markov chain with eigenvalue gap ϵ starting from an initial distribution q. Let f be a non-negative function on the state space of M, and let $F_n := \sum_{i \in [n]} f(X_n)$. By the convergence to stationarity of the Markov chain, we know that $\lim_{n \to \infty} F_n/n = \mathrm{E}[f]$. The following theorem due independently to Gillman [36] and Kahale [48] gives a quantitative bound on this convergence.

Theorem 3.6. *Let $X_1, X_2, \ldots, X_n$ be a sequence generated by a Markov chain with eigenvalue gap ϵ starting from an initial distribution q. For a non-negative function f on the state space of M, let $F_n := \sum_{i \in [n]} f(X_n)$. Then*

$$\Pr[|F_n - n\mathrm{E}[f]| > t] \le C_{\gamma,\epsilon,n,q} \exp\left(-\epsilon \frac{t^2}{cn}\right),$$

where c is an absolute constant and $C_{\gamma,\epsilon,n,q}$ is a rational function. In particular, taking $f := \chi_S$, the characteristic function of a subset S of the state space, and letting $T_n := \sum_{i \in [n]} \chi_S(X_i)$ denote the number of times the chain is in state S,

$$\Pr[|T_n - n\pi(S)| > t] \le C_{\gamma,\epsilon,n,q} \exp\left(-\epsilon \frac{t^2}{cn}\right).$$

Note that this is very similar to the usual Chernoff bound, except for the rational term and, more importantly, the appearance of the eigenvalue gap in the exponent.

3.5.3 Application: Probability Amplification

Let $f : \{0, 1\}^n \to \{0, 1\}$ be a function that is computed by a randomized algorithm A that takes as input the argument $x \in \{0, 1\}$ at which f has to be evaluated and also a sequence r of n random bits. Suppose the algorithm A is guaranteed to compute f correctly with a constant probability bounded away from $1/2$, say,

$$\Pr_r[A(x, r) = f(x)] \geq 3/4.$$

We want to *amplify* the success probability, that is, provide an algorithm $\hat{A}$ that computes f correctly with probability arbitrarily close to 1.

The standard way to do this is by repetition: make k runs of algorithm A and take the majority outcome. Each run of the algorithm is independent of the previous one and uses n fresh independent random bits. What is the success probability of the resulting algorithm? Recall the standard application of the Chernoff bound in the previous chapter: let $X_1, \ldots, X_n$ be indicator random variables with $X_i = 1$ if and only if algorithm A computes f correctly on the ith invocation, and set $X := \sum_i X_i$. The Chernoff bound yields

$$\Pr[X < k/2] \leq e^{-k/8}.$$

Thus to achieve an error probability of at most δ, we can take $k = O(\log \frac{1}{\delta})$.

We shall now describe an algorithm that achieves similar amplification of probability, but with the advantage that the algorithm will be significantly more efficient in its use of randomness as a resource. The preceding algorithm uses a total of nk random bits. The algorithm we describe next will use only $O(n + k)$ random bits to achieve very similar error probability.

To do this we start with an *expander* graph G on the vertex set $\{0, 1\}^n$, the underlying probability space of the original algorithm A. Expander graphs are very useful in many different areas of algorithms and complexity. This example is typical and can be viewed as an introduction to their uses. Here, we will only state the properties we need. The expander graph G is regular of constant degree d. The expansion property is that any subset A of the vertices of size at most $|V(G)|/2$ has a neighbourhood of size at least $\gamma |A|$ for some positive constant γ.

There is an equivalent algebraic characterisation which is more directly of use to us here. Consider the simple random walk on the graph G: start at any vertex and choose the next vertex uniformly at random from all the neighbours. This defines a Markov chain $M(G)$ with state space consisting of the vertices of G whose unique stationary distribution is the uniform distribution. The expansion property of G translates equivalently into the property that the Markov chain $M(G)$ has an eigenvalue gap $\epsilon > 0$; that is, the first eigenvalue is 1 and the second is bounded from above by $1 - \epsilon$.

We are now in a position to state our algorithm and analyse it using the Chernoff–Hoeffding bound for Markov chains. The algorithm $\tilde{A}$ is as follows:

1. Pick a point $r_1 := \in \{0, 1\}$ at random. Then starting at r_1, execute a random walk on G: $r_1, r_2, \ldots, r_k$.
2. Run algorithm A for k times, using these bits as the random source,

$$A(x, r_1), A(x, r_2), \ldots, A(x, r_k),$$

and take the majority outcome.

To analyse the success probability of the algorithm $\tilde{A}$, we introduce, as before, the indicators X_i', $i \in [k]$, with $X_i' = 1$ if the algorithm is correct on trial i and 0 otherwise. Now, since r_1 is picked according to the stationary distribution, the marginal distribution of each r_i, $i \in k$, separately is also the stationary distribution which is uniform. Hence, $\Pr[X_i' = 1] \geq 3/4$ for each $i \in [k]$, and so if $X' := \sum_{i \in [k]} X_i'$, then $E[X'] \geq 3/4k$. So far the analysis is identical to what we saw before.

The hitch is in the fact that whereas the indicators $X_1, \ldots, X_k$ were independent before due to the fresh choice of random bits every time the algorithm A is rerun, this time, the indicators $X_1', \ldots, X_k'$ are *not* independent because the sequence $r_1, \ldots, r_k$ is chosen by a random walk; thus, each r_i depends heavily on its predecessor r_{i-1}. This is the place where Theorem 3.6 kicks in. Let $S := \{r \in \{0, 1\}^n \mid A(x, r) = f(x)\}$. Note that since the stationary distribution π is uniform, $\pi(S) \geq 3/4$. Applying Theorem 3.6, we get

$$\Pr[X' < 1/2k] \leq e^{-c\epsilon k},$$

for some constant $c > 0$. This is essentially the same error probability as we had for algorithm $\hat{A}$ with the independent repetitions except for constant factors in the exponent. However, in this case, the number of random bits used by algorithm $\tilde{A}$ is $O(n + k)$ compared with nk bits needed by algorithm $\hat{A}$.

Exercise 3.8. *Work out the number of bits used by algorithm $\tilde{A}$ and compare with the naive one (i.e. k independent runs of algorithm A). Note the role played by the fact that G is a constant-degree graph.*

Exercise 3.9. *Work out the constant in the exponent of the error bound in terms of the constants in Theorem 3.6.*

3.6 Pointers to the Literature

The results in Section 3.1 are from [27], where negative dependence is treated at greater length. A plethora of versions of Chernoff–Hoeffding bounds for limited independence are given in [83], with applications to reducing randomness requirements of algorithms. Stronger versions of Theorem 3.2 are given in [44] with more applications. Gillman [36] gives more applications of Theorem 3.6. Kahale [48] gives almost tight versions of the bound for Markov chains and compares them with the bounds of Gillman. The applications of Examples 3.2 and 3.3 are from [76] and [42], while that of Example 3.4 is from [16]. The results of Section 3.2 are from [44].

3.7 Problems

Problem 3.1. Let $X_i, i \in [n]$, be random variables such that for any subset $I \subseteq [n]$ and any $t > 0$, the distribution of $X_i, i \in I$, conditioned on $\sum_{i \in I} X_i = t$ is

- conditionally independent of any other variables,
- *stochastically increasing* in t; that is, for any non-decreasing f,
  $\mathrm{E}[f(X_i, i \in I) \mid \sum_{i \in I} X_i = y]$ is increasing in t.

Further, suppose the distribution of $X_i, i \in [n]$, is concentrated on the event $\sum_{i \in [n]} X_i = c$ for some constant c; that is, these are the only points with non-zero probability mass. Then $X_i, i \in [n]$, are negatively associated. Deduce that the arc variables $L_i, i \in [n]$, in Example 3.4 are negatively associated. ▽

Problem 3.2 (Negative regression). A set of random variables $X_1, \ldots, X_n$ satisfy the *negative regression* condition $(-R)$ if for any two disjoint index sets $I, J \subseteq [n]$ and any non-decreasing function f,

$$\mathrm{E}[f(X_i, i \in I) \mid X_j = a_j, j \in J] \tag{3.8}$$

is non-increasing in each $a_j, j \in J$.

1. Show that if $(-R)$ holds, then $\mathrm{E}\left[\prod_i f_i(X_i)\right] \leq \prod_i \mathrm{E}[f_i(X_i)]$ for any non-decreasing functions $f_i, i \in [n]$.

2. Deduce that the Chernoff–Hoeffding bound applies to variables satisfying $(-R)$. ▽

Problem 3.3 (Permutations). Recall the following problem on permutations encountered in the analysis of treaps (Problem 2.7): a position i in a permutation σ of $[n]$ is "checked" if $\sigma(j) < \sigma(i)$ for all $j < i$. Let σ be a permutation chosen uniformly at random, and let X_i, $i \in [n]$, be indicator variables for whether a position is checked. Show that these variables satisfy $(-R)$. ▽

Problem 3.4. Prove Theorem 3.5. Also derive a bound on the lower tail. ▽

Problem 3.5 (Subgraph counts). Consider the random graph $G(n, p)$ and let us consider the number of occurrences $X(H)$ of the number of occurrences of H in G. Define

$$\phi_H = \phi_H(n, p) := \min\{E[X_{H'}] \mid H' \subseteq H, e_{H'} > 0\}.$$

Note that $\phi_H \approx \min_{H' \subseteq H, e_{H'} > 0} n^{v'_H} p^{e'_H}$, where v_H is the number of vertices and e_H the number of edges of a graph H. Show that for any fixed graph H (with at least one edge), $\Pr[X_H = 0] \leq \exp(-\Theta(\phi_H))$. ▽

Problem 3.6 (Sampling with reduced randomness [83]). Recall the problem of estimating the fraction $f^* := |W|/|U|$ of elements of a special subset W of a large universal set U. The approach is to take a random sample S from U and estimate f^* by $\hat{f} := |W \cap S|/|S|$. Investigate the possibility of reducing the randomness requirements of this algorithm using Theorem 3.5 or Theorem 3.6. ▽

Problem 3.7 (Fractional chromatic number of Kneser graphs). Consider the *Kneser graphs* $K(n, d)$ whose vertex set is $\binom{[n]}{d}$ and whose edge set is $\{(A, B) \mid A \cap B = \emptyset\}$. Compute bounds on $\Delta(K(n, d))$, $\chi(K(n, d))$ and $\chi^*(K(n, d))$. ▽

4

Interlude: Probabilistic Recurrences

Karp [49] developed an attractive framework for the analysis of randomized algorithms. Suppose we have a randomized algorithm that, on input x, performs "work" $a(x)$ and then produces a subproblem of size $H(x)$, which is then solved by recursion. One can analyse the performance of the algorithm by writing down a "recurrence":

$$T(x) = a(x) + T(H(x)). \tag{4.1}$$

Superficially this looks just the same as the usual analysis of algorithms via recurrence relations. However, the crucial difference is that in contrast with deterministic algorithms, the size of the subproblem produced here, $H(x)$ is a random variable, and so (4.1) is a *probabilistic recurrence* equation.

What does one mean by the solution of such a probabilistic recurrence? The solution $T(x)$ is itself a random variable and we want as much information about its distribution as possible. While a complete description of the exact distribution is usually neither possible nor really necessary, the "correct" useful analogue to the deterministic solution is a concentration of measure result for $T(x)$. Of course, to do this, one needs some information on the distribution of the subproblem $H(x)$ generated by the algorithm. Karp gives a very easy-to-apply framework that requires only the bare minimum of information on the distribution of $H(x)$, namely, (a bound on) the expectation, and yields a concentration result for $T(x)$. Suppose that in (4.1), we have $E[H(x)] \leq m(x)$ for some function $0 \leq m(x) \leq x$. Consider the "deterministic" version of (4.1) obtained by replacing the random variable $H(x)$ by the deterministic bound $m(x)$:

$$u(x) = a(x) + u(m(x)). \tag{4.2}$$

The solution to this equation is $u(x) = \sum_{i \geq 0} a(m^i(x))$, where $m^0(x) := 0$ and $m^{i+1}(x) = m(m^i(x))$. Karp gives a concentration result around this value $u(x)$.

Theorem 4.1 (Karp's first theorem). *Suppose that in (4.1), we have* $E[H(x)] \leq m(x)$ *for some function* $0 \leq m(x) \leq x$ *and such that* $a(x), m(x), m(x)/x$ *are all non-decreasing. Then*

$$\Pr[T(x) > u(x) + ta(x)] \leq \left(\frac{m(x)}{x}\right)^t.$$

We have stated the result in the simplest memorable form that captures the essence and is essentially correct. However, technically, the statement of Theorem 4.1 is actually not quite accurate and we have omitted some continuity conditions on the functions involved. These conditions usually hold in all cases where we apply the theorem. Moreover, as shown in [18], some of these conditions can be discarded at the cost of only slightly weakening the bound. For instance, we can discard the condition that $m(x)/x$ is non-decreasing; in that case, the bound on the right-hand side can be essentially replaced by $\left(\max_{0 \leq y \leq x} \frac{m(y)}{y}\right)^t$.

Also, in the preceding formulation, we assumed that the distribution of $H(x)$, the size of the derived subproblem, depends only on the input size x. Karp [49] gives a more general formulation where the subproblem is allowed to depend on the actual input instance. Suppose we have a "size" function s on inputs, and on processing an input z, we expend work $a(s(z))$ and get a subproblem $H(z)$ such that $E[s(H(z))] \leq m(s(z))$. The probabilistic recurrence is now

$$T(z) = a(s(z)) + T(H(z)).$$

By considering $T'(x) := \max_{s(z)=x} T(z)$, one can bound this by a recurrence of the earlier form and apply the theorem to give exactly the same solution. Thus we can apply the theorem per se even in this more general situation.

We illustrate the ease of applicability of this cookbook-style recipe by some examples (taken from Karp's paper).

Example 4.1 (Selection). Hoare's classic algorithm for finding the kth smallest element in an n-element set S proceeds as follows: Pick a random element $r \in S$ and by comparing each element in $S \setminus r$ with r, partition $S \setminus r$ into two subsets $L := \{y \in S \mid y < r\}$ and $U := \{y \in S \mid y > r\}$. Then,

- If $|L| \geq k$, recursively find the kth smallest element in L.
- If $|L| = k - 1$, then return r.
- If $|L| < k - 1$, then recursively find the $k - 1 - |L|$th smallest element in U.

The partitioning step requires $n - 1$ comparisons. It can be shown that the expected size of the subproblem, namely, the size of L or U, is at most $3n/4$, for all k. Thus Karp's theorem can be applied with $m(x) = 3x/4$. We compute

$u(x) \leq 4x$. Thus, if $T(n, k)$ denotes the number of comparisons performed by the algorithm, we have the following concentration result: For all $t \geq 0$,

$$\Pr[T(n, k) > 4n + t(n - 1)] \leq \left(\frac{3}{4}\right)^t.$$

This bound is nearly tight as showed by the following simple argument: Define a *bad* splitter to be one where $n/|U| \geq \log\log n$ or $n/|L| \geq \log\log n$. The probability of this is greater than $2/\log\log n$. The probability of picking $\log\log n$ consecutive bad splitters is $\Omega(1/(\log\log n)^{\log\log n})$. The work done for $\log\log n$ consecutive bad splitters is

$$n + n\left(1 - \frac{1}{\log\log n}\right) + n\left(1 - \frac{1}{\log\log n}\right)^2 + \cdots + n\left(1 - \frac{1}{\log\log n}\right)^{\log\log n},$$

which is $\Omega(n\log\log n)$. Compare this with the previous bound using $t = \log\log n$. $\triangledown$

Example 4.2 (Luby's maximal independent set algorithm). Luby [57] gives a randomized parallel algorithm for constructing a maximal independent set in a graph. The algorithm works in stages: at each stage, the current independent set I (initially the empty set) is augmented by a set of vertices S, and the vertices in S with their neighbours are deleted form the graph. The algorithm terminates when we arrive at the empty graph. Here is the description of one stage of the algorithm:

- Create a set of candidates S as follows: Each vertex v, in parallel, enters S with probability $1/\deg(v)$.
- For every edge uv in the current graph, if both endpoints are in S, discard (i.e. take away from S) the one of lower degree. (Ties are resolved arbitrarily.) The resulting set S is added to the current independent set I.
- All vertices from S and their neighbours are deleted from the graph.

Clearly the algorithm produces a maximal independent set I. The work performed at each iteration is proportional to the number of edges in the current graph. Luby showed that at each stage, the expected number of edges deleted is at least one-eighth of the number of edges in the graph. If $T(G)$ is the number of stages the algorithm runs and $T'(G)$ is the total amount of work done, then we get the concentration results:

$$\Pr[T(G) > \log_{8/7} n + t] \leq \left(\frac{7}{8}\right)^t,$$

$$\Pr[T'(G) > (8 + t)n] \leq \left(\frac{7}{8}\right)^t. \qquad \triangledown$$

Example 4.3 (Tree contraction). Miller and Reif [71] give a randomized *tree contraction* algorithm that starts with an n-node tree representing an arithmetic expression and repeatedly applies a randomized contraction operation that provides a new tree representing a modified arithmetic expression. The input is a binary (or any constant-degree) rooted tree. The algorithm performs a set of contraction steps, each consisting of a rake operation and a compress operation in any order. The rake operation deletes all the leaf nodes in parallel. The compress operation finds an independent set of unary nodes and splices out the selected nodes. The process eventually reaches a one-node tree and terminates.

The work performed in the contraction step can be taken to be proportional to the number of nodes in the tree. Miller and Reif show that when applied to a tree with n nodes, the contraction step results in a tree of size at most $4n/5$. However the distribution of the size may depend on the original tree, not just the original size. Define the size function here to be the number of nodes in the tree in order to apply the more general framework. Let $T(z)$ and $T'(z)$ denote the number of iterations and the total work respectively when the contraction algorithm is applied to tree z. Then, Karp's theorem gives the measure concentration results:

$$\Pr[T(z) > \log_{5/4} n + t] \le (4/5)^t$$

and

$$\Pr[T'(z) > (5 + t)n] \le (4/5)^t. \qquad\qquad \triangledown$$

Under the weak assumptions on the distribution of the input, Karp's first theorem is essentially tight. However, if one has additional information on the distribution of the subproblem, say, some higher moments, then one can get sharper results.

Karp also gives an extension of the framework for the very useful case when the algorithm might generate more than one subproblem. Suppose we have an algorithm that, on input x, performs work $a(x)$ and then generates a fixed number $k \ge 1$ subproblems $H_1(x), \dots, H_k(x)$, each a random variable. This corresponds to the probabilistic recurrence:

$$T(x) = a(x) + T(H_1(x)) + \cdots + T(H_k(x)). \qquad (4.3)$$

To obtain a concentration result in this case, Karp uses a different method which requires a certain condition.

Theorem 4.2 (Karp's second theorem). *Suppose that in (4.3), we have that for all possible values* $(x_1, \ldots, x_k)$ *of the tuple* $(H_1(x), \ldots, H_k(x))$, *we have*

$$E[T(x)] \geq \sum_i E[T(x_i)]. \tag{4.4}$$

Then, we have the concentration result: for all x and all t > 0,

$$\Pr[T(x) > (t+1)E[T(x)]] < e^{-t}.$$

Condition (4.4) says that the expected work in processing *any* subproblems that can result from the original one can never exceed the expected cost of processing the original instance. This is a very strong assumption and, unfortunately, in many cases of interest, for example in computational geometry, it does not hold. Consequently, the theorem is somewhat severely limited in its applicability. A rare case in which the condition is satisfied is for the following.

Example 4.4 (Quicksort). Hoare's quicksort algorithm is a true classic in computer science: to sort a set S of n items, we proceed as in the selection algorithm given earlier: select a random element $r \in S$ and by comparing it with every other element, partition S as into the sets L of elements less than x and U, the set of elements at least as big as r. Then, recursively, sort L and U. Let $Q(n)$ denote the number of comparisons performed by quicksort on a set of n elements. Then $Q(n)$ satisfies the probabilistic recurrence:

$$T(n) = n - 1 + Q(H_1(n)) + Q(H_2(n)),$$

where $H_1(n) = |L|$ and $H_2(n) = |U|$. For quicksort we have "closed-form" solutions for $q_n := E[Q(n)]$, which imply that $q_n \geq q_i + q_{n-i-1} + n - 1$ for any $0 \leq i < n$, which is just the condition needed to apply Karp's second theorem. Thus we get the concentration result:

$$\Pr[Q(n) > (t+1)q_n] \leq e^{-t}.$$

Actually one can get a much stronger bound by applying Karp's first theorem suitably. Charge each comparison made in quicksort to the non-pivot element, and let $T(\ell)$ denote the number of comparisons charged to a fixed element when quicksort is applied to a list ℓ. Use the natural size function $s(\ell) := |\ell|$, which gives the number of elements in the list. Then we have the recurrence $T(\ell) = 1 + T(H(\ell))$, where $s(H(\ell)) = |\ell|/2$ since the sublist containing the fixed element (when it is not the pivot) has size uniformly distributed in $[0, |\ell|]$. So applying Karp's first theorem, we have that for $t \geq 1$,

$$\Pr[T(\ell) > (t+1)\log|\ell|] \leq (1/2)^{t\log|\ell|} = |\ell|^{-t}.$$

Thus any fixed element in a list of n elements is charged at most $(t+1)\log n$ comparisons with probability at least $1 - n^{-t}$. The total number of comparisons is therefore at most $(t+1)n\log n$ with probability at least $1 - n^{t-1}$.

In a later section we shall get a somewhat stronger and provably optimal bound on the concentration. ∇

It would naturally be of great interest to extend the range of Karp's second theorem by eliminating the restrictive hypothesis. For instance, it would be of interest to extend the theorem under the kind of assumptions in Karp's first theorem.

4.1 Problems

Problem 4.1. Consider the following parallel and distributed vertex-colouring algorithm [58]. Every vertex u in a graph G initially has a list of colours $L_u := [\Delta(G)]$. The algorithm is in rounds. In each round the following happens:

- Every vertex not yet coloured wakes up with probability $1/2$.
- Every vertex that woke up picks a tentative colour uniformly at random from its own list of colours.
- If t_u is the tentative colour picked by u, and no neighbour of u picked t_u, then u colours itself with t_u.
- The colour list of each uncoloured vertex in the graph is updated by removing all colours successfully used by neighbours.
- All uncoloured vertices go back to sleep.

(a) Show that the algorithm computes a legal colouring.
(b) Show that in every round, each uncoloured vertex colours itself with probability at least $1/4$.
(c) Show that within $O(\log|V(G)|)$ many rounds the graph will be coloured with high probability. ∇

Problem 4.2. Let $X_0, X_1, \ldots$ be positive integer random variables such that $X_0 = N$ and such that

$$E[X_i | X_{i-1}] \leq cX_{i-1} \quad \text{for all } i > 1 \text{ and some } c \in (0, 1).$$

Show

- $E[X_t] \leq c^t N$. (HINT: $E[X] = E[E[X|Y]]$; see Chapter 5.)
- With high probability, $X_t = 0$ for $t = O(\log N)$. (HINT: Use Markov's inequality.)
- Compare your result with the theory developed in this chapter. $\triangledown$

5

Martingales and the Method of Bounded Differences

The Chernoff–Hoeffding bounds provide very sharp concentration estimates when the random variable X under consideration can be expressed as the sum $X = X_1 + \cdots + X_n$ of independent and bounded random variables. However in many applications, to do this might be very difficult or impossible. It would therefore be useful to obtain sharp concentration results for the case when X is some complicated function of not necessarily independent variables. Such a generalisation would be useful in many diverse contexts but especially in the analysis of randomized algorithms where the parameters that characterise the behaviour of the algorithm are the result of a complicated interaction among a base set of (often non-independent) random variables. Our goal then is to study the case when

$$X := f(X_1, X_2, \ldots, X_n),$$

where f is a function that may not even be explicitly specified in a "closed form". We seek a set of conditions on f so that one can assert that the probability of a large deviation of f from its expected value is exceedingly small – ideally, exponentially small in the amount of the deviation. In general, we want to be able to do this even without assuming that the X_i's are independent.

We will present a number of such inequalities, all of which rest upon a well-studied concept of probability theory known as *martingales*. We shall see that once the appropriate concept to replace independence is properly formulated, the proofs of these inequalities are quite similar to the basic structure of the proofs of the Chernoff–Hoeffding bounds we have already seen.

5.1 Review of Conditional Probabilities and Expectations

The concept of a martingale requires a good understanding of the notions of conditional probability and expectation, so we first provide a quick review from an elementary standpoint. The reader familiar with these concepts can skip this section entirely.

Given two events $\mathcal{E}$ and $\mathcal{F}$ in a probability space with measure $\Pr$, the *conditional probability* of $\mathcal{E}$ with respect to $\mathcal{F}$ is defined by

$$\Pr[\mathcal{E} \mid \mathcal{F}] := \frac{\Pr[\mathcal{E} \wedge \mathcal{F}]}{\Pr[\mathcal{F}]},$$

provided that $\Pr[\mathcal{F}] \neq 0$. If $\Pr[\mathcal{F}] = 0$, then by convention we shall set $\Pr[\mathcal{E} \mid \mathcal{F}] = 0$.

Often we will be interested in events of the form $X = a$, that a random variable X takes the value a or that a sequence $X_1, \ldots, X_n$ takes the values $a_1, \ldots, a_n$ respectively. For economy of notation, we shall use the vector bold-face notation to stand for a finite or infinite sequence of the appropriate type. Thus a sequence of variables $X_1, X_2, \ldots$ will be denoted by $\boldsymbol{X}$ and a sequence of real values $a_1, a_2, \ldots$ by $\boldsymbol{a}$. When given such a sequence, we shall use the subscript n to denote the prefix of length n; thus, $\boldsymbol{X}_n$ will denote $X_1, \ldots, X_n$ and $\boldsymbol{a}_n$ will denote $a_1, \ldots, a_n$. If n is less than the starting index of the sequence under consideration, the prefix sequence is empty. With these conventions the event $X_1 = a_1, \ldots, X_n = a_n$ can be abbreviated by $\boldsymbol{X}_n = \boldsymbol{a}_n$. We can always assume that such an event occurs with non-zero probability by discarding from the domain the values for which it is zero.

Likewise we will make use of the shorthand notation $\boldsymbol{X}^n$ (respectively $\boldsymbol{a}^n$) to denote the remainder of a (possibly infinite) sequence; that is, $\boldsymbol{X}^n = X_n, X_{n+1}, \ldots$ (respectively $\boldsymbol{a}^n = a_n, a_{n+1}, \ldots$).

The *conditional expectation* of a random variable Y with respect to an event $\mathcal{E}$ is defined by

$$\mathrm{E}[Y \mid \mathcal{E}] := \sum_b b \cdot \Pr[Y = b \mid \mathcal{E}]. \tag{5.1}$$

In particular, if the event $\mathcal{E}$ is $X = a$, this equation defines a function f, namely,

$$f(a) := \mathrm{E}[Y \mid X = a].$$

Thus, $\mathrm{E}[Y \mid X]$ is a random variable, namely, the variable $f(X)$. In the same way, if the event $\mathcal{E}$ in (5.1) is $\boldsymbol{X} = \boldsymbol{a}$, we have a multivariate function

$$f(\boldsymbol{a}) := \mathrm{E}[Y \mid \boldsymbol{X} = \boldsymbol{a}],$$

and $\mathrm{E}[Y \mid \boldsymbol{X}]$ can be regarded as the random variable $f(\boldsymbol{X})$.

Regarding $E[Y \mid X]$ as a random variable, we can ask what is its expectation? The answer involves some fundamental properties of conditional expectation that are listed in the next proposition and whose verification we leave as an exercise.

Proposition 5.1. *Let X, Y and Z be random variables defined on a probability space. Then, for arbitrary functions f and g,*

$$E[E[f(X)g(X, Y) \mid X]] = E[f(X)E[g(X, Y)] \mid X].$$

Also,

$$E[X] = E[E[X|Y]]$$

and

$$E[X \mid Z] = E[E[X \mid Y, Z] \mid Z].$$

The formal verification of these is left as an exercise to the reader. Nevertheless it is perhaps appropriate to give an intuitive justification of these formulae that at first might appear somewhat obscure. The first equality is based on the simple fact that

$$E[f(X)g(X, Y) \mid X = a] = f(a)E[g(X, Y) \mid X = a],$$

which simply says that once the value of X is given, $f(X)$ becomes a constant and can be taken out of the expectation. The second equality states that there are two ways to compute an average. Suppose that X is a random variable representing the height of individuals of a given population, say, of all people in the world. And suppose that Y is the country of an individual. In order to compute $E[X]$ – the average height of a human being – we can either do it directly or proceed as follows: First, compute the average height of people living in each country. For a given country y this is given by $E[X|Y = y]$. Second, compute the average of these average heights. If p_i is the fraction of the world population living in country y_i, then this average of averages is

$$E[E[X|Y]] = \sum_i p_i E[X|Y = y_i] = E[X].$$

The third equality is the same as the second one, restricted to a particular subspace. In our example Z could represent the sex of an individual. Thus, $E[X|Z]$ is the average height of a human being of a given sex. Again, this can be computed either directly or on a country-by-country basis:

$$E[E[X \mid Y, Z] \mid Z] = \sum_i p_i E[X|Y = y_i, Z] = E[X|Z].$$

Proposition 5.1 generalises smoothly to the multivariate case. Once again we leave the verification as an exercise.

Proposition 5.2 (Fundamental facts about conditional expectation). *Let X, Y and Z be random variables defined on a probability space. For arbitrary functions f and g,*

$$E[E[f(X)g(X, Y) \mid X]] = E[f(X)E[g(X, Y) \mid X]]. \tag{5.2}$$

Also,

$$E[X] = E[E[X \mid Y]] \tag{5.3}$$

and

$$E[X \mid Z] = E[E[X \mid Y, Z] \mid Z]. \tag{5.4}$$

These facts will be heavily used in this chapter.

5.2 Martingales and Azuma's Inequality

Martingales are a well-studied concept in classical probability. Here we will develop them in a discrete setting in the simplest form, which is sufficient for our purposes.

Definition 5.1. *A* martingale *is a sequence of random variables $X_0, X_1, \ldots$ such that*

$$E[X_i \mid X_0, X_1, \ldots, X_{i-1}] = X_{i-1}, \quad i \geq 1.$$

With the vector notation, the martingale condition is succinctly expressed as

$$E[X_i \mid X_{i-1}] = X_{i-1}, \quad i \geq 1.$$

The next examples and exercises should help clarify this definition.

Example 5.1. A fair coin is flipped n times. Let $X_i \in \{-1, 1\}$ denote the outcome of the ith trial. Let $S_0 := 0$ and $S_n := \sum_{i \leq n} X_i$. The variables $S_i, i \geq 0$, define a martingale. First, observe that they satisfy the so-called Markov property, $E[S_n \mid S_0, \ldots, S_{n-1}] = E[S_n \mid S_{n-1}]$, which intuitively says that the future outcome depends only on the current state. Hence,

$$
\begin{aligned}
E[S_n|S_0, \ldots, S_{n-1}] &= E[S_n|S_{n-1}] \\
&= E[S_{n-1} + X_n|S_{n-1}] \\
&= S_{n-1} + E[X_n|S_{n-1}] \\
&= S_{n-1} + E[X_n], \quad \text{by independence of the coin tosses} \\
&= S_{n-1}, \quad \text{since } E[X_n] = 0.
\end{aligned}
$$

Think of a gambler who starts with an initial fortune of $S_0 := 0$ and repeatedly bets an amount of 1 unit on a coin toss. Thus his fortune can go up or down by 1 unit equiprobably on each toss. His fortune after n tosses is S_n. Think of the sequence $S_0, S_1, \ldots$ as a sequence of dependent random variables. Before his nth wager, the gambler knows only the numerical values of $S_0, \ldots, S_{n-1}$, but can only guess at the future $S_n, S_{n+1}, \ldots$. If the game is fair, then conditional on the past information, he will expect no change in his present capital on average. This is exactly the martingale condition.   ▽

The following definition is central.

Definition 5.2 (Bounded differences). *Let* $X_0, X_1, \ldots$ *be a martingale. The* X_i's *satisfy the* bounded difference condition *with parameters* a_i *and* b_i *if*

$$
a_i \le X_i - X_{i-1} \le b_i
$$

for some reals $a, b_i, i > 0$.

Exercise 5.1. *Consider the infinite lattice* $N \times N$. *A pebble starting from the origin walks at random, each time moving equiprobably to one of the four neighbours. Let* X_i *be the distance from the origin, measured as the number of hops (Manhattan distance). Show that this defines a martingale sequence satisfying the bounded difference condition.*

The following concentration result for martingales is known as the Azuma–Hoeffding inequality. It will provide us with a basic tool for our generalisation.

Theorem 5.1 (Azuma–Hoeffding inequality). *Let* $X_0, X_1, \ldots$ *be a martingale satisfying the bounded difference condition with parameters* $a_i, b_i, i \ge 1$. *Then,*

$$
\Pr(X_n > X_0 + t), \Pr(X_n < X_0 - t) \le \exp\left(-\frac{2t^2}{\sum_{i \in [n]}(b_i - a_i)^2}\right).
$$

Before proving this theorem some comments are in order. First, note that there is no assumption of independence. Second, if we think of a martingale sequence as keeping track of a process evolving through time – where X_i is the measurement at time i – the bounded difference condition roughly states that the process does not make big jumps. The Azuma–Hoeffding inequality roughly says that if this is so, then it is unlikely that the process wanders very far from its starting point. Note also that $\sum_{i \in [n]} (b_i - a_i)^2$ appears in the denominator, which means that the smaller the values $(b_i - a_i)$, the sharper the concentration.

In the proof of Azuma's inequality we shall use several ideas already encountered in the derivation of various forms of the Chernoff–Hoeffding bounds. The assumption of independence will be replaced by the martingale property, while the assumption that the summands are bounded is replaced by the bounded difference condition.

Now to the proof. We shall prove the statement for the upper tail; the proof for the lower tail is symmetrical with the martingale X replaced by $-X$. To start with, we can assume without loss of generality that $X_0 := 0$. Otherwise we can define the translated sequence $X_i' := X_i - X_0$, which satisfies the conditions equally well. We then apply the Chernoff method starting with Markov's inequality:

$$\Pr(X_n > t) = \Pr(e^{\lambda X_n} > e^{\lambda t}) \tag{5.5}$$
$$\leq \frac{\mathrm{E}[e^{\lambda X_n}]}{e^{\lambda t}}$$

for all $\lambda > 0$. Now we focus on the numerator $\mathrm{E}[e^{\lambda X_n}]$: we want to find a good upper bound in terms of λ and then find the value of λ that minimises the ratio $\mathrm{E}[e^{\lambda X_n}]/e^{\lambda t}$.

We define the *martingale difference sequence*:

$$Y_i := X_i - X_{i-1}, \quad i \geq 1.$$

Note that

$$\mathrm{E}[Y_i \mid X_{i-1}] = 0.$$

Applying the basic equality (5.3), we get

$$\mathrm{E}[e^{\lambda X_n}] = \mathrm{E}[\mathrm{E}[e^{\lambda X_{n-1}} e^{\lambda Y_n} | X_{n-1}]] = \mathrm{E}[e^{\lambda X_{n-1}} \mathrm{E}[e^{\lambda Y_n} | X_{n-1}]]. \tag{5.6}$$

The last equality follows from (5.2).

Now the proof continues by looking for a good upper bound for $\mathrm{E}[e^{\lambda Y_n} | X_{n-1}]$. There are two different ways to find such good upper bounds. The first, to be used in the next lemma, is based on the convexity of the e^x function – a fact already exploited to derive the Hoeffding generalisation of the Chernoff bounds. The second uses a different idea, which we used in section 1.7. This second approach leads to another useful generalisation of the

Chernoff–Hoeffding bounds which we shall call the *the method of bounded variances*, and to which we return in a later chapter.

Lemma 5.1. *Let Z be a random variable such that $E[Z] = 0$ and $a \leq Z \leq b$ for some reals a and b. Then, $E[e^{\lambda Z}] \leq e^{\lambda^2(b-a)^2/8}$.*

Proof. We observe that $e^{\lambda x}$ is convex in the interval (a, b) for any $\lambda > 0$ and hence its graph lies entirely below the line joining $P_a := (a, e^{\lambda a})$ and $P_b := (b, e^{\lambda b})$. Thus, for $a \leq Z \leq b$,

$$e^{\lambda Z} \leq \frac{Z - a}{b - a}e^{\lambda b} + \frac{b - Z}{b - a}e^{\lambda a}.$$

Taking expectations,

$$\begin{aligned}
E[e^{\lambda Z}] &\leq \frac{b}{b - a}e^{\lambda a} - \frac{a}{b - a}e^{\lambda b} \\
&= (1 - p)e^{-py} + pe^{(1-p)y} \\
&= e^{-py}(1 - p + pe^y) \\
&=: e^{f(y)},
\end{aligned}$$

where $p := -a/(b - a)$, $y := \lambda(b - a)$ and $f(x) := -px + \ln(1 - p + pe^x)$.

Now, for some calculus applied to f, we compute $f'(x) = -p + \frac{p}{p+(1-p)e^{-x}}$ and $f''(x) = \frac{p(1-p)e^{-x}}{(p+(1-p)e^{-x})^2} \leq \frac{1}{4}$ (since the geometric mean of p and $(1 - p)e^{-x}$ is at most their arithmetic mean). Also, $f(0) = 0 = f'(0)$ and hence by Taylor's theorem with remainder,

$$f(y) = f(0) + f'(0)y + f''(\xi)\frac{t^2}{2} \leq \frac{1}{8}y^2 = \frac{1}{8}\lambda^2(b - a)^2,$$

where $0 < \xi < y$, which yields the desired inequality. ∎

Proof (Azuma–Hoeffding inequality). We apply the lemma to the random variable

$$Z := (Y_n | X_{n-1}).$$

Z satisfies the hypotheses of the lemma since

$$E[Z] = E[Y_n | X_{n-1}] = E[X_n - X_{n-1} | X_{n-1}] = 0$$

by the martingale property, and the bounded difference condition holds by hypothesis. Therefore,

$$E[e^{\lambda Y_n} | X_{n-1}] \leq e^{\lambda^2(b_n - a_n)^2/8},$$

which, after substituting into Equation (5.6), yields by induction

$$\begin{aligned}
E[e^{\lambda X_n}] &= E[e^{\lambda X_{n-1}} E[e^{\lambda Y_n} | \Sigma_{n-1}]] \\
&\leq E[e^{\lambda X_{n-1}}] \cdot e^{\lambda^2 (b_n - a_n)^2 / 8} \\
&= \prod_{i=1}^{n} e^{\lambda^2 (b_i - a_i)^2 / 8} =: e^{\lambda^2 c / 8},
\end{aligned}$$

where

$$c := \sum_{i=1}^{n} (b_i - a_i)^2.$$

A straightforward application of calculus shows that the ratio $e^{\lambda^2 c / 8} / e^{\lambda t}$ attains the minumum when $\lambda = 4t/c$. Therefore, substituting into Equation (5.5),

$$\begin{aligned}
\Pr(X_n > t) &\leq \min_{\lambda > 0} \frac{E[e^{\lambda X_n}]}{e^{\lambda t}} \\
&\leq \min_{\lambda > 0} e^{\lambda^2 c / 8 - \lambda t} \\
&= \exp\left(-\frac{2t^2}{c}\right),
\end{aligned}$$

which ends the proof of Theorem 5.1. ∎

Exercise 5.2. *Consider the two-dimensional random walk of Exercise 5.1. Compute the probability that after n steps the pebble is at distance $>100\sqrt{n}$ from the origin.*

Exercise 5.3. *If $X := X_1 + \cdots + X_n$ is the sum of n independent random variables with $a_i \leq X_i \leq b_i$ for each $i \in [n]$, then rework the basic Chernoff bound argument using Lemma 5.1 to show that*

$$\Pr[X > E[X] + t], \Pr[X < E[X] - t] \leq \exp\left(-2t^2 / \sum_i (b_i - a_i)^2\right).$$

5.3 Generalising Martingales and Azuma's Inequality

It is useful to generalise the definition of martingale to the case when the random variables under study might depend on another set of random variables.

Definition 5.3. *A sequence of random variables* $Y := Y_0, Y_1, \ldots$ *is a* martingale with respect to another sequence $X := X_0, X_1, \ldots$ *if for each* $i \geq 0$,

$$Y_i = g_i(X_i),$$

for some function g_i, *and*

$$\mathrm{E}[Y_i | X_{i-1}] = Y_{i-1}, \quad i \geq 1.$$

Example 5.2. Suppose that $X_i \in \{0, 1\}$ equiprobably for each $i \in [n]$. Now it is no longer true that $\mathrm{E}[X_i] = 0$. Nevertheless, a martingale can be defined by letting $S_k := \sum_{i \leq k} X_i - k/2$ with $S_0 := 0$. This is a martingale with respect to the sequence $X_1, \ldots, X_n$. The straightforward verification is left as an exercise. ▽

Exercise 5.4. *Let* $X_i \in \{0, 1\}$ $(1 \leq i \leq n)$ *be a set of n variables such that* $\Pr[X_i = 1] = p_i$. *Can you generalise Example 5.2?*

A very important example of this general definition of a martingale is provided by the following definition and lemma.

Definition 5.4. *The* Doob sequence of a function f with respect to a sequence of random variables $X_1, \ldots, X_n$ is defined by

$$Y_i := \mathrm{E}[f | X_i], \quad 0 \leq i \leq n.$$

In particular, $Y_0 := \mathrm{E}[f]$ and $Y_n = f(X_1, \ldots, X_n)$.

Proposition 5.3. *The Doob sequence of a function defines a martingale. That is,*

$$\mathrm{E}[Y_i | X_{i-1}] = Y_{i-1}, \quad 0 \leq i \leq n.$$

This proposition is an immediate consequence of (5.4).

Example 5.3 (Edge exposure martingale). An important special case of Definition 5.4 occurs in the context of the *random graph* $G_{n,p}$. This is the graph with vertex set $[n]$ and each edge $ij, i \neq j$, is present with probability p independently of all other edges. Let $f : \binom{[n]}{2} \to \mathbb{R}$ be a function on the edge set of the complete graph K_n. For instance, f could be the chromatic number or the size of the largest clique. Number the edges from 1 to $\binom{n}{2}$ in some arbitrary order and let $X_j := 1$ if the jth edge is present and 0 otherwise. The Doob sequence of f with respect to the variables $X_j, j \in [\binom{n}{2}]$, is called the *edge exposure martingale*. Intuitively, we are exposing the edges one by one and observing the average value of f under this partial information. ▽

Azuma's inequality can be generalised to a sequence Y which is a martingale with respect to another sequence X of random variables.

Theorem 5.2 (Azuma–Hoeffding inequality – general version). *Let $Y_0, Y_1, \ldots$ be a martingale with respect to the sequence $X_0, X_1, \ldots$. Suppose also that the Y satisfies the bounded difference condition with parameters $a_i, b_i i, i \geq 1$. Then,*

$$\Pr(Y_n > Y_0 + t), \Pr(Y_n < Y_0 - t) \leq \exp\left(-\frac{2t^2}{\sum_{i \in [n]}(b_i - a_i)^2}\right).$$

Proof. The proof is almost identical to that of Theorem 5.1. Assume without loss of generality that $Y_0 := 0$ and define the martingale difference sequence $D_i := Y_i - Y_{i-1}, i \geq 1$. Then $Y_n = Y_{n-1} + D_n$. As before,

$$\Pr(Y_n > t) \leq \min_{\lambda > 0} \frac{E[e^{\lambda Y_n}]}{e^{\lambda t}}.$$

Focus on the numerator $E[e^{\lambda Y_n}]$.

$$\begin{aligned}
E[e^{\lambda Y_n}] &= E[e^{\lambda(Y_{n-1}+D_n)}] \\
&= E[E[e^{\lambda(Y_{n-1}+D_n)} \mid X_{n-1}]] \\
&= E[e^{\lambda Y_{n-1}} E[e^{\lambda D_n} | X_{n-1}]].
\end{aligned}$$

The last line, the only place where the proof differs from that of Theorem 5.1, follows from (5.2) because $Y_{n-1} = g_{n-1}(X_{n-1})$. The proof now proceeds identical to that of Theorem 5.1, provided Lemma 5.1 is invoked for the variables $Z := (D_n | X_{n-1})$. The verification that Z satisfies the hypotheses of Lemma 5.1 is straightforward and is left as an exercise. ∎

Exercise 5.5 (Chernoff bounds for Bernoulli trials). *Let $X_1, \ldots, X_n, X_i \in \{0, 1\}$, be independent trials such that $\Pr[X_i = 1] = p$. Derive the Chernoff–Hoeffding bounds for $X := \sum_{i=1}^{n} X_i$ using Theorem 5.2.*

Exercise 5.6 (Chernoff bounds for Poisson trials). *Let $X_1, \ldots, X_n, X_i \in \{0, 1\}$, be independent trials such that $\Pr[X_i = 1] = p_i$. Derive the Chernoff–Hoeffding bounds for $X := \sum_{i=1}^{n} X_i$ using Theorem 5.2.*

5.4 The Method of Bounded Differences

We shall now see how to apply Azuma's inequality to obtain a very powerful and useful generalisation of the Chernoff–Hoeffding bounds. The link is provided by the Doob martingale from which the following theorem emerges naturally.

Theorem 5.3 (The method of averaged bounded differences). *Let $X_1, \ldots, X_n$ be an arbitrary set of random variables and let f be a function satisfying the property that for each $i \in [n]$, there is a non-negative c_i such that*

$$|E[f|X_i] - E[f|X_{i-1}]| \le c_i. \qquad (5.7)$$

Then,

$$\Pr[f > Ef + t] \le \exp\left(-\frac{2t^2}{c}\right)$$

and

$$\Pr[f < Ef - t] \le \exp\left(-\frac{2t^2}{c}\right),$$

where $c := \sum_{i \le n} c_i^2$.

This theorem is just a restatement of Theorem 5.2 for the special case of the Doob sequence $Y_i := E[f|X_i], 0 \le i \le n$. *Note that the X_i's are not assumed to be independent.*

Some weaker, but often more convenient, versions of this bound will now be deduced.

Definition 5.5 (Averaged Lipschitz condition). *A function f satisfies the* averaged Lipschitz condition *(henceforth ALC) with parameters $c_i, i \in [n]$, with respect to the random variables $X_1, \ldots, X_n$ if for any a_i, a_i',*

$$|E[f|X_{i-1}, X_i = a_i] - E[f|X_{i-1}, X_i = a_i']| \le c_i \qquad (5.8)$$

for $1 \le i \le n$.

In words, the condition ALC in (5.8) states, fix the first $i - 1$ variables to some values, let the ith variable take two different values and set the remaining variables at random (according to the given distribution conditioned on the previous settings). Then the difference between the two corresponding partial averages of f must be bounded uniformly by c_i.

Corollary 5.1 (The method of averaged bounded differences: Alternate take). *Let f satisfy the* ALC *condition with respect to the variables $X_1, \ldots, X_n$ with parameters $c_i, i \in [n]$. Then*

$$\Pr[f > Ef + t] \le \exp\left(-\frac{2t^2}{c}\right)$$

and

$$\Pr[f < Ef - t] \le \exp\left(-\frac{2t^2}{c}\right),$$

where $c := \sum_{i \le n} c_i^2$.

Proof. We shall show that if (5.8) holds then so does (5.7). To see this, expand using total conditional probability,

$$E[f \mid X_{i-1}] = \sum_a E[f \mid X_{i-1}, X_i = a] \Pr[X_i = a \mid X_{i-1}]$$

and write

$$E[f \mid X_i] = \sum_a E[f \mid X_i] \Pr[X_i = a \mid X_{i-1}].$$

Hence,

$$|E[f \mid X_{i-1}] - E[f \mid X_i]|$$

$$= \left| \sum_a (E[f \mid X_{i-1}, X_i = a] - E[f \mid X_i]) \Pr[X_i = a \mid X_{i-1}] \right|$$

$$\leq \sum_a \left| E[f \mid X_{i-1}, X_i = a] - E[f \mid X_i] \right| \Pr[X_i = a \mid X_{i-1}]$$

$$\leq \sum_a c_i \cdot \Pr[X_i = a \mid X_{i-1}]$$

$$= c_i. \qquad \blacksquare$$

Exercise 5.7. *Show that if for each $i \in [n]$,*

$$|E[f \mid X_i] - E[f \mid X_{i-1}]| \leq c_i,$$

then for any a_i, a_i',

$$|E[f \mid X_{i-1}, X_i = a_i] - E[f \mid X_{i-1}, X_i = a_i']| \leq 2c_i.$$

That is, the two alternate takes of the method of averaged bounded differences are virtually the same but for a factor of 2.

A further significant simplification obtains from the following definition.

Definition 5.6. *A function $f(x_1, \ldots, x_n)$ satisfies the* Lipschitz property *or the* bounded differences condition *with constants d_i, $i \in [n]$, if*

$$|f(a) - f(a')| \leq d_i, \qquad (5.9)$$

whenever a and a' differ in just the ith coordinate, $i \in [n]$.

In words, the bounded difference condition states, the difference between the values of f on two inputs that differ in only the ith coordinate is bounded uniformly by d_i. This is exactly like the usual Lipschitz condition in the setting where the underlying metric is the Hamming distance.

Corollary 5.2 (Method of bounded differences). *If f satisfies the Lipschitz property with constants $d_i, i \in [n]$, and $X_1, \ldots, X_n$ are independent random variables, then*

$$\Pr[f > \mathrm{E}f + t] \leq \exp\left(-\frac{2t^2}{d}\right)$$

and

$$\Pr[f < \mathrm{E}f - t] \leq \exp\left(-\frac{2t^2}{d}\right),$$

where $d := \sum_{i \leq n} d_i^2$.

Proof. Recall that X^{i+1} is a shorthand notation for the sequence $X_{i+1}, \ldots, X_n$, and that $X^{i+1} = a^{i+1}$ denotes the componentwise equality for the two sequences. We show that if f satisfies the Lipschitz condition with parameters $c_i, i \in [n]$, then (5.8) holds. To see this, expand using total conditional probability to get

$$\mathrm{E}[f \mid X_{i-1}, X_i = a]$$

$$= \sum_{a_{i+1},\ldots,a_n} \mathrm{E}[f \mid X_{i-1}, X_i = a, X^{i+1} = a^{i+1}]\Pr[X^{i+1} = a^{i+1} \mid X_{i-1}, X_i = a]$$

$$= \sum_{a_{i+1},\ldots,a_n} \mathrm{E}[f \mid X_{i-1}, X_i = a, X^{i+1} = a^{i+1}]$$

$$\times \Pr[X^{i+1} = a^{i+1}], \quad \text{by independence,}$$

$$= \sum_{a_{i+1},\ldots,a_n} f(X_{i-1}, a, a_{i+1}, \ldots, a_n)\Pr[X^{i+1} = a^{i+1}].$$

Put $a := a_i, a_i'$ successively and take the difference. Then

$$|\mathrm{E}[f \mid X_{i-1}, X_i = a_i] - \mathrm{E}[f \mid X_{i-1}, X_i = a_i']|$$

$$= \left| \sum_{a_{i+1},\ldots,a_n} f(X_{i-1}, a_i, a^{i+1}) - f(X_{i-1}, a_i', a^{i+1})\Pr[X^{i+1} = a^{i+1}] \right|$$

$$\leq \sum_{a_{i+1},\ldots,a_n} |f(X_{i-1}, a_i, a_{i+1}, \ldots, a_n)$$

$$- f(X_{i-1}, a_i', a_{i+1}, \ldots, a_n)|\Pr[X^{i+1} = a^{i+1}]$$

$$\leq \sum_{a_{i+1},\ldots,a_n} c_i \cdot \Pr[X^{i+1} = a^{i+1}], \quad \text{by the Lipschitz property,}$$

$$= c_i. \qquad \blacksquare$$

Some comments are in order about the three different versions of the "method of bounded differences".

Corollary 5.2 is usually referred to in the literature as *the* method of bounded differences. This is because it is the most convenient one to apply. The bounded difference condition is very attractive and easy to check. It also makes the result intuitive: if f does not depend on any one argument, then it is not likely to be far from its expectation when the inputs are set at random. However, there are two drawbacks: first the variables $X_1, \ldots, X_n$ must be independent. Second, the parameters d_i in the bounded difference condition might be too large and consequently the bound might turn out too weak to be useful.

It might be the case that the bounded difference condition holds for f with small parameters d_i except for a small set of exceptional instances. In that case, it is unfair to "penalise" f with the "worst-case" larger parameters strictly demanded by the bounded difference condition. Rather, one should take an average, and this is the purpose of the ALC condition. The parameters c_i required for the ALC condition are always bounded by the parameters d_i required for the bounded difference condition, and often $c_i \ll d_i$. In the latter case, the bound obtained from Corollary 5.1, the method of average bounded differences, will be significantly better than that from Corollary 5.2, the method of bounded differences.

Theorem 5.3 is the most powerful version of the method: the parameters required for the martingale differences condition are always bounded by the parameters required by the ALC condition, and hence the probability bound is always stronger.

The price to be paid, however, is that both the martingale differences condition and the ALC condition can be quite difficult to check for an arbitrary f compared with the simple bounded difference condition. If f can be decomposed as a sum, linearity of expectation can be used to simplify the computation, as we shall demonstrate with some examples in the next chapter. We will also introduce a powerful technique called *coupling* which can often be used to check such a condition.

Note, crucially, that in both Theorem 5.3 and Corollay 5.1, *the variables are not required to be independent*. This greatly increases the scope of their applicability, as we shall demonstrate in several examples in the next chapter.

We now develop familiarity with these tools by applying them to several different situations in the next chapter.

5.5 Pointers to the Literature

Martingales are a classic subject treated in many standard texts on probability, such as Grimmett and Stirzaker ([40], chap. 7, 12). The method of bounded differences and its applications to problems of combinatorics and discrete mathematics are covered in a well-known survey of the same name by McDiarmid [65]. This is now updated and supplanted by McDiarmid's own more recent survey [67], which is an authoritative and complete account of these techniques. All of these are however couched in measure-theoretic terminology, which can be a bit forbidding. A more elementary account can be found in Alon and Spencer [2].

5.6 Problems

Problem 5.1. Show that bounded difference condition (5.9) does not imply the average Lipschitz condition (5.7) or (5.8).   ▽

Problem 5.2. Let $X_0, X_1, \ldots$ be random variables such that the partial sums $S_n := X_1 + \cdots + X_n$ determine a martingale with respect to X. Show that $E[X_i X_j] = 0$ if $i \neq j$.   ▽

Problem 5.3 (Sampling without replacement). Consider an urn containing N balls, out of which M are red. Balls are drawn without replacement. Show that the sequence of random variables denoting the fraction of red balls remaining in the urn defines a martingale. Derive a concentration result.   ▽

Problem 5.4. Let $X_0, X_1, \ldots$ be a sequence of random variables with finite means, satisfying

$$E[X_{n+1} \mid X_0, \ldots, X_n] = aX_n + bX_{n-1}, \quad n \geq 1,$$

where $0 < a, b < 1$ and $a + b = 1$. Find a value of α for which $S_n := \alpha X_n + X_{n-1}$ determines a martingale with respect to X.   ▽

Problem 5.5. We shall generalise the definition of a martingale even further to be able to define the so-called vertex exposure martingale in a random graph.

Definition 5.7. *A sequence $Y := Y_0, Y_1, \ldots$ is a martingale with respect to a sequence $X := X_0, X_1, \ldots$ if there is an increasing sequence $0 \leq k_0 \leq k_1 \leq \cdots$ such that $Y_i = g_i(X_{k_i}), i \geq 0$, for some function g_i and $E[Y_i \mid X_{k_{i-1}}] = Y_{i-1}$.*

- (Vertex exposure martingale) Use Definition 5.7 to define a martingale in the random graph $G_{n,p}$ corresponding to revealing the edges in n stages where at the ith stage we reveal all edges incident on the first i vertices.
- (Azuma generalised further) Show that Azuma's inequality can be generalised to apply to the Definition 5.7 of a martingale.   ▽

Problem 5.6 (Azuma and centering sequences [66]). A sequence of random variables X_i, $i \geq 0$, is called a *centering sequence* if $E[X_{i+1} - X_i \mid X_i = t]$ is a non-increasing function of t.

(a) Show that Azuma's inequality applies to a centering sequence with bounded differences.
(b) Let X_i, $i \geq 0$, be the number of red balls in a random sample of size i picked without replacement from n objects, of which r are red. Show that the X_i, $i \geq 0$, form a centering sequence and derive a concentration result on X_k for any $k \leq n$. ▽

Problem 5.7 (Negative regression and method of bounded differences [27]).

(a) Show that the method of bounded differences applies when the underlying variables satisfy the negative regression condition (3.8).
(b) Consider a random sample of size k drawn from n objects, of which r are red, and let X_i, $i \leq k$, be the indicator for whether the ith draw was red. Show that $X_1, \ldots, X_k$ satisfy negative regression and deduce a sharp concentration on the number of red balls in the sample. ▽

Problem 5.8 [87]. A sequence of random variables $A_0, A_1, \ldots$ is (n, N)-bounded if

$$A_i - n \leq A_{i+1} \leq A_i - N \quad \text{for all } i.$$

Prove the following:

(a) Suppose $n \leq N/2$ and $r < nm$. If $\emptyset \equiv A_0, A_1, \ldots$ is an (n, N)-bounded submartingale then

$$P_r(A_m \leq -r) \leq \exp\left(\frac{-r^2}{3nmN}\right).$$

(b) Suppose $n \leq N/10$ and $r < mn$. If $\emptyset \equiv A_0, A_1, \ldots$ is an (n, N)-bounded supermartingale then

$$P_r(A_m \geq r) \leq \exp\left(\frac{-r^2}{3nmN}\right). \qquad ▽$$

6

The Simple Method of Bounded Differences in Action

In this chapter we shall see the "method of bounded differences", namely, Corollary 5.2 in action by applying it to various examples of increasing sophistication.

6.1 Chernoff–Hoeffding Revisited

Let $X_1, \ldots, X_n$ be independent variables taking values in $[0, 1]$, and consider $f(x_1, \ldots, x_n) := \sum_i x_i$. Then, of course, f has the Lipschitz property with each $d_i = 1$ in (5.9), and by Corollary 5.2, we get for $X := X_1 + \cdots + X_n$ the classical Chernoff–Hoeffding bound

$$\Pr[|X - \mathrm{E}[X]| > t] \leq 2e^{-2t^2/n}.$$

6.2 Stochastic Optimisation: Bin Packing

The bin-packing problem is a well-studied combinatorial optimisation problem: we are given n items of sizes in the interval $[0, 1]$ and are required to pack them into the fewest number of unit-capacity bins as possible. In the stochastic version, the item sizes are independent random variables in the interval $[0, 1]$. Let $B_n = B_n(x_1, \ldots, x_n)$ denote the optimum value, namely, the minimum number of bins that suffice. Then clearly the Lipschitz condition holds with constant 1 and we get the concentration result:

$$\Pr[|B_n - \mathrm{E}[B_n]| > t] \leq 2e^{-2t^2/n}.$$

Exercise 6.1. *Show that* $\lim_{n\to\infty} \mathrm{E}[B_n]/n = \beta$ *for some constant* $\beta > 0$ *by using sub-additivity (see [84]).*

From this exercise we deduce that $\Pr[|B_n - \mathrm{E}[B_n]| > \epsilon \mathrm{E}[B_n]]$ decreases exponentially in n. This straightforward application of the martingale technique vastly improved previous results on this problem.

Exercise 6.2. *Let B_n^{FF} denote the number of bins that would be needed if one applied the* first-fit *heuristic. Give a sharp concentration result on B_n^{FF}. (The first-fit heuristic places the items one by one, with the current item being placed in the first available bin.)*

6.3 Balls and Bins

In the classical balls-and-bins experiment, m balls are thrown independently at random into n bins (usually $m \geq n$) and we are interested in various statistics of the experiment, for instance, the number of empty bins. Let Z_i, $i \in [n]$, denote the indicator variables

$$Z_i := \begin{cases} 1, & \text{if bin } i \text{ is empty}, \\ 0, & \text{otherwise}. \end{cases}$$

Then, the variable we are interested in is the sum $Z := \sum_i Z_i$.

Exercise 6.3. *Show that $\mu := \mathrm{E}[Z] = n(1 - 1/n)^m \approx n e^{-m/n}$.*

Exercise 6.4. *Show that the Z_i's are not independent.*

In view of Exercise 6.4 we cannot apply the Chernoff bounds. In order to get a sharp concentration result, we can use the method of bounded difference in simple form. Consider Z as a function $Z(X_1, \ldots, X_m)$, where for $k \in [m]$, X_k is a random variable taking values in the set $[n]$ and indicating the bin in which ball k lands.

Let us check that the function Z satisfies the Lipschitz condition with constant 1. Denoting by b_k the bin into which the kth balls falls, the condition

$$|Z(b_1, \ldots, b_{i-1}, b_i, b_{i+1}, \ldots, b_m) - Z(b_1, \ldots, b_{i-1}, \hat{b}_i, b_{i+1}, \ldots, b_m)| \leq 1$$

simply states that if the ith ball is moved from one bin to another, keeping all other balls where they are, the number of empty bins can at most either go up by 1 or down by 1. Hence, again by Corollary 5.2, we have the bound

$$\Pr[|Z - \mathrm{E}[Z]| > t] \leq 2 \exp\left(\frac{-2t^2}{m}\right). \tag{6.1}$$

6.4 Distributed Edge Colouring: Take 1

The edge-colouring problem is one of the most studied in the theory of algorithms and combinatorics. Given a graph G we are asked to colour the edges of the graph in such a way that adjacent edges receive different colours, using as few colours as possible. This minimal number of colours is called the chromatic index and denoted as $\chi'(G)$. If Δ denotes the maximum degree of G, then clearly $\chi'(G) \geq \Delta$. A classic result of Vizing shows that every graph can be edge coloured in polynomial time with $\Delta + 1$ colours. Interestingly, whether a graph G really needs $\Delta + 1$ colours is an NP-complete problem.

Here we want to consider a very simple, distributed procedure applied to bipartite graphs. Let G be a Δ-regular bipartite graph. Each edge e has a list $L_e := [\Delta]$ of Δ colours. Consider the following simple step:

> Every edge e picks a tentative colour $t_e \in L_e$ uniformly at random (UAR), independently of other edges. If $t_e \neq t_f$ for all edges f adjacent to e, then t_e becomes the final colour of e.

Iterating this procedure raises some interesting and difficult questions. Here we only want to analyse what happens to the degree of a vertex after the preceding simple step. Fix a vertex u and let Z be the number of edges incident on u that get a final colour. We want a good bound on the probability that Z deviates far from its expectation. Our goal is to show a bound of the form

$$\Pr(|Z - \mathrm{E}Z| > t) \leq 2e^{-\Theta(t^2/\Delta)}. \tag{6.2}$$

Let us begin by computing $\mathrm{E}Z$. For every $e \ni u$, let

$$Z_e := \begin{cases} 1, & e \text{ colours itself,} \\ 0, & \text{otherwise.} \end{cases}$$

Now, since the tentative colours are chosen independently,

$$\Pr(Z_e = 1) = \left(1 - \frac{1}{\Delta}\right)^{2\Delta-2} \sim \frac{1}{e^2},$$

and therefore $\Delta e^{-2} \sim \mathrm{E}Z = \Theta(\Delta)$. This says that the bound of Equation (6.2) is $e^{-\Theta(\Delta)}$ when $t = \epsilon \Delta$, for $\epsilon > 0$. This is what one needs for repeated applications of the aforementioned basic step.

Exercise 6.5. *Show that the random variables Z_e, $e \ni u$, are not independent.*

In view of this exercise we cannot apply the Chernoff–Hoeffding bounds directly to Z. Let $e_1, \ldots, e_\Delta$ denote the edges incident on u and let $e_i := uv_i$. Let e_i^j, $1 \leq j \leq \Delta - 1$, denote an edge incident on v_i ($e_i \neq e_i^j$). Please refer to

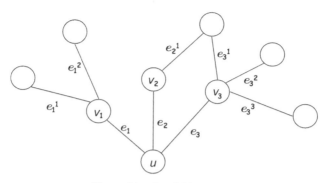

Figure 6.1. u's neighbourhood.

Figure 6.1. Similarly, let T_i denote the tentative colour of edge e_i and T_i^j that of edge e_i^j. Z can be expressed as a function of these $\Delta(\Delta - 1)$ variables,

$$Z := f(T_1 \ldots T_\Delta, T_1^1 \ldots T_1^{\Delta-1}, \ldots, T_\Delta^1 \ldots T_\Delta^{\Delta-1}).$$

It might seem that a straightforward application of the method of bounded differences in simple form, Corollary 5.2, would suffice. The T_i's and T_i^j's are independent, and changing T_i can have an effect of 2, while changing T_i^j can have an effect of 1. The catch is that f depends on $\Theta(\Delta^2)$ variables and the sum of their effects (squared) will also be $c = \Theta(\Delta^2)$. This leads to the bound

$$\Pr(|Z - EZ| > t) \le 2e^{-\Theta(t^2/\Delta^2)},$$

which is much weaker than what we want. An elegant way out is to consider, for each i, the vector $Y_i := (T_i^1, \ldots, T_i^{\Delta-1})$ as just one variable, so that

$$Z := f(T_1, \ldots, T_\Delta, Y_1, \ldots, Y_\Delta).$$

The Y_i's are independent because G is bipartite. Furthermore,

$$|f(T_1 \ldots T_i \ldots T_\Delta, Y_1 \ldots Y_\Delta) - f(T_1 \ldots T_i' \ldots T_\Delta, Y_1 \ldots Y_\Delta)| \le 2$$

and

$$|f(T_1 \ldots T_\Delta, Y_1 \ldots Y_i \ldots Y_\Delta) - f(T_1 \ldots T_\Delta, Y_1 \ldots Y_i' \ldots Y_\Delta)| \le 1,$$

which gives $c = 5\Delta$ and bound (6.2).

6.5 Models for the Web Graph

A lot of research focusing on the Web concerns stochastic generative models for the Web graph. This is the graph defined by Webpages as vertices and by the links among them as directed edges. Modelling of the Web tries to reproduce some of its noteworthy features. For instance, it is well-known that the in-degree distribution of Webpages follows a power law, and one would want the model to be able to reproduce this aspect. An intriguing set of papers by Boldi and Vigna [7, 8] shows that the real Web graph is highly compressible: it can be stored in such a way that each edge requires only a small constant number – between two and four – of bits on average; a more recent experimental study confirms these findings [15]. These results suggest the intriguing possibility that the Web might require just $O(1)$ bits per edge on average. In this section we present a graph model for the Web that exhibits the usual power-law distribution of the in-degrees together with a power-law distribution of the "lengths" of the links. In both cases the exponent of the power law is greater than 1. In the case of the length distribution this implies that the graph has low entropy. A very similar property of the real Web was exploited in [7, 8] to attain the high compression (see [20]).

Let $k > 2$ be a fixed positive integer. The model creates a simple graph (i.e. no self-loops or multiedges) by means of the following iterative process:

- The process starts at time t_0, with a simple directed *seed graph* G_{t_0} whose nodes are arranged on a line. The graph, G_{t_0}, has t_0 nodes, each of out-degree k. Here, G_{t_0} could be, for instance, a complete directed graph with $t_0 = k + 1$ nodes.
- At time $t > t_0$, an existing node y is chosen uniformly at random (UAR):

  1. A new node x is placed to the immediate left of y.
  2. A directed edge $x \rightarrow y$ is added to the graph.
  3. $k - 1$ edges are "copied" from y; that is, $k - 1$ successors of y, say, $z_1, \ldots, z_{k-1}$, are chosen UAR (without replacement) and the directed edges $x \rightarrow z_1, \ldots, x \rightarrow z_{k-1}$ are added to the graph.

In this model, the following can be shown:

- The fraction of nodes of in-degree i is asymptotic to $\Theta(i^{-2-\frac{1}{k-1}})$; this power law is often referred to as "the rich get richer".
- The fraction of edges of length ℓ, in the given embedding, is asymptotic to $\Theta(\ell^{-1-\frac{1}{k}})$; analogously, we refer to this as "the long get longer". (The length of an edge $x \rightarrow y$ is the number of nodes below this edge in the layout.)

The first property is a consequence of the preferential attachment mechanism: the higher your in-degree now, the more likely it is to grow later. It is commonly considered to be a basic requirement that all stochastic models for behavioural graphs should satisfy. The second property is noteworthy because it implies that a graph with n nodes that is generated by our model can be represented by using only $O(n)$ bits, with high probability. We shall not be concerned with proving these statements on the expectations here. Our focus here is to show that the in-degree distribution is tightly concentrated by establishing the Lipschitz property for it. In the problem session we will do the same for the length distribution.

Let X_i^t denote the number of nodes of in-degree i at time t. We now prove that each random variable X_i^t satisfies the $(2k)$-Lipschitz property.

The key is to give a different, but equivalent, description of the random process that generates the graph. The model can be interpreted as the following stochastic process: at step t, two independent dice, with $t - 1$ and k faces respectively, are thrown. Let Q_t and R_t be the corresponding random variables. The new node x will position itself to the immediate left of the node y that was added at time Q_t. This is just another way to choose one node UAR. Suppose that the (ordered) list of successors of y is $(z_1, \ldots, z_k)$. The ordered list of successors of x will be composed of y followed by the nodes $z_1, \ldots, z_k$ with the exception of node z_{R_t}. Thus, the number of nodes X_i^t of in-degree i at time t can be interpreted as a function of the trials $(Q_1, R_1), \ldots, (Q_t, R_t)$.

We want to show that changing the outcome of any single trial (Q_τ, R_τ) changes the random variable X_i^t (for fixed i) by an amount not greater than $2k$. Suppose we change (q_τ, r_τ) to (q_τ', r_τ') going from graph G to G'. Let x be the node added at time τ with the choice (q_τ, r_τ), and x' be the node added with the choice (q_τ', r_τ'). And let S and S' be the set of successors of x in G and x' in G', respectively.

Before time τ, G and G' are identical. Let $d_i^t(G)$ denote the in-degree that the node inserted at step i has in G at time $t \geq i$. (We can use the convention that $d_i^t(G) = 0$ for $t < i$, so that these quantities are always defined.) Clearly, if $t < \tau$, the in-degree sequences of G and G' at time t are the same. At time τ they might differ only for the vertices in S and S'. Let us define the *Hamming distance* between two sequences as the number of position where they differ. Thus the Hamming distance between the in-degree sequence of G and G' is zero at time $t < \tau$ and is $\leq 2k$ at time τ. Let (Q_t, R_t) be the insertion at time $t > \tau$. How can the Hamming distance change? The set of vertices that receive a new incoming edge at time t is the same in G and G' and therefore $d_i^t(G) = d_i^{t-1}(G) + 1$ if and only if $d_i^t(G') = d_i^{t-1}(G') + 1$, for all i. Thus, the

Hamming distance between the two sequences can never be more than $2k$ so that $|X_i^t(G) - X_i^t(G')| \leq 2k$ at all times t.

6.6 Game Theory and Blackwell's Approachability Theorem

Consider a non-collaborative two-player game given by a matrix M with n rows and m columns. There are two players, the row player and the column player. The row player chooses a row i and, simultaneously, the column player chooses a column j. The selected entry $M(i, j)$ is the *loss* suffered by the row player. We assume for simplicity that the entries in M are bounded in the range $[0, 1]$.

By standard game-theoretic terminology, the (deterministic) choice of a specific row or column is called a *pure* strategy and a probability distribution over the rows or columns is called a *mixed* strategy. We will use P to denote the strategy of the row player and Q to denote the strategy of the *column* player. $P(i)$ denotes the probability with which row i is selected and similarly $Q(j)$ denotes the probability with which column j is selected. We write $M(P, Q) := P^T M Q$ to denote the expected loss of the row player when the two players use the strategies P and Q respectively.

Consider now a *repeated* play of the game. That is, the two players play a series of *rounds* of interactions. At round $t \geq 0$, the row player picks a row I_t using strategy P independently of the earlier rounds and, simultaneously, the column player picks a column J_t using strategy Q independently. The total loss suffered by the row player after T rounds is $\sum_{0 \leq t \leq T} M(I_t, J_t)$, whose expectation is $T M(P, Q)$. Since each entry of M is bounded in $[0, 1]$, changing any one of the underlying choices changes the total loss by at most 1. Hence, applying the method of bounded differences,

$$\Pr\left[\left| \sum_{0 \leq t \leq T} M(I_t, J_t) - T M(P, Q) \right| > \epsilon T \right] \leq 2e^{-2\epsilon^2 T},$$

for any $\epsilon > 0$.

6.6.1 Games with Vector Pay-Offs

A non-cooperative game G with vector pay-offs is given by strategy sets $A_i, i = 1, 2$, for the two players and utility functions $u_i(i, j), i = 1, 2$, whose range is R^n; that is, the pay-offs are n-dimensional vectors.

For a subset $S \subseteq R^n$ and a point $x \in R^n$, let

$$d(x, S) := \inf_{s \in S} \|x - s\|.$$

Let G be a vector pay-off game such that the range of the utilities is a bounded subset of R^n. A subset $S \subseteq R^N$ is said to be *approachable* (by player 1) if there exists a randomized algorithm to choose $i_1, i_2, \ldots$ such that for any adaptive adversary strategy choosing $j_1, j_2, \ldots$, we have

$$\lim_{T \to \infty} d\left(\frac{1}{T} \sum_{t=1}^{T} u_1(i_t, j_t), S\right) = 0.$$

In words, a subset S is approachable if no adversary can prevent player 1 from choosing strategies such that the average pay-off converges to the set S as the time horizon tends to infinity.

For given $a, b \in R^n$, consider the half-space $S := \{u \mid au \geq b\}$. To determine when this half-space is approachable, consider the corresponding scalar-valued game aG whose pay-off to player 1 is just au_1 instead of u_1.

Proposition 6.1. *The half-space $S := \{u \mid au \geq b\}$ is approachable if and only if the value of the game aG is at least b.*

Proof. Since we assume that the pay-off vectors in the original game G belong to a bounded subset of R^n, we may assume without loss of generality that $-1 \leq au(i, j) \leq 1$ for all i, j.

First, let us assume that the value of the game aG is at least b. By von Neumann's theorem, we know that there exists a mixed strategy for player 1 which guarantees him an expected pay-off of at least b. Let player 1 choose $i_1, i_2, \ldots$ by independently sampling from this strategy.

To analyse the outcome, define $X_t := \sum_{s=1}^{t}(au(i_s, j_s) - b)$. Since the expected pay-off guaranteed for player 1 is at least b, we have $E[X_t] \geq 0$. Moreover, by the boundedness assumption, the result of changing any i_s changes the value of X by at most 2. So, applying the method of bounded differences,

$$\Pr[X_t \leq -\lambda\sqrt{t}] \leq e^{-\frac{\lambda^2}{2}}.$$

Taking $\lambda := 2\sqrt{\log t}$ gives

$$\Pr[X_t \leq -2\sqrt{t \log t}] \leq 1/t^2.$$

Thus with probability at least $1 - 1/t^2$, $X_t > -2\sqrt{t \log t}$; that is,

$$\frac{1}{t} \sum_{s=1}^{t} au(i_s, j_s) \geq b - 2\sqrt{\frac{\log t}{t}}.$$

The right-hand side goes to b as $t \to \infty$, which shows that if the value of the game aG is at least b, then the half-space S is approachable.   ∎

Exercise 6.6. *Show that if the half-space S is not approachable if the value of the game is less than b.*

A powerful generalisation of this result due to Blackwell ([5]; see also [31, 32]) examines the corresponding question for general convex subsets.

Theorem 6.1 (Blackwell's approachability theorem). *A closed convex subset is approachable if and only if every half-space containing it is approachable.*

Some of the preceding ideas can be applied again. However, a major significant difference is that one cannot apply the method of bounded differences, but must use an extension of Azuma's inequality for supermartingales (see Problem 6.6 where we outline a proof).

6.7 Pointers to the Literature

Modelling of the Web graph is an active area of research (see for instance [1, 9, 12, 20, 55] and references therein). A discussion of Blackwell's approachability theorem is in section 7.7 in [17].

6.8 Problems

Problem 6.1 (From [2], p. 103). Let ρ be the Hamming metric on $H := \{0, 1\}^n$. For $A \subseteq H$, let $B(A, s)$ denote the set of $y \in H$, so that $\rho(x, y) \le s$ for some $x \in A$. ($A \subseteq B(A, s)$ as we may take $x = y$.) Show that if $\epsilon, \lambda > 0$ satisfy $e^{-\lambda^2/2} = \epsilon$, then

$$|A| \ge \epsilon 2^n \implies |B(A, 2\lambda\sqrt{n})| \ge (1 - \epsilon)2^n. \qquad \triangledown$$

Problem 6.2 (From [2], p. 103). Let B be a normed space and let $v_1, \ldots, v_n \in B$ with $|v_i| \le 1$ for each $i \in [n]$. Let $\epsilon_1, \ldots, \epsilon_n$ be independent and uniform in $\{-1, +1\}$. Set $f := |\sum_i \epsilon_i v_i|$. Show that f is Lipschitz and deduce a sharp concentration result. Can you improve this by using the method of bounded martingale differences? $\qquad \triangledown$

Problem 6.3. Let G be a d-uniform, bipartite *multigraph*; that is, parallel edges are allowed. Each edge selects a tentative colour in $[d]$ independently at random. An edge colours successfully if and only if its tentative colour is not chosen by any of the incident edges. For a fixed vertex u, let Z_u be the number of edges incident on u that colour successfully.

- Estimate $E[Z_u]$.
- Show that Z_u is sharply concentrated around its mean.
- Can you generalise your result to the case when G is not uniform and has maximum degree d? And to the case when G is not bipartite?   ▽

Problem 6.4. In this exercise we will derive the Lipschitz property for the distribution of lengths of the Web graph model of Section 6.5. Recall that the graphs generated by the model are laid out on the line and that the *length* of an arc $x \to y$ is the number of nodes below the arc, that is, the number of nodes between x and y in the layout (plus 1). For simplicity, assume x to be to the left of y. An edge $x_a \to x_b$ is said to *pass* over two consecutive nodes x_c and x_{c+1} if $a < c$ and $c + 1 < b$.

1. Let x_a, x_b, and x_c be three nodes such that $a < b < c$ and $t(x_c) > t(x_b)$. ($t(x)$ denotes the arrival time of x in the graph.) Show that it is impossible for the edge $x_a \to x_c$ to exist.
2. Let x_a, x_b, x_c, and x_d be four nodes such that $a < b < c < d$ and $x_a \to x_c$ and $x_b \to x_d$. Show that, given this, then there exists an edge $x_c \to x_d$.
3. Show the following: At any time during the evolution of the graph, given any two consecutive nodes x and x', and any edge length ℓ, the number of edges of length ℓ that pass over x or x' (or both) is at most $C = (t_0 + 1)k + 1$, where t_0 denotes the cardinality of the vertex set of the initial seed graph.
4. Let Y_ℓ^t denote the number of edges of length ℓ at time t. Show that each random variable Y_ℓ^t satisfies the $(k(t_0 + 1) + 2t_0 + 1)$-Lipschitz property.   ▽

Problem 6.5 (Azuma for supermartingales). A sequence of random variables $X_0, X_1, \ldots, X_n$ is called a *supermartingale* if for all $k \geq 1$,

$$E[X_k \mid X_1, X_2, \ldots, X_{k-1}] \leq X_{k-1}.$$

Prove that Azuma's inequality is valid also for supermartingales.   ▽

Problem 6.6 (Blackwell's approachability theorem). We outline a proof of Blackwell's theorem (Theorem 6.1).

As before, we assume that all pay-off vectors lie in the unit sphere and that the closed convex subset S also lies in the unit sphere.

Given the hypothesis, we describe a simple algorithm to approach S: let x_t and y_t denote the strategies chosen at time t, and let $u_t := u(x_t, y_t)$ be the pay-off at time t. Let $A_T := \frac{1}{T} \sum_{t=1}^{T} u_t$ be the average pay-off until time T. If

$A_T \in S$, then player 1 plays an arbitrary strategy at time T; else let B_T denote the point in S closest to A_T. By elementary geometry, S is contained in the half-space $\{v \mid v(A_T - B_T) \leq 0\}$. By assumption, there is a mixed strategy for player 1 to approach this half-space. The algorithm plays this strategy.

Let $d_t := \|A_t - B_t\|$.

(a) Show that

$$E[d_{t+1}^2 \mid x_1, \ldots, x_t, y_1, \ldots, y_t] \leq \frac{t^2}{(t+1)^2} d_t^2 + \frac{4}{(t+1)^2}.$$

(b) Let $Z_t := t^2 d_t^2 - 4t$. Show that $Z_0, Z_1, \ldots, Z_T$ is a supermartingale.
(c) Show that

$$|Z_{t+1} - Z_t| \leq 8(t+1).$$

(d) Apply Azuma's inequality for supermartingales to deduce that

$$\Pr\left[d_T > 4\left(\frac{\ln T}{T}\right)^{1/4}\right] \leq 1/T^2.$$

Hence deduce Blackwell's theorem (Theorem 6.1).   ▽

Problem 6.7. Let $X = (X_1 \ldots X_n)$ be a point in $\mathbb{R}^n$ such that every X_i is independently and uniformly drawn at random from $[0, 1]$. Let $Z := \|X\|^2$ and let $W := \|X - Y\|^2$, where Y is distributed like X.

(a) Compute $E[Z]$ and give a concentration bound for Z.
(b) Do the same with $E[W]$ and W.   ▽

7

The Method of Averaged Bounded Differences

Sometimes, the function f for which we are trying to show a concentration result does not satisfy the conditions needed to apply the simple method of bounded differences: the Lipschitz coefficients are simply too large in the *worst case*. The function is not "smooth". In such cases, the method of average bounded differences can be deployed, needing only an *averaged* smoothness condition. That is, we need a bound of the form

$$\left| E[f \mid X_{i-1}, X_i = a_i] - E[f \mid X_{i-1}, X_i = a_i'] \right|, \tag{7.1}$$

or the similar

$$\left| E[f \mid X_{i-1}, X_i = a_i] - E[f \mid X_{i-1}] \right|. \tag{7.2}$$

At first glance, getting a handle on this appears formidable, and indeed it is often non-trivial. We illustrate three main approaches to this:

1. Direct computation is sometimes possible (using linearity of expectation for example).
2. *Coupling* which is a very versatile tool for comparing two closely related distributions such as in (7.1) or (7.2).
3. Bounding the difference by conditioning on the non-occurrence of some rare "bad" events.

7.1 Hypergeometric Distribution

The hypergeometric distribution describes the number of red balls drawn in an experiment where n balls are sampled without replacement from a bin containing N balls, M of which are red. This can be regarded as a function $f(X_1, \ldots, X_n)$, where $X_1, \ldots, X_n$ are independent random variables, the variable X_i taking values in the set $[N - i + 1]$ for $i \in [n]$ giving the number of the ball drawn on the ith trial. To estimate $|E[f \mid X_i] - E[f \mid X_{i-1}]|$, let N_{i-1} be the total number of balls and M_{i-1} the number of red balls at the stage when the ith ball is drawn, for $i \in [n]$. Thus, $N_0 = N$, $M_0 = M$ and $N_i = N - i$. Observe that

$$E[f \mid X_i] = (M - M_i) + \frac{M_i}{N_i}(n - i)$$

and, furthermore, that $M_{i-1} - M_i \leq 1$. From this, we conclude that

$$|E[f \mid X_i] - E[f \mid X_{i-1}]| \leq \max\left(\frac{M_{i-1}}{N_{i-1}}, 1 - \frac{M_{i-1}}{N_{i-1}}\right)\frac{N - n}{N - i}$$

$$\leq \frac{N - n}{N - i}.$$

Furthermore,

$$\sum_i \left(\frac{N - n}{N - i}\right)^2 = (N - n)^2 \sum_i \frac{1}{(N - i)^2}$$

$$= (N - n)^2 \sum_{N-n \leq j \leq N-1} \frac{1}{j^2}$$

$$\approx (N - n)^2 \int_{N-n}^{N-1} \frac{1}{x^2}dx$$

$$= (N - n)\frac{n - 1}{N - 1}.$$

Thus, by Theorem 5.3, we get the bound

$$\Pr[|f - E[f]| > t] \leq \exp\left(\frac{-2(N - 1)t^2}{(N - n)(n - 1)}\right).$$

Thus with $t := \epsilon E[f]$ and $E[f] = \frac{M}{N}n$, we get

$$\Pr\left[\left|f - \frac{M}{N}n\right| > \epsilon\frac{M}{N}n\right] \leq \exp\left(-2(1 - o(1))\epsilon^2\frac{M}{N}\frac{M}{N - n}n\right).$$

7.2 Occupancy in Balls and Bins

Recall the bound that we derived in Section 6.3:

$$\Pr[|Z - E[Z]| > t] \leq 2\exp\left(\frac{-t^2}{2m}\right) \tag{7.3}$$

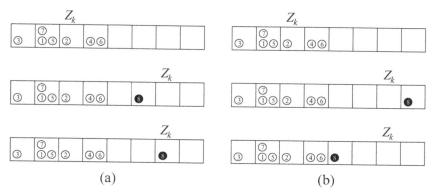

Figure 7.1. The white balls represent the first $i - 1$ choices, while the ith choice, which is different in the two situations (a) and (b), is represented by the black ball. In the example $i = 8$.

on the concentration of the number of empty bins when we throw m balls independently and uniformly at random into n bins. A better bound can be obtained by applying the method of bounded average differences. We make use of the notation developed in Section 6.3. Now we need to compute

$$c_i := |E[Z \mid X_{i-1}, X_i = b_i] - E[Z \mid X_{i-1}, X_i = b'_i]|$$

for each ball $i \in [m]$. By linearity of expectation, this reduces to computing for each bin $k \in [n]$, $c_{i,k} := |E[Z_k \mid X_{i-1}, X_i = b_i] - E[Z_k \mid X_{i-1}, X_i = b'_i]|$.

Let us therefore consider for each bin $k \in [n]$, and for some fixed set of bins $b_1, \ldots, b_i, b'_i$ ($b_i \neq b'_i$),

$$c_{i,k} = |E[Z_k \mid X_{i-1} = b_{i-1}, X_i = b_i] - E[Z_k \mid X_{i-1} = b_{i-1}, X_k = b'_i]|.$$

Let $S := \{b_1, \ldots, b_{i-1}\}$ and refer to Figure 7.1.

- (Figure 7.1 – top) If $k \in S$, then, of course,

$$E[Z_k \mid X_{i-1} = b_{i-1}, X_i = b_i] = E[Z_k \mid X_{i-1} = b_{i-1}, X_k = b'_i] = 0$$

and so $c_{i,k} = 0$.

- (Figure 7.1 – middle) If $k \notin S$ and $k \neq b_i, b'_i$, then

$$E[Z_k \mid X_{i-1} = b_{i-1}, X_i = b_i] = E[Z_k \mid X_{i-1} = b_{i-1}, X_i = b'_i]$$
$$= (1 - 1/n)^{m-i}.$$

Hence, we have again $c_{i,k} = 0$.

- (Figure 7.1 – bottom) Finally, if $k = b_i \notin S$, then of course

$$E[Z_k \mid X_{i-1} = b_{i-1}, X_i = b_i] = 0,$$

but if $b_i' \notin S$,

$$E[Z_k \mid X_{i-1} = b_{i-1}, X_i = b_i'] = (1 - 1/n)^{m-i}.$$

Hence, $c_{i,k} = (1 - 1/n)^{m-i}$ in this case.

Overall, we see that $c_i = \sum_k c_{i,k} \leq (1 - 1/n)^{m-i}$ and

$$\sum_i c_i^2 \leq \frac{1 - (1 - 1/n)^{2m}}{1 - (1 - 1/n)^2} = \frac{n^2 - \mu^2}{2n - 1},$$

where $\mu := E[Z]$ as customary. By Corollary 5.1 this gives the bound

$$\Pr[|Z - E[Z]| > t] \leq 2\exp\left(-\frac{4t^2(n - 1/2)}{n^2 - \mu^2}\right).$$

Asymptotically in terms of $r := m/n$, this is

$$2\exp\left(-\frac{4t^2}{n(1 - e^{-2r})}\right) = 2e^{-\Theta(t^2/n)}.$$

If $m \geq n$, this is stronger than the previous $e^{-\Theta(t^2/m)}$ bound of (7.3) that was derived by means of the method of bounded differences in simple forms (see also Exercise 7.6).

7.3 Stochastic Optimisation: Travelling Salesman Problem

A travelling salesman is required to visit n towns and must choose the shortest route to do so. This is a notoriously difficult combinatorial optimisation problem. A stochastic version in two dimensions asks for the shortest route when the points $P_i := (X_i, Y_i), i \in [n]$, are chosen uniformly and independently in the unit square, $[0, 1]^2$ (i.e. each X_i and Y_i is distributed uniformly and independently in $[0, 1]$).

Let $T_n = T_n(P_i, i \in [n])$ denote the length of the optimal tour. A celebrated result shows that $E[T_n] = \beta\sqrt{n}$ for some $\beta > 0$. What about a sharp concentration result? A straightforward approach is to observe that T_n has the Lipschitz property with constant at most $2\sqrt{2}$. (Imagine that all except one point are in one corner and the last is in the opposite corner.) Hence,

$$\Pr[|T_n - E[T_n]| > t] \leq e^{-t^2/4n}. \tag{7.4}$$

Note that since $E[T_n] = \beta\sqrt{n}$, this bound is no good for small deviations around the mean, that is, for $t = \epsilon E[T_n]$.

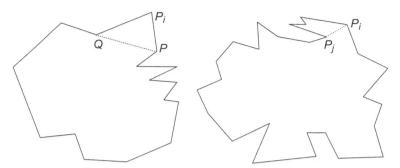

Figure 7.2. Tours.

For a better bound, we shall turn to the method of bounded martingale differences. Let $T_n(i)$ denote the length of the shortest tour through all points except the ith for $i \in [n]$.

Now we observe the crucial inequality that

$$T_n(i) \leq T_n \leq T_n(i) + 2Z_i, \quad i < n, \tag{7.5}$$

where Z_i is the shortest distance from point P_i to one of the points P_{i+1} through P_n. The first inequality follows because (refer to Figure 7.2 – left), denoting the neighbours of P_i in T_n by P and Q, the tour obtained by joining P and Q directly excludes P_i and, by the triangle inequality, has length less than T_n. For the second inequality (refer to Figure 7.2 – right), suppose P_j, $j > i$, is the closest point to P_i. Now take an optimal tour of all points except P_i and convert it into a tour including P_i by visiting P_i after reaching P_j and returning to P_j. This is not a tour but can be converted into one by taking a shortcut to the next point after P_j. The length of the resulting tour is no more than $T_n(i) + 2Z_i$ by the triangle inequality. Taking conditional expectations in (7.5), we get

$$\mathrm{E}[T_n(i) \mid \boldsymbol{P}_{i-1}] \leq \mathrm{E}[T_n \mid \boldsymbol{P}_{i-1}] \leq \mathrm{E}[T_n(i) \mid \boldsymbol{P}_{i-1}] + 2\mathrm{E}[Z_i \mid \boldsymbol{P}_{i-1}],$$
$$\mathrm{E}[T_n(i) \mid \boldsymbol{P}_i] \leq \mathrm{E}[T_n \mid \boldsymbol{P}_i] \leq \mathrm{E}[T_n(i) \mid \boldsymbol{P}_i] + 2\mathrm{E}[Z_i \mid \boldsymbol{P}_i].$$

Note that $\mathrm{E}[T_n(i) \mid \boldsymbol{P}_i] = \mathrm{E}[T_n(i) \mid \boldsymbol{P}_{i-1}]$. Hence, we conclude

$$|\mathrm{E}[T_n \mid \boldsymbol{P}_i] - \mathrm{E}[T_n \mid \boldsymbol{P}_{i-1}]| \leq 2\max(\mathrm{E}[Z_i \mid \boldsymbol{P}_{i-1}], \mathrm{E}[Z_i \mid \boldsymbol{P}_i]), \quad i \leq n.$$

Computing $\mathrm{E}[Z_i \mid \boldsymbol{P}_i]$ is the following question: given a point Q in $[0, 1]$, what is its shortest distance to one of a randomly chosen set of $n - i$ points? Computing $\mathrm{E}[Z_i \mid \boldsymbol{P}_{i-1}]$ is the same, except the point Q is also picked at random. This exercise is relegated to Problem 7.9. The answer is that

$\mathrm{E}[Z_i \mid \boldsymbol{P}_i], \mathrm{E}[Z_i \mid \boldsymbol{P}_{i-1}] \le c/\sqrt{n-i}$ for some constant $c > 0$. Finally, taking the trivial bound $|\mathrm{E}[T_n \mid \boldsymbol{P}_n] - \mathrm{E}[T_n \mid \boldsymbol{P}_{n-1}]| \le 2\sqrt{2}$, we get

$$\Pr[|T_n - \mathrm{E}[T_n]| > t) \le 2\exp\left(\frac{-2t^2}{8 + \sum_{i<n} 4c^2/(n-i)}\right)$$

$$\le 2\exp\left(\frac{-at^2}{\log n}\right), \tag{7.6}$$

for some $a > 0$. Compare (7.6) with (7.4); in particular, note that the former together with $\mathrm{E}[T_n] = \beta\sqrt{n}$ yields

$$\Pr[|T_n - \beta\sqrt{n}| > \epsilon\sqrt{n}] \le 2\exp\left(\frac{-b\epsilon^2 n}{\log n}\right),$$

for some $b > 0$ and all $\epsilon > 0$.

We shall see later that this bound can be further improved by removing the $\log n$ factor. But that will need a new method!

7.4 Coupling

Consider the following two scenarios. In the first we throw m balls uniformly at random into n bins, while in the second we throw $m' \ge m$ balls uniformly at random into the same number n of bins. Denoting with Z and Z' the number of *non*-empty bins in the two situations, it is intuitively compelling to assert that, for all k, $\Pr[Z > k] \le \Pr[Z' > k]$. This intuition is correct but surprisingly difficult to prove by direct calculation. An elegant proof, devoid of any calculations, can be given by resorting to the concept of coupling. For notational convenience, assume that the balls are numbered as $1, 2, \ldots, m$ in the first scenario and as $1', 2', \ldots, m'$ in the second. Consider the following equivalent way to perform the experiment. First, throw the m balls $1, 2, \ldots, m$ of the first scenario. Let X be the number of non-empty bins in the first scenario. To realise the second scenario, place first (deterministically) ball i' in the same bin where ball i landed, $1 \le i \le m$. Then throw the remaining $m' - m$ balls uniformly at random. Let Y be the number of non-empty bins in the second scenario under this experiment. Clearly, $Y \ge X$. Now, note that X has the same distribution of Z and that Y has the same distribution of Z'. Therefore for any k,

$$\Pr[Z' > k] = \Pr[Y > k] \ge \Pr[X > k] = \Pr[Z > k].$$

What we have done is to exhibit a *coupling* between the distributions of Z and Z': that is, a joint distribution $\pi(X, Y)$ such that the marginal distribution X, denoted as $\pi(X)$, coincides with the distribution of Z, and the marginal

$\pi(Y)$ has the same distribution of Z'. A basic property of a coupling $\pi(X_1, X_2)$ of two distributions Z_1 and Z_2 that we will use is the following: For any function f,

$$E_\pi[f(X_i)] = E_{Z_i}[f(Z_i)]. \tag{7.7}$$

Exercise 7.1. *Prove formally Equation (7.7).*

Exercise 7.2. *Suppose the balls are not identical: ball number k has a probability $p_{k,i}$ of falling into bin number i. Extend the preceding argument to this situation.*

The next example formalises the intuition used in Exercise 1.1. Suppose we perform two independent trials of tossing a coin n times, the first with a coin of bias p of turning up heads and the second with bias $p' \geq p$. Intuitively, it is clear that we expect to get more heads in the second case. To make this rigorous, let $X_1, \ldots, X_n$ be the indicator variables corresponding to getting a head with the first coin and $X'_1, \ldots, X'_n$ the corresponding ones for the second coin. We assert that for any $t \geq 0$,

$$\Pr[X_1 + \cdots + X_n > t] \leq \Pr[X'_1 + \cdots + X'_n > t].$$

To do this, we will introduce a coupling of the two distributions; that is, we will define a joint distribution $\pi(Z_1, \ldots, Z_n, Z'_1, \ldots, Z'_n)$ such that $\pi(Z_1, \ldots, Z_n)$ has the same distribution as $(X_1, \ldots, X_n)$ and $\pi(Z'_1, \ldots, Z'_n)$ has the same distribution as $(X'_1, \ldots, X'_n)$, and moreover, at each point of the sample space, $Z_i \leq Z'_i, i \in [n]$. Then

$$\begin{aligned}
\Pr[X_1 + \cdots + X_n > t] &= \Pr_\pi[Z_1 + \cdots + Z_n > t] \\
&\leq \Pr_\pi[Z'_1 + \cdots + Z'_n > t] \\
&= \Pr[X'_1 + \cdots + X'_n > t].
\end{aligned}$$

Now for the construction of the coupling, recall that $\Pr[X_i = 1] = p \leq p' = \Pr[X'_i = 1]$ for each $i \in [n]$. We define the joint distribution $\pi(Z_1, \ldots, Z_n, Z'_1, \ldots, Z'_n)$ by specifying the distribution of each pair (Z_i, Z'_i) independently for each $i \in [n]$. The distribution π is the product of these marginal distributions. For each $i \in [n]$, first toss a coin with bias p of turning up heads. If it shows heads, set $Z_i = 1 = Z'_i$. Otherwise, set $Z_i = 0$, and to determine the value of Z'_i, toss another coin with bias $\frac{p'-p}{1-p}$ of showing up heads. If this turns up heads, set $Z'_i = 1$; otherwise set $Z'_i = 0$.

It is easy to see that in the distribution π, $Z_i \leq Z'_i$ for each $i \in [n]$.

Exercise 7.3. *Check that the marginal distributions are as claimed before: that is, for each i, $\Pr[Z_i] = p$ and $\Pr[Z'_i = 1] = p'$.*

Exercise 7.4. *Generalise the preceding example in two steps:*

(a) *Suppose the probabilities* $\Pr[X_i] = p_i \leq p_i' = \Pr[X_i']$ *are not necessarily all equal. Give the required modification in the preceding coupling to prove the same result.*

(b) *Suppose* $X_1, \ldots, X_n$ *and* $X_1', \ldots, X_n'$ *are distributed in* $[0, 1]$ *and not necessarily identically. However,* $E[X_i] \leq E[X_i']$ *for each* $i \in [n]$. *What further modifications are needed now?*

Exercise 7.5. *Use coupling to prove the following fact used in Exercise 1.1: Let* $X_1, \ldots, X_n$ *be independent random variables distributed in* $[0, 1]$ *with* $E[X_i] = p_i$ *for each* $i \in [n]$. *Let* $Y_1, \ldots, Y_n$ *and* $Z_1, \ldots, Z_n$ *be independent random variables with* $E[Y_i] = q_i$ *and* $E[Z_i] = r_i$ *for each* $i \in [n]$. *Now suppose* $q_i \leq p_i \leq r_i$ *for each* $i \in [n]$. *Then, if* $X := \sum_i X_i$, $Y := \sum_i Y_i$ *and* $Z := \sum_i Z_i$, *for any* t,

$$\Pr[X > t] \leq \Pr[Z > t] \quad and \quad \Pr[X < t] \leq \Pr[Y < t].$$

Exercise 7.6 (Empty bins revisited). *Rework the balls-and-bins problem of Section 7.2 via coupling and the method of average bounded differences.*

7.4.1 How to Use Coupling with Method of Average Bounded Differences

Coupling can be used very effectively to get good bounds on

$$\left| E[f \mid X_{i-1} = a_{i-1}, X_i = a_i] - E[f \mid X_{i-1} = a_{i-1}, X_i = a_i'] \right|. \tag{7.8}$$

The idea is to find a "good" coupling π of the two conditional distributions $(\cdot \mid X_{i-1} = a_{i-1}, X_i = a_i)$ and $(\cdot \mid X_{i-1} = a_{i-1}, X_i = a_i')$. Let us denote by $Y_{i+1}, \ldots, Y_n$ and $Y_{i+1}', \ldots, Y_n'$ the pair of random variables in the coupling π. Then, in (7.8), we have

$$
\begin{aligned}
&\left| E[f \mid X_{i-1} = a_{i-1}, X_i = a_i] - E[f \mid X_{i-1} = a_{i-1}, X_i = a_i'] \right| \\
&= \left| E_\pi[f(a_{i-1}, a_i, Y_{i+1}, \ldots, Y_n)] - E_\pi[f(a_{i-1}, a_i', Y_{i+1}', \ldots, Y_n')] \right| \\
&= \left| E_\pi[f(a_{i-1}, a_i, Y_{i+1}, \ldots, Y_n) - f(a_{i-1}, a_i', Y_{i+1}', \ldots, Y_n')] \right| \\
&\leq E_\pi[\left| f(a_{i-1}, a_i, Y_{i+1}, \ldots, Y_n) - f(a_{i-1}, a_i', Y_{i+1}', \ldots, Y_n') \right|]. \tag{7.9}
\end{aligned}
$$

Now, suppose the coupling π is chosen to have the property that it concentrates all the mass on points where the two vectors $Y_{i+1}, \ldots, Y_n$ and $Y_{i+1}', \ldots, Y_n'$ differ on very few coordinates. Suppose, for concreteness, that the (weighted) Hamming distance (with weight c_i in coordinate i) of

$(a_i, Y_{i+1}, \ldots, Y_n)$ and $(a'_i, Y'_{i+1}, \ldots, Y'_n)$ at any point with non-zero probability is at most c. Then, if f is 1-Lipschitz in the weighted Hamming metric, we can continue in (7.9):

$$\left| E[f \mid X_{i-1} = a_{i-1}, X_i = a_i] - E[f \mid X_{i-1} = a_{i-1}, X_i = a'_i] \right|$$
$$\leq E_\pi \left[\left| f(a_{i-1}, a_i, Y_{i+1}, \ldots, Y_n) - f(a_{i-1}, a'_i, Y'_{i+1}, \ldots, Y'_n) \right| \right]$$
$$\leq c.$$

The next exercise asks you to carry out this programme in two very commonly occurring distributions.

Exercise 7.7. *Let f be a function that satisfies the Lipschitz condition with coefficients c_i, $i \in [n]$. Use coupling to show the following:*

(a) If $X_1, \ldots, X_n$ are independent, then

$$|E[f|X_{i-1}, X_i = a_i] - E[f|X_{i-1}, X_i = a'_i]| \leq c_i.$$

(b) If $X_1, \ldots, X_n$ are distributed as uniform permutations over a finite set, then

$$|E[f|X_{i-1}, X_i = a_i] - E[f|X_{i-1}, X_i = a'_i]| \leq c_i + \sum_{j>i} c_j/(n-i).$$

In particular, if all $c_i = c$, then the right-hand side is $2c$.

7.4.2 Distributed Edge Colouring: Take 2

Recall the simple distributed procedure from Section 6.4: Every edge e of a Δ-regular, bipartite graph G picks a tentative colour T_e independently at random from its own list $L_e := [\Delta(G)]$ of available colours. Colour T_e becomes final if none of the adjacent edges picks it. As before we focus on a vertex u to prove a concentration bound of the form

$$\Pr(|Z - E[Z]| > t) \leq 2e^{-\Theta(t^2/\Delta)}, \tag{7.10}$$

where Z is the number of edges incident on u that successfully colour. We now want to do this removing the assumption that G is bipartite. The discussion is a nice illustration of the power of the method of bounded differences in averaged form.

First, let us see why the previous analysis falls apart. Please refer to Figure 7.3. Fix a vertex u and let Z be the number of edges incident on u that are coloured. Let $N_1(u) := \{e_1, \ldots, e_\Delta\}$ denote the edges incident on u and let $e_i := uv_i$. Let $N_2(u) := \{e_i^j, 1 \leq j \leq \Delta - 1\}$ denote the set of edges incident on the neighbours $v_1, \ldots, v_\Delta$ of u ($e_i \neq e_i^j$). We used T_i and T_i^j to

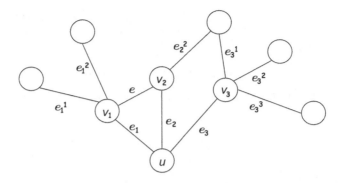

Figure 7.3. Colours around v_1 are given by the choices of (e_1^1, e_1^2, e) and colours around v_2 are those of (e, e_2^2). These two vectors of choices are not independent.

denote the tentative colours of these edges and defined the random vectors $Y_i := (T_i^1, \ldots, T_i^{\Delta-1})$ so that Z can be expressed as a function of 2Δ variables,

$$Z := f(T_1, \ldots, T_\Delta, Y_1, \ldots, Y_\Delta).$$

These variables are independent if G is bipartite, but they are not if G contains triangles. Thus, we cannot use the method in its simple form.

Instead, we will express Z as a function of $\Theta(\Delta^2)$ independent variables,

$$Z := f\left(T_e, e \in N_1(u) \bigcup N_2(u)\right),$$

and prove by a more careful analysis that the effect of each T_e, $e \in N_2(u)$, is $\sim 1/\Delta$.

Let us number the edges in $N_1(u) \bigcup N_2(u)$ as $e_1, e_2, \ldots,$ so that the edges in $N_2(u)$ come before those in $N_1(u)$. As usual, denoting the tentative colour choice of edge e_i by T_i, we want to estimate

$$c_i := |\mathrm{E}[f|T_1, \ldots, T_{i-1}, T_i = a] - \mathrm{E}[f|T_1, \ldots, T_{i-1}, T_i = a']|.$$

The plan will be, as outlined in Section 7.4.1, to find a "good" coupling of the two distributions

$$(T_j, j > i \mid T_1, \ldots, T_{i-1}, T_i = a) \quad \text{and} \quad (T_j, j > i \mid T_1, \ldots, T_{i-1}, T_i = a'),$$

that is, a joint distribution π over variables

$$(Y_j \mid j > i) \quad \text{and} \quad (Y_j' \mid j > i),$$

such that the marginals satisfy

$$\pi(Y_j, j > i) \sim (T_j, j > i \mid T_1, \ldots, T_{i-1}, T_i = a)$$

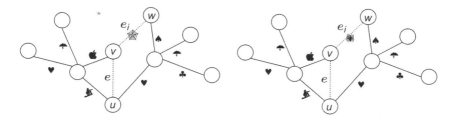

Figure 7.4. The two conditionings differ only for the assignment to e_i. The fate of e under the two conditionings differs only if $T_e = T_{e_i}$ in one scenario and $T_e \neq T_{e_i}$ in the other.

and

$$\pi(Y_j', j > i) \sim (T_j', j > i \mid T_1, \ldots, T_{i-1}, T_i = a),$$

and the coupled variables $(Y_j \mid j > i)$ and $(Y_j' \mid j > i)$ differ in very few co-ordinates, that is, here, in the colours of very few edges. (The notation $X \sim Y$ denotes the fact that the two random variables have the same distribution.)

The coupling is rather trivial.

Coupling For each $j > i$, colour Y_j is picked independently according to its distribution and Y_j' is set equal to Y_j. Trivially, the marginals are as asserted.

This coupling has the following important property.

Property 7.1. *In both colourings, all edges have the same colour except possibly the edge e_i.*

Now, let us bound

$$c_i = |E[f \mid T_1, \ldots, T_{i-1}, T_i = a_i] - E[f \mid T_1, \ldots, T_{i-1}, T_i = a_i']|$$
$$\leq E_\pi \left[\left| f(a_{i-1}, a_i, Y_j, j > i) - f(a_{i-1}, a_i', Y_j', j > i) \right| \right]. \quad (7.11)$$

There are two cases to consider:

Direct edge If $e_i \in N_1(u)$, then by property (7.1), we note that the term inside the expectation in (7.11) is at most 2; hence, $c_i \leq 2$.

Indirect edge (refer to Figure 7.4) If $e_i := vw \in N_2(u)$, then by property (7.1), the only direct edge that could suffer a different fate under the two colourings is $e = uv$. Furthermore, this happens only if $T_e \in \{a_i, a_i'\}$, an event that happens with probability at most $2/\Delta$. Since in the worst case only edge e is affected, we have the bound $c_i \leq 2/\Delta$.

Putting these together,

$$\sum_i c_i^2 = \sum_{i \in N_1(u)} 4 + \sum_{i \in N_2(u)} \frac{4}{\Delta^2} \leq 4(\Delta + 1).$$

Hence we have the bound

$$\Pr[|Z - \mathrm{E}[Z]| > t] \leq 2 \exp\left(-t^2/2(\Delta + 1)\right),$$

which, for $t = \epsilon \Delta$ for fixed $\epsilon > 0$, gives a bound exponentially decreasing in Δ.

7.4.3 Distributed Edge Colouring: Take 3

We now illustrate a more sophisticated use of coupling. Again, we consider the edge-colouring problem for bipartite graphs. The algorithm we consider now is the one described in Example 3.2, which we recall for the sake of convenience. Refer to the two sides of the bipartition, respectively, as the *top vertices* and the *bottom vertices*. The graph is Δ-regular, and each vertex knows to which side of the bipartition it belongs. Let $N_1(u)$ and $N_2(u)$, respectively, denote the edges incident on u and those incident on its neighbours. The algorithm treats the two sides of the bipartition differently:

- Every bottom vertex u, in parallel, assigns tentative colours simultaneously to every incident edge by means of a random permutation $\pi_u : N_1(u) \rightarrow [\Delta]$. These random permutations are independent.
- Every top vertex v, in parallel, resolves colour conflicts as follows: If an edge e incident on v has tentative colour $T(e) = c$, and no other edge has this tentative colour, then c becomes the final colour of e. Otherwise, vertex v arbitrarily selects an edge e_c among those with tentative colour c. Edge e_c final colour is c, while all other edges do not get a final colour.

In Example 3.2 we were able to analyse the degrees of the top vertices by means of negative dependence. Alternatively, one could use the method of bounded differences (see Problem 7.1). Here we will tackle the much more difficult problem given by the bottom vertices. That is, we focus now on a bottom vertex u to prove a concentration bound of the form

$$\Pr(|Z - \mathrm{E}[Z]| > t) \leq 2e^{-\Theta(t^2/\Delta)}, \tag{7.12}$$

where Z is the number of edges incident on u that successfully colour.

Exercise 7.8. *Show that the expected number of edges that are coloured around top and bottom vertices is* $\sim \Delta/e$. *Then, for* $t = \epsilon\Delta$, *get a concentration for a top vertex that is exponential in* Δ.

The problem in estimating Z for a bottom vertex is that changing the tentative colour of one edge can potentially have large effects, since tentative colours around a vertex are assigned by means of a permutation. The key to disentangle the situation is to use a coupling.

As in the last section, we will express Z as a function of $\Theta(\Delta^2)$ independent variables,

$$Z := f\left(T_e, e \in N_1(u) \bigcup N_2(u)\right).$$

The judicious choice of the coupling is in particular needed in order to prove that the effect of each T_e, $e \in N_2(u)$, is $\sim 1/\Delta$.

Exercise 7.9. *Show that the permutations can be realised by means of a set of independent random variables.*

As before, let us number the edges so that the edges in $N_2(u)$ come before those in $N_1(u)$. We want to estimate

$$c_i := |\mathrm{E}[f \,|\, T_{i-1} = a_{i-1}, T_i = \heartsuit] - \mathrm{E}[f \,|\, T_{i-1} = a_{i-1}, T_i = \spadesuit]|.$$

The plan will be, as outlined in Section 7.4.1, to find a "good" coupling of the two distributions

$$(T_j, j > i \,|\, T_{i-1} = a_{i-1}, T_i = \heartsuit) \quad \text{and} \quad (T_j, j > i \,|\, T_{i-1} = a_{i-1}, T_i = \spadesuit),$$

that is, a joint distribution π over variables

$$(Y_j \,|\, j > i) \quad \text{and} \quad (Y'_j \,|\, j > i),$$

such that the marginals satisfy

$$\pi(Y_j, j > i) \sim (T_j, j > i \,|\, T_{i-1} = a_{i-1}, T_i = \heartsuit)$$

and

$$\pi(Y'_j, j > i) \sim (T'_j, j > i \,|\, T_{i-1} = a_{i-1}, T_i = \spadesuit),$$

and the coupled variables $(Y_j \,|\, j > i)$ and $(Y'_j \,|\, j > i)$ differ in very few coordinates, that is, here, in the colours of very few edges.

The coupling now is more involved than in the previous section because the edge colours are not independent:

> **Coupling** For each set of edges incident on a bottom vertex whose colours are not fixed, pick a uniform permutation of the colours available at that

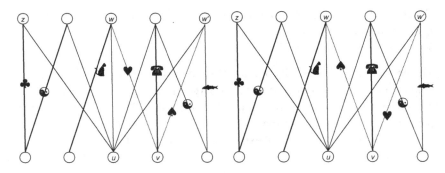

Figure 7.5. The coupled colourings (left) and (right). The edges $e_i = vw$ and $e_{i'} = vw'$, whose colours are switched, are dotted. Here, $e' = uw'$. The solid lines represent the edges whose tentative choices are exposed so far.

vertex. These are the colours Y_j, $j > i$. Set $Y'_j = Y_j$ *except for two edges*: the edge $e_i = vw$ and the edge $e_{i'} = vw'$. Under Y_j, $j > i$, their colours are $Y_i = \heartsuit$ and $Y_{i'} = \spadesuit$, respectively. While under Y'_j, $j > i$, they are swapped: $Y'_i = \spadesuit$ and $Y'_{i'} = \heartsuit$.

Exercise 7.10. *Check that this is a valid coupling; that is, the marginals are as required.*

This coupling has the following important property.

Property 7.2. *In both colourings, all edges have the same colour except two edges: e_i and some other edge e_j incident on the same bottom vertex for which the colours $\heartsuit$ and $\spadesuit$ are swapped.*

Now, let us bound

$$c_i = |\mathrm{E}[f|T_1, \ldots, T_{i-1}, T_i = \heartsuit] - \mathrm{E}[f|T_1, \ldots, T_{i-1}, T_i = \spadesuit]|$$
$$\leq \mathrm{E}_\pi \left[\left| f(a_{i-1}, \heartsuit, Y_j, j > i) - f(a_{i-1}, \spadesuit, Y'_j, j > i) \right| \right]. \qquad (7.13)$$

Again, there are two cases to consider:

Direct edge If $e_i \in N_1(u)$, then by property (7.2), we note that the term inside the expectation in (7.13) is at most 2; hence, $c_i \leq 2$.

Indirect edge (Refer to Figure 7.5) Suppose $e_i = vw \in N_2(u)$ is incident on bottom vertex v (so uw is one of the edges around u). By property (7.2), the two colourings differ only in the colours of the two edges e_i and some other edge $e_{i'} = vw'$ incident on v. In the worst case, $e_{i'}$ is also adjacent to an edge incident on u, say, $e' = uw'$. Now, from property (7.2), we note that the only possible edges around u that could suffer different fates under the two colourings are $e = uw$ and $e' = uw'$. Furthermore, this would happen only if the tentative colours of these edges are one of the colours ♠ or ♡. Thus, the maximum effect is 2, and the probability that e or e' uses spade or heart is at most $4/\Delta$. Thus, we have the bound $c_i \leq 8/\Delta$.

Putting these together,

$$\sum_i c_i^2 = \sum_{i \in N_1(u)} 4 + \sum_{i \in N_2(u)} \frac{64}{\Delta^2} \leq 4\Delta + 64.$$

Hence we have the bound

$$\Pr[|Z - \mathrm{E}[Z]| > t] \leq 2 \exp\left(-t^2/2\Delta + 32\right),$$

which, for $t = \epsilon \Delta$ for fixed $\epsilon > 0$, gives a bound exponentially decreasing in Δ. The analysis can be improved somewhat (see Problem 7.1).

7.5 Handling Rare Bad Events

In some situations, one can apply the method of average bounded differences successfully by bounding the "maximum effect" coefficients but for certain pathological circumstances. Such rare "bad events" can be handled using the following version of the method of average bounded differences.

Theorem 7.1. *Let f be a function of n random variables $X_1, \ldots, X_n$, each X_i taking values in a set A_i, such that $\mathrm{E}f$ is bounded. Assume that*

$$m \leq f(X_1, \ldots, X_n) \leq M.$$

Let $\mathcal{B}$ any event, and let c_i be the maximum effect of f assuming $\mathcal{B}^c$:

$$|\mathrm{E}[f \,|\, X_{i-1}, X_i = a_i, \mathcal{B}^c] - \mathrm{E}[f \,|\, X_{i-1}, X_i = a_i', \mathcal{B}^c]| \leq c_i.$$

Then

$$\Pr[f > \mathrm{E}[f] + t + (M - m)\Pr(\mathcal{B})] \leq \exp\left(-\frac{2t^2}{\sum_i c_i^2}\right) + \Pr[\mathcal{B}]$$

and

$$\Pr[f < \mathrm{E}[f] - t - (M - m)\Pr(\mathcal{B})] \leq \exp\left(-\frac{t^2}{\sum_i c_i^2}\right) + \Pr[\mathcal{B}].$$

Proof. We prove the statement for the upper tail. The proof for the lower tail is analogous. For any value $t > 0$,

$$\Pr(f > \mathrm{E}[f] + t) \le \Pr(f > \mathrm{E}[f] + t \mid \mathcal{B}^c) + \Pr[\mathcal{B}]. \qquad (7.14)$$

To bound $\Pr(f > \mathrm{E}[f] + t \mid \mathcal{B}^c)$, we apply Theorem 5.3 to $(f \mid \mathcal{B}^c)$ and get

$$\Pr(f > \mathrm{E}[f] + t \mid \mathcal{B}^c) \le \exp\left(-\frac{2t^2}{\sum_i c_i^2}\right). \qquad (7.15)$$

Note that all c_i's are computed in the subspace obtained by conditioning on $\mathcal{B}^c$. To conclude the proof we show that $\mathrm{E}[f]$ and $\mathrm{E}[f \mid \mathcal{B}^c]$ are very close. Now, since

$$\mathrm{E}[f] = \mathrm{E}[f \mid \mathcal{B}]\Pr[\mathcal{B}] + \mathrm{E}[f \mid \mathcal{B}^c]\Pr[\mathcal{B}^c]$$

and $m \le f \le M$, we have that

$$\mathrm{E}[f \mid \mathcal{B}^c] - (\mathrm{E}[f \mid \mathcal{B}^c] - m)\Pr[\mathcal{B}] \le \mathrm{E}[f]$$
$$\le \mathrm{E}[f \mid \mathcal{B}^c] + (M - \mathrm{E}[f \mid \mathcal{B}^c])\Pr[\mathcal{B}]$$

so that

$$|\mathrm{E}[f] - \mathrm{E}[f \mid \mathcal{B}^c]| \le (M - m)\Pr[\mathcal{B}].$$

The claim follows: ∎

The error term $(M - m)\Pr[\mathcal{B}^c]$ in practice is going to be small and easy to estimate. However, using some tricky technical arguments, one can prove ([66], Theorem 3.7) the following cleaner statement:

Theorem 7.2. *Let f be a function of n random variables $X_1, \ldots, X_n$, each X_i taking values in a set A_i, such that $\mathrm{E}f$ is bounded. Let $\mathcal{B}$ be any event, and let c_i be the maximum effect of f assuming $\mathcal{B}^c$:*

$$|\mathrm{E}[f \mid X_{i-1}, X_i = a_i, \mathcal{B}^c] - \mathrm{E}[f \mid X_{i-1}, X_i = a_i', \mathcal{B}^c]| \le c_i.$$

Then if $t \ge 0$

$$\Pr(f > \mathrm{E}[f] + t) \le \exp\left(-\frac{2t^2}{\sum_i c_i^2}\right) + \Pr[\mathcal{B}], \qquad (7.16)$$

where, again, the maximum effects c_i are those obtained conditioned on $\mathcal{B}^c$.

7.6 Quicksort

We shall sketch the application of the method of average bounded differences to quicksort. This application is interesting because it is a very natural application of the method and yields a provably optimal tail bound. While conceptually simple, the details required to obtain the tightest bound are messy, so we shall confine ourselves to indicating the basic method.

Recall that quicksort can be modelled as a binary tree T, corresponding to the partition around the pivot element performed at each stage. With each node v of the binary tree, we associate the list L_v that needs to be sorted there. At the outset, the root r is associated with $L_r = L$, the input list, and if the the pivot element chosen at node v is X_v, the lists associated with the left and right children of v are the sublists of L_v consisting of, respectively, all elements less than X_v and all elements greater than X_v. (For simplicity, we assume that the input list contains all distinct elements.) Now, the number of comparisons performed by quicksort on the input list L, Q_L, is a random variable given by some function f of the random choices made for the pivot elements, $X_v, v \in T$:

$$Q_L = f(X_v, v \in T).$$

We shall now expose the variables $X_v, v \in T$, in the natural top-down fashion: level by level and left to right within a level, starting with the root. Let us denote this (inorder) ordering of the nodes of T by $<$. Thus, to apply the method of martingale differences, we merely need to estimate for each node $v \in T$,

$$|E[Q_L \mid X_w, w < v] - E[Q_L \mid X_w, w \le v]|.$$

A moment's reflection shows that this difference is simply

$$|E[Q_{L_v}] - E[Q_{L_v} \mid X_v]|,$$

where L_v is the list associated with v as a result of the previous choices of the partitions given by $X_w, w < v$. That is, the problem reduces to estimating the difference between the expected number of comparisons performed on a given list when the first partition is specified and when it is not. Such an estimate is readily available for quicksort via the recurrence satisfied by the expected value $q_n := E[Q_n]$, the expected number of comparisons performed on a input list of length n. If the first partition (which by itself requires $n - 1$ comparisons) splits the list into a left part of size $k, 0 \le k < n$, and a right part of size $n - 1 - k$, the expected number of comparisons is $n - 1 + q_k + q_{n-1-k}$ and the estimate is

$$|q_n - (n - 1 + q_k + q_{n-k-1})| \le n - 1.$$

We shall plug this estimate into the method of bounded differences: thus, if $\ell_v := |L_v|$ is the length of the list associated with node v, then we need to estimate $\sum_v \ell_v^2$. This is potentially problematical, since these lengths are themselves random variables. Suppose that we restrict attention to levels $k \geq k_1$ for which we can show that

1. $\ell_v \leq \alpha n$ for some parameter α to be chosen later, and
2. k_1 is small enough that the difference between the real process and the one obtained by fixing the values upto level k_1 arbitrarily is negligibly small.

Then summing over all levels $\geq k_1$, level by level, and denoting the height of a vertex v by $h(v)$,

$$
\begin{aligned}
\sum_v \ell_v^2 &= \sum_{k \geq k_1} \sum_{h(v)=k} \ell_v^2 \\
&\leq \sum_{k \geq k_1} \sum_{h(v)=k} \alpha n \ell_v \\
&= \sum_{k \geq k_1} \alpha n \sum_{h(v)=k} \ell_v \\
&\leq \sum_{k \geq k_1} \alpha n^2.
\end{aligned}
$$

Next we are faced with yet another problem: the number of levels, which itself is again a random variable. Suppose we can show, for some $k_2 > k_1$, that the tree has height no more than k_2 with high probability. Then the previously computed sum reduces to $(k_2 - k_1)\alpha n^2$.

Finally we can apply Theorem 7.2. Here the "bad events" we want to exclude are the events that after k_1 levels, the list sizes exceed α, and that the height of the tree exceeds k_2. All that remains is to choose the parameters with care. Suppose the maximum size of the list associated with a node at height at least k_1 exceeds αn with probability at most p_1 and that the overall height of the tree exceeds k_2 with probability at most p_2. (One can estimate these probabilities in an elementary way by using the fact that the size of the list at a node at depth $k \geq 0$ is explicitly given by $n \prod_{1 \leq i \leq k} Z_i$, where each Z_i is uniformly distributed in $[0, 1]$.) Then the final result, applying Theorem 7.2, will be

$$
\Pr[Q_n > q_n + t] < p_1 + p_2 + \exp\left(\frac{-2t^2}{(k_2 - k_1)\alpha n^2}\right).
$$

(If we applied Theorem 7.1, we would have an additional error term: if we use pessimistic estimates of the maximum and minimum values of the number of comparisons as n^2 and 0, respectively, then the error term is $n^2(p_1 + p_2)$, which is $o(1)$.)

We choose the parameters to optimise this sum of three terms. The result whose details are messy (see [64]) is as follows:

Theorem 7.3. *Let $\epsilon = \epsilon(n)$ satisfy $1/\ln n < \epsilon \leq 1$. Then as $n \to \infty$,*

$$\Pr[|Q_n/q_n - 1| > \epsilon] < n^{-2\epsilon(\ln \ln n - \ln(1/\epsilon) + O(\ln \ln \ln n))}.$$

This bound is slightly better than an inverse polynomial bound and can be shown to be essentially tight [64].

7.7 Pointers to the Literature

The stochastic travelling salesman problem is discussed in [84]. The use of coupling with the method of average bounded differences is from [29], which simplifies considerably the much more complicated analysis of [76]. For edge- and vertex-colouring problems, see also [28, 38, 39] and the book [73]. The use of the method of average bounded differences for quicksort is from [64].

7.8 Problems

Problem 7.1. Consider the edge-colouring algorithm of Section 7.4.3.

(a) Let Z be the number of edges incident on a top vertex that successfully colour. Show that

$$\Pr(|Z - EZ| > t) \leq 2e^{-\Theta(t^2/\Delta)}. \qquad (7.17)$$

(b) Show by a tighter analysis of a bottom vertex that

$$c_i := |E[Z|T_1 \cdots T_{i-1}, T_i = a] - E[Z|T_1 \cdots T_{i-1}, T_i = b]| \leq \frac{2}{\Delta},$$

and hence strengthen the concentration bound (by a constant factor in the exponent). $\triangledown$

Problem 7.2 (FKG/Chebyshev correlation inequality). Show that for any non-decreasing functions f and g and for any random variable X,

$$E[f(X)g(X)] \geq E[f(X)]E[g(X)].$$

(HINT: Let Y be distributed identical to X but independent of it. Consider $E[(f(X) - f(Y))(g(X) - g(Y))]$. Argue this is non-negative and simplify it using linearity of expectation.) $\triangledown$

Problem 7.3 (Kryptographs [78, 79]). The following graph model arises in the context of cryptographically secure sensor networks [77, 78]. We are given a *pool* of cryptographic keys that can be identified with the finite set $P := [m]$ and a set of n vertices. Each vertex i is given a *key ring* S_i generated by sampling P with replacement k times. Two vertices i and j are joined by an edge if and only if $S_i \cap S_j \neq \emptyset$. In the following we assume that $k = \Theta(\log n)$ and $m = \Theta(n \log n)$.

(a) Show that the graph is connected with probability at least $1 - 1/n^2$.
    (HINT: Show that given a set S of vertices, the size of the union of the key rings of vertices in S is not far from its expectation. Using this, show that it is unlikely that G has a cut.)
(b) Using coupling show that the graph is connected with at least the same probability when the key rings are generated without replacement.   ▽

Problem 7.4 (Concentration for permutations). Let $f(x_1, \ldots, x_n)$ be a Lipschitz function with constant c; that is, changing any coordinate changes the value of f by at most c. Let σ be a permutation of $[n]$ chosen uniformly at random. Show a strong concentration for $f(\sigma(1), \ldots, \sigma(n))$. (HINT: Use a natural coupling to bound $\left| E[f \mid X_{i-1}, X_i = a_i] - E[f \mid X_{i-1}, X_i = a_i'] \right|$.)
    ▽

Problem 7.5. Consider the edge-colouring algorithm of Section 7.4.2. Fix an edge e and suppose that after one step of the algorithm, the final colours chosen by the edge incident on e are removed from e's colour list. Let X_e be the random variable denoting the number of colours that remain in e's list. Compute $E[X_e]$ and show that X_e is sharply concentrated around its mean. Can you do the same for the algorithm of Section 7.4.3?
    ▽

Problem 7.6. Let $G = (V, E)$ be a d-regular graph with n vertices. Consider the following algorithm for computing independent sets. Let $p : V \to [n]$ be a random permutation of the vertices. A vertex i enters the independent set if and only if $p_i < p_j$ for every j neighbour of i. (The set so computed is clearly independent.) Let X denote the size of the resulting independent set. Compute $E[X]$ and show that X is concentrated around its expectation.   ▽

Problem 7.7 [70]. The following problem arises in the context of routing with optical switches. We have a graph with $n := k^2$ nodes V partitioned into $k = \sqrt{n}$ many groups. The group to which a node u belongs is denoted as S_u. There is also a fixed permutation $\pi : V \to V$ (denoting the fact that node u is to send a message to π_u). The set of pairs $u\pi_u$ is the set of edges of the graph.

Consider the following simple procedure: each node u picks a random colour $c_u \in [k]$ with which it colours the edge $u\pi_u$. A colour is *successful* if (a) no other edge leaving group S_u has the same colour, and (b) no other edge entering group S_{π_u} has the same colour. An edge is successful if its colour is also successful. Let X be the number of successful edges.

- Compute $E[X]$ and show a concentration result for X.
- Consider now the following procedure: All successful edges are removed from the graph. The remaining edges pick again a colour, and so on, until there are no edges left. Using the techniques of Chapter 4 show that all edges are removed within $O(\log n)$ rounds, with high probability.
- Can you show that they are in fact all removed within $O(\log \log n)$ many rounds, with high probability? ▽

Problem 7.8 (From [73]). First toss a fair coin. Now, for $i \geq 1$, if the ith toss is head, for the $(i + 1)$st toss, use a biased coin which shows head with probability $2/3$, and if ith toss is tail, for the $(i + 1)$th toss, use a biased coin which shows tail with probability $2/3$. Let X be no of heads with a total of n tosses.

- Show that $E[X] = n/2$.
- Show strong concentration. ▽

Problem 7.9 (Geometric probability). Let Q be a given point in the unit square $[0, 1]^2$ and let $P_1, \ldots, P_l$ be l points chosen uniformly and independently at random in the unit square. Let Z denote the shortest distance from Q to one of the points $P_1, \ldots, P_l$.

(a) Observe that if $Z > x$, then no P_i lies within the circle $C(Q, x)$ centered at Q with radius x. Note that $x \leq \sqrt{2}$.
(b) Argue that there is a constant c such that for all $x \in (0, \sqrt{2}]$, the intersection of $C(Q, x)$ with the unit square has area at least cx^2. Hence deduce that

$$\Pr[Z > x] \leq (1 - cx^2)^l, \quad x \in (0, \sqrt{2}].$$

(c) Integrate to deduce that $E[Z] \leq d/\sqrt{l}$ for some constant $d > 0$. ▽

8

The Method of Bounded Variances

In this chapter we describe a tail bound similar in flavour to the method of bounded differences. This new bound too rests on a martingale inequality similar to Azuma's. In the previous chapters we saw how, given a function $f(X_1, \ldots, X_n)$, the strength of the method of bounded differences depends on our ability to bound the absolute increments of the Doob martingale sequence $Z_i := E[f|X_1, \ldots, X_i]$. In doing this, we would expose the variables $X_1, \ldots, X_n$ one at a time and consider the expected change of f when X_i is revealed, conditioned on the values of the $X_1, \ldots, X_{i-1}$ exposed so far, and take the maximum value among all assignments to the first $i - 1$ variable. That is, we would look for a bound c_i as small as possible, such that

$$|E[f|X_1, \ldots, X_i] - E[f|X_1, \ldots, X_{i-1}]| \le c_i$$

for all possible assignments to $X_1, \ldots, X_i$. The resulting bound was

$$\Pr[|X - E[X]| > t] \le 2 \exp\left\{-\frac{t^2}{2\sum_i c_i^2}\right\}.$$

We will see in this chapter that basically the same result obtains if we consider the sum of variances of the increments, conditioned on the variables exposed so far:

$$v_i := var(E[f|X_1, \ldots, X_i] - E[f|X_1, \ldots, X_{i-1}]).$$

The resulting bound will be

$$\Pr[|X - E[X]| > t] \le 2 \exp\left\{-\frac{t^2}{4\sum_i v_i^2}\right\},$$

assuming some mild conditions on t. Since the variance factors in the probability with which jumps occur, this estimate is often quite sharp. What we will see in this chapter resembles quite closely what we saw in Chapter 1, where we derived the variance bound

$$\Pr[|X - \mathrm{E}[X]| > t] \leq 2 \exp\left\{-t^2/4\sigma^2\right\}.$$

This bound can be much stronger than the original Chernoff bound and in fact it essentially subsumes it. In practice, we will see that good estimates of the variance are not hard to compute. In a sense, the method can be viewed as a quick-and-dirty version of the method of bounded differences. We begin by proving the basic underlying martingale inequality.

8.1 A Variance Bound for Martingale Sequences

We make use of the basic definitions of martingales and their properties developed in Chapter 5. Recall that given a vector X, the notation X_i denotes the truncated vector consisting of the first i coordinates of X_i.

Theorem 8.1. *Let $Z_0, Z_1, \ldots, Z_n$ be a martingale with respect to the sequence $X_0, X_1, \ldots, X_n$, satisfying the bounded difference condition*

$$|Z_i - Z_{i-1}| \leq c_i$$

for some set of non-negative values c_i. Let

$$V := \sum_{i \leq n} v_i,$$

where

$$v_i = \sup var(Z_i - Z_{i-1}|X_{i-1}),$$

where the sup is taken over all possible assignments to X_{i-1}. Then

$$\Pr(Z_n > Z_0 + t) \leq \exp\left(-\frac{t^2}{4V}\right)$$

and

$$\Pr(Z_n < Z_0 - t) \leq \exp\left(-\frac{t^2}{4V}\right),$$

provided that

$$t \leq 2V/\max_i c_i. \tag{8.1}$$

Proof. The initial part of the proof is identical to that of Theorem 5.2 but we reproduce it here for ease of exposition. It suffices to prove the statement for the upper tail. The proof for the lower tail is symmetrical with the martingale Z replaced by $-Z$.

Assume without loss of generality that $Z_0 := 0$ and define the martingale difference sequence $D_i := Z_i - Z_{i-1}, i \geq 1$. Then $Z_n = Z_{n-1} + D_n$. Note that $E[D_i] = 0$, for all i. By Markov's inequality,

$$\Pr(Z_n > t) \leq \min_{\lambda > 0} \frac{E[e^{\lambda Z_n}]}{e^{\lambda t}}. \tag{8.2}$$

With foresight we set

$$\lambda := \frac{t}{2V}. \tag{8.3}$$

As usual we focus on the numerator $E[e^{\lambda Z_n}]$ and seek a good upper bound for it.

$$E[e^{\lambda Z_n}] = E[e^{\lambda(Z_{n-1}+D_n)}]$$
$$= E[E[e^{\lambda(Z_{n-1}+D_n)} \mid X_{n-1}]]$$
$$= E[e^{\lambda Z_{n-1}} E[e^{\lambda D_n} \mid X_{n-1}]].$$

We now show that for all i,

$$E[e^{\lambda D_i} \mid X_{i-1}] \leq e^{\lambda^2 v_i}. \tag{8.4}$$

Assuming this, it follows by induction that

$$E[e^{\lambda Z_n}] = E[e^{\lambda Z_{n-1}} E[e^{\lambda D_n} \mid X_{n-1}]]$$
$$\leq E[e^{\lambda Z_{n-1}}] e^{\lambda^2 v_n}$$
$$\leq e^{\lambda^2 V}.$$

The base case is the trivial case $Z_0 = 0$. Using our choice for λ and the bound on the numerator, it follows that

$$\Pr(Z_n > t) \leq \min_{\lambda > 0} \frac{E[e^{\lambda Z_n}]}{e^{\lambda t}}$$
$$\leq \frac{e^{\lambda^2 V}}{e^{\lambda t}}$$
$$= e^{-t^2/2V}.$$

The crux then is to establish (8.4). This follows from the well-known inequalities $1 + x \leq e^x$, valid for all x, and $e^x \leq 1 + x + x^2$, valid for $|x| \leq 1$.

Since Z is a martingale with respect to X, $E[D_i|X_{i-1}] = 0$. Now, if $\lambda|D_i| \leq 1$, then

$$E[e^{\lambda D_i}|X_{i-1}] \leq E[1 + \lambda D_i + (\lambda D_i)^2|X_{i-1}]$$
$$= 1 + \lambda^2 E[D_i^2|X_{i-1}]$$
$$= 1 + \lambda^2 v_i$$
$$\leq e^{\lambda^2 v_i}.$$

The condition $\lambda|D_i| \leq 1$ follows, for all i, from hypothesis (8.1) and Equation (8.3). The claim follows. ∎

A couple of observations are in order. First, the term V is related to the variance of Z_n in the following way: $E[V] = var(Z_n)$ (see Problem 8.1). Second, the condition on t roughly says that this inequality is a bound for deviations that are "not too large." By using Bernstein's estimate (1.2) it is possible to obtain the following slightly sharper bound without making any assumptions on t:

$$\Pr(Z_n > Z_0 + t) \leq \exp\left(-\frac{t^2}{2V(1 + bt/3V)}\right). \tag{8.5}$$

The term b is defined as the $\max_k dev_k$, where $dev_k := \sup\{(Z_k - Z_{k-1}|X_1 = x_1, \ldots, X_{k-1} = x_{k-1}\}$. In some situations the error term bt/V is negligible, and (8.5) yields a slightly sharper bound than that of Theorem 8.2. The interested reader can refer to [67].

The next step is to package this inequality in a form suitable for the applications. Note that the ground variables X_i's need not be independent for the next theorem to hold.

Theorem 8.2 (The method of bounded variances). *Let $X_1, \ldots, X_n$ be an arbitrary set of random variables and let $f := f(X_1, \ldots, X_n)$ be such that $\mathbf{E}f$ is finite. Let*

$$D_i := E[f|X_i] - E[f|X_{i-1}]$$

and let $c_1, \ldots, c_n$ be such that

$$|D_i| \leq c_i. \tag{8.6}$$

And let

$$V := \sum_{i=1}^{n} v_i,$$

where

$$v_i := \sup var\,(D_i | X_{i-1}),$$

with the sup *taken over all possible assignment to* X_{i-1}. *Then*

$$\Pr[f > Ef + t] \le \exp\left(-\frac{t^2}{4V}\right)$$

and

$$\Pr[f < Ef - t] \le \exp\left(-\frac{t^2}{4V}\right),$$

provided that $t \le 2V / \max_i c_i$.

Proof. Apply Theorem 8.1 to the Doob martingale sequence $Z_i := E[f | X_i]$ (see Problem 8.3). ∎

Intuitively, when applying this inequality we will expose, or *query*, the values of the variables X_i one by one, starting from $E[f]$ and ending with $f(X_1, \ldots, X_n)$. As we shall see, the power of this inequality derives from the fact that it is possible, and sometimes easy, to give good estimates of the v_i's. Note that one has the freedom to decide the sequence according to which the variables are exposed. This will be put to good effect in the applications to follow.

Notation 8.3. *In the sequel we shall refer to* V *as the* variance *of* f *and to* c_i *as the* maximum effect *of the* ith query.

8.2 Applications

As usual, the best approach to understand the method is by means of examples of increasing sophistication. For the method to be useful one needs simple ways to bound the variance. A simple but useful bound is the following: Assume that a random variable X is such that $E[X] = 0$ and $|X| \le r$. Then

$$var(X) \le \frac{r^2}{4} \tag{8.7}$$

(see Problem 8.2).

With this we can essentially recover the basic version of the method of bounded differences (Theorem 5.3). Assume that we are given a function $f(X_1, \ldots, X_n)$ satisfying the conditions

$$|f(X) - f(X')| \le c_i$$

for each i, whenever X and X' differ only in the ith coordinate. We apply (8.7) to the random variable $D_i := \mathrm{E}[f|X_1, \ldots, X_i] - \mathrm{E}[f|X_1, \ldots, X_{i-1}]$, which has zero mean. Thus,

$$v_i = var(D_i) \leq \frac{c_i^2}{4}. \tag{8.8}$$

Therefore $V \leq \frac{1}{4} \sum_i c_i^2$ and by Theorem 8.2,

$$\Pr[f > \mathrm{E}f + t] \leq \exp\left(-\frac{t^2}{4V}\right) \leq \exp\left(-\frac{t^2}{\sum_i c_i^2}\right),$$

provided that $t \leq 2V/\max_i c_i$.

Exercise 8.1. *Establish the basic Chernoff–Hoeffding bounds by using the method of bounded variances.*

The next example is to derive the variance bound of the basic Chernoff–Hoeffding bounds that we developed in Section 1.7. We are given n independent random variables $X_i \in [0, 1]$ and we want to prove that

$$\Pr[X > \mathrm{E}X + t] \leq \exp\left(-\frac{t^2}{4\sigma^2}\right),$$

where $X := \sum_i X_i$, $\sigma^2 := \sum_i \sigma_i^2$ and $\sigma_i^2 := var(X_i)$. We apply the method to $f(X_1, \ldots, X_n) := \sum_i X_i$. Now, if we set

$$Z_i := \mathrm{E}[f|X_1, \ldots, X_i],$$

we have that

$$|Z_i - Z_{i-1}| \leq 1.$$

Furthermore, by independence we get

$$D_i := Z_i - Z_{i-1} = X_i - \mathrm{E}[X_i]$$

and

$$var(D_i) = var(X_i),$$

and thus $V = \sum_i var(X_i) = \sigma^2$. Therefore, by invoking Theorem 8.2,

$$\Pr[f > \mathrm{E}f + t] \leq \exp\left(-\frac{t^2}{4V}\right) = \exp\left(-\frac{t^2}{4\sigma^2}\right)$$

if $t \leq 2V$. In the case when $\Pr[X_i = 1] = p$, for all i, we have by independence that $\sigma^2 = np(1-p)$ and the bound becomes

$$\Pr[f > \mathrm{E}f + t] \leq e^{-t^2/4np(1-p)}.$$

The variance is maximised when $p = 1/2$ so that $\sigma^2 \le n/4$, which gives

$$\Pr[f > \mathrm{E}f + t] \le \exp^{-t^2/n} .$$

This bound loses a factor of 2 in the exponent. By applying the slightly sharper bound (8.5) one essentially recovers (1.6).

8.2.1 Bounding the Variance

We saw that (8.7) gives a simple but useful bound for the variance that always applies. A common situation that arises when studying a function $f(X_1, \ldots, X_n)$ is when each X_i takes on two types of values: a "good" value, corresponding to a set of choices with total probability p_i, with probability p_i and a "bad" value with total probability $1 - p_i$, corresponding to the remaining set of choices. In this case, assuming that X_i takes values in a finite set A_i, we get the following useful bound:

$$v_i \le p_i(1 - p_i)c_i^2 \tag{8.9}$$

so that

$$\Pr[f > \mathrm{E}f + t] \le \exp^{-t^2/\sum_i p_i(1-p_i)c_i^2} \tag{8.10}$$

and

$$\Pr[f < \mathrm{E}f - t] \le \exp^{-t^2/\sum_i p_i(1-p_i)c_i^2} . \tag{8.11}$$

Bound (8.9) follows from elementary, but non-trivial, computations (see Problem 8.10).

8.2.2 Edge Colouring: Take 4

Let us apply this bounding technique to the edge-colouring problem of Section 7.4.2. Recall the algorithm. Every edge e of a graph G picks a tentative colour t_e independently at random from its own list $L_e := [\Delta(G)]$ of available colours. Colour t_e becomes final if none of the adjacent edges picks it. We focus on a vertex u to prove a concentration bound of the form

$$\Pr(|Z - \mathrm{E}Z| > t) \le 2e^{-\Theta(t^2/\Delta)}, \tag{8.12}$$

where Z is the number of edges incident on u that successfully colour. In Section 7.4.2 we used the method of bounded differences in averaged form and a somewhat lengthy case analysis. The argument simplifies considerably if one uses the method of bounded variances. In Section 7.4.2 we exposed the edge choices in this order: first the edges in $N_2(u)$ (those incident on neighbours

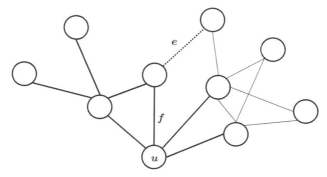

Figure 8.1. Solid edges are exposed, while thin edges are not. The choice of edge e can affect only edge f, and this happens with probability $1/\Delta$.

of u) and then those in $N_1(u)$ (incident on u). Now we will do the reverse. The goal now, as before, is to show that the total variation, in this case the variance, of these choices is $O(\Delta)$. Each edge in $N_1(u)$ can affect the final degree by at most 2, for a total contribution to V of Δ in view of (8.8). When we expose the random choices of the remaining edges, the key observation is the following: Let $e \in N_2(u)$ be the edge whose effect we are considering, and let $f \in N_1(u)$ denote the edge incident on u that touches e (refer to Figure 8.1). Note that when we expose e's tentative choice, f has already been queried. The choice of e can affect f (and only f), but only if e picks the same colour chosen by f, and this happens with probability $1/|L_e| = 1/\Delta$. Therefore, by (8.9), the maximum effect of this choice is 1 and its variance is at most

$$1 \times \frac{1}{\Delta} \times \left(1 - \frac{1}{\Delta}\right) \le \frac{1}{\Delta}.$$

(e can touch two edges incident on u, but its effect can be at most 1. Why?) Therefore, we can bound the total variance as follows:

$$V \le \Delta + \Delta(\Delta - 1)\frac{1}{\Delta} \le 2\Delta,$$

which gives, for $t \le 2V/\max_i c_i = V$,

$$\Pr[|Z - \mathrm{E}[Z]| > t] \le 2\exp(t^2/8\Delta). \tag{8.13}$$

Note that while in Section 7.4.2 the overall effect of edges in $N_2(u)$ was estimated to be $O(1)$, here the estimate is $O(\Delta)$. This is good enough however, since in any case the overall effect of the edges in $N_1(u)$ is also $O(\Delta)$.

8.2.3 Dealing with Unlikely Circumstances

Sometimes the effect of a random variable X_i on the value of a function $f(X_1, \ldots, X_n)$ can be quite large, but only with very low probability. In other words, it might be the case that for most outcomes of $X_1, \ldots, X_n$ the variance of f is very small. In dealing with such situations the following result comes handy. In the statement of the next theorem the event $\mathcal{B}$ is to be understood as a set of exceptional outcomes of very low probability.

Theorem 8.4. *Let f be a function of n random variables $X_1, \ldots, X_n$, each X_i taking values in a set A_i, such that $E[f]$ is bounded. Assume that*

$$m \leq f(X_1, \ldots, X_n) \leq M.$$

Let $\mathcal{B}$ be any event, and let V and c_i be, respectively, the variance and the maximum effects of f assuming $\mathcal{B}^c$. Then

$$\Pr[f > E[f] + t + (M - m)\Pr(\mathcal{B})] \leq \exp\left(-\frac{t^2}{4V}\right) + \Pr(\mathcal{B})$$

and

$$\Pr[f < E[f] - t - (M - m)\Pr(\mathcal{B})] \leq \exp\left(-\frac{t^2}{4V}\right) + \Pr(\mathcal{B}).$$

Proof. We prove the statement for the upper tail. The proof for the lower tail is analogous. For any t,

$$\Pr(f > E[f] + t) \leq \Pr(f > E[f] + t \mid \mathcal{B}^c) + \Pr(\mathcal{B}). \qquad (8.14)$$

To bound $\Pr(f > E[f] + t \mid \mathcal{B}^c)$ we apply Theorem 8.2 to $(f \mid \mathcal{B}^c)$ and get

$$\Pr(f > E[f \mid \mathcal{B}^c] + t \mid \mathcal{B}^c) \leq \exp\left(-\frac{t^2}{4V}\right) \qquad (8.15)$$

for every $t \leq 2V / \max c_i$, provided that V and all c_i's are computed in the subspace obtained by conditioning on $\mathcal{B}^c$. To conclude the proof we show that $E[f]$ and $E[f \mid \mathcal{B}^c]$ are very close. Now,

$$E[f] = E[f \mid \mathcal{B}]\Pr(\mathcal{B}) + E[f \mid \mathcal{B}^c]\Pr(\mathcal{B}^c)$$

$$\geq m\Pr(\mathcal{B}) + E[f \mid \mathcal{B}^c](1 - \Pr(\mathcal{B}))$$

$$= E[f \mid \mathcal{B}^c] - (E[f \mid \mathcal{B}^c] - m)\Pr(\mathcal{B}).$$

Likewise,

$$E[f] \leq E[f \mid \mathcal{B}^c] + (M - E[f \mid \mathcal{B}^c])\Pr(\mathcal{B}),$$

so that

$$|E[f] - E[f|\mathcal{B}^c]| \leq (M - m)\Pr(\mathcal{B}).$$

The claim follows. ∎

The error term $(M - m)\Pr[\mathcal{B}^c]$ in practice is going to be $o(1)$ and easy to estimate, as the next example will make clear.

It is possible to prove the following cleaner statement [67]: For any $t \leq 2V/\max c_i$,

$$\Pr(f > E[f] + t) \leq \exp\left(-\frac{t^2}{4V}\right) + \Pr[\mathcal{B}], \tag{8.16}$$

where V is the variance and the maximum effects c_i are those obtained conditioned on $\mathcal{B}^c$. The proof however is not as simple as that of Theorem 8.4, while this formulation in practice is not any stronger, at least for the kind of applications that one normally encounters in the analysis of algorithms.

Let us see a non-trivial application of Theorem 8.4. We have a d-regular graph G in which each vertex is given a list of c colours. We consider the same simple distributed algorithm of the previous section, this time applied to the vertices: every vertex u has a list of L_u of c colours. It picks a tentative colour at random from its list, which becomes final only if no neighbour picks the same colour. It is possible to prove that by iterating this algorithm (each time removing from the lists the final colours chosen by the neighbours) computes a vertex-colouring with high probability in $O(\log n)$ many rounds, provided that G has no triangles, $d \gg \log n$ and $c = \Omega(d/\ln d)$ [39]. Note that c can be much smaller than d. More generally, it is known that such good colourings exist for triangle-free graphs and that this is the best that one can hope for, since there are infinite families of triangle-free graphs whose chromatic number is $\Omega(d/\ln d)$ [10, 51]. In what follows we assume for simplicity that $c = d/\log_2 d$.

Here we analyse what happens to the degree of a vertex after one round and show that it is sharply concentrated around its expectation. As with the previous example this will exemplify some of the difficulties of the full analysis. Let us fix a vertex u and let Z be the number of neighbours of u which colour themselves successfully. We first compute $E[Z]$. The probability that a vertex colours itself is

$$\left(1 - \frac{1}{c}\right)^d \sim e^{-d/c}$$

so that

$$E[Z] \sim de^{-d/c}.$$

We are interested in a bound on the probability that the new degree $d' := d - Z$ is far from its expectation. We will show that this happens only with inverse polynomial probability in d. As with the edge-colouring example the value of Z depends not only on the tentative colour choices of the neighbours of u but also on those of the neighbours of the neighbours – $\Theta(d^2)$ choices in total. To compound the problem, vertices at distance 2 can now have very large effects. Assume for instance that all neighbours of u pick colour a tentatively. If a vertex w at distance 2 from u also picks a, the effect can be as large as $|N_u \cap N_w|$, which, in general, can be as large as d. We can get around this problem using the fact that it is unlikely that "many" neighbours of u will pick the same colour.

Let $N_i(u)$ denote the set of vertices at distance i from u. Z depends on the choices of vertices in $\{u\} \cup N_1(u) \cup N_2(u)$. We expose the colour choices in this order: first u, then the vertices in $N_1(u)$ (in any order) and finally those in $N_2(u)$ (in any order). The first query does not affect the variance. The next d queries can each affect the final outcome of Z by 1, but note that this is possible only if the vertex selects the same tentative colour of u, an event that occurs with probability $1/c$. The total variance after these queries is then at most

$$0 + \sum_{x \in N_1(u)} v_x \leq \frac{d}{c}.$$

So far so good, but we now need to estimate the total variance of vertices in $N_2(u)$ and we know that this can be extremely large in the worst case. We exploit the fact that the tentative colour choices of the neighbours of u are binomially distributed. Fix $w \in N_2(u)$ and let

$$x := |N_u \cap N_w|.$$

Moreover, let x_a denote the number of vertices in $N_u \cap N_w$ that choose colour a tentatively. For each colour a, the expected number of u-neighbours that pick a is d/c. The set of "bad" events $\mathcal{B}$ that we are going to consider is when there exists a colour that is chosen more than $r_\delta := (1 + \delta)d/c$ times. By the Chernoff and the union bounds, for any $\delta > 2e - 1$, the probability of $\mathcal{B}$ is at most $c2^{-r_\delta} = c2^{-(1+\delta)d/c}$. Note that this gives an "error term" of at most $d \Pr[\mathcal{B}] = dc2^{-(1+\delta)d/c} = o(1)$.

We now want to estimate the variance assuming the "good" event $\mathcal{B}^c$. Let

$$d_a := |\mathrm{E}[Z|X_1, \ldots, X_w = a] - \mathrm{E}[Z|X_1, \ldots, X_{w-1}]| \leq x_a$$

and thus

$$v_w = \sum_a \Pr[X_w = a]d_a^2 \leq \frac{1}{c}\sum_a x_a^2.$$

This sum of squares is subject to

$$x = \sum_a x_a,$$

and by the previous assumption,

$$0 \leq x_a \leq r_\delta.$$

The maximum is therefore attained at the extreme point, when there are x/r_δ terms, each equal to r_δ^2 (see Section 8.4). Therefore,

$$v_w \leq \frac{1}{c}\frac{x}{r_\delta}r_\delta^2 = \frac{(1+\delta)xd}{c^2}.$$

The total variance of vertices in $N_2(u)$ is $\sum_{w\in N_2(u)} v_w$. If we assign a weight of v_w/x on each edge between w and $N_1(u)$, we then have

$$\sum_{w\in N_2(u)} v_w = \sum_{wv:w\in N_2(u),v\in N_1(u)} \frac{v_w}{x} \leq d(d-1)\frac{(1+\delta)d}{c^2}$$

for a total variance of

$$V \leq 0 + \frac{d}{c} + d(d-1)\frac{(1+\delta)d}{c^2} \leq \frac{(1+\delta)d^3}{c^2}.$$

Therefore, if $\delta \geq 2e - 1$,

$$\Pr[Z - E[Z] > t + o(1)] \leq e^{-t^2/4V} + c2^{-(1+\delta)d/c},$$

provided that $t \leq 2V$. If $c = \Theta(d/\ln d)$ and $t = \Theta(V \ln d)$, this says that Z deviates from its expectation by more than $\Theta(\sqrt{d \ln^3 d})$ with inverse polynomial probability. An analogous derivation establishes the result for the lower tail.

8.3 Pointers to the Literature

The inequality we presented here is from [37], which generalises a similar inequality of [3] for a function f of 0/1 random variables. Our presentation does away with some superfluous conditions stated in [37], notably the fact that f is defined on a product space, that is, f be a function of independent random variables $X_1, \ldots, X_n$. McDiarmid's survey presents a treatment of some of the inequalities that we discussed, with several useful variations on the theme [67]. The edge-colouring application is from [38]. A good source for colouring problems of the type discussed here is the book of Molloy and Reed [73].

8.4 Problems

Problem 8.1. With reference to the statement of Thereom 8.1, show that

$$E[V] = var(Z_n).$$ ▽

Problem 8.2. Prove that if a random variable X satisfies $EX = 0$ and $a \leq X \leq b$, then

$$var(X) \leq (b - a)^2/4.$$ ▽

Problem 8.3. Prove Theorem 8.2 (HINT: Define the Doob martingale sequence $Z_i := E[f|X_0, \ldots, X_i]$ and observe that $(D_i|X_{i-1}) = D_i$. Apply Theorem 8.1.)   ▽

Problem 8.4. Prove Equation (8.9), that is,

$$v_i := \sum_{a \in A_i} \Pr[X_i = a](D_i^2|X_i = a) \leq p(1 - p)c_i^2,$$

under the hypothesis that A_i can be partitioned into two disjoint regions G and B, such that $\Pr[X_i \in G] = p$.   ▽

Problem 8.5. Work out Problem 7.6 using the method of bounded variances.   ▽

Problem 8.6. Show a bound similar to Equation (8.13) for the edge-colouring problem discussed in Section 7.4.3.   ▽

Problem 8.7. Carry on the analysis of Section 8.2.3 under the hypothesis $c = (1 + \epsilon)d$.   ▽

Problem 8.8. Show that

$$\max \sum_i x_i^2$$

subject to $\sum_i x_i = n$ and $0 \leq x_i \leq c$ is attained when $\lfloor \frac{n}{c} \rfloor$ terms are set equal to c and the remaining terms are set to 0.   ▽

Problem 8.9. Let $X_1, \ldots, X_n$ be independent, with $a_k \leq X_k \leq b_k$ for each k, where a_k and b_k are constants, and let $X := \sum_i X_i$. Prove that then, for any $t \geq 0$,

$$\Pr[|X - \mathbf{E}X| \geq t] \leq 2\exp\left\{-2t^2 / \sum_i (b_i - a_i)^2\right\}. \qquad \triangledown$$

Problem 8.10. Prove Equation (8.9). $\triangledown$

Problem 8.11. Consider the edge-colouring algorithm described in Section 8.2.2.

- Compute the expected number of colours that remain available for an edge.
- Show that this number is sharply concentrated around its expectation.
- Do the same for the intersection of the colour lists of two edges incident on the same vertex.
- Can you get the same bounds using the method of (averaged) bounded differences? $\triangledown$

Problem 8.12. Let G be a d-regular graph and consider the following randomized algorithm to compute a matching in the graph. Every edge enters a set S with probability $1/d$. If an edge in S does not have any neighbouring edges in S, it enters the matching M. Edges in M and all their neighbours are removed from G.

- Compute the expected degree of a vertex that is not matched.
- Use the method of bounded variances to prove that the degree of a vertex that is not matched is concentrated around its expectation. Can you use the method of bounded differences in its simplest form?
- Show that the same is true if the preceding algorithm is repeated. How large a value of d (as a function of n) is needed for concentration to hold?

The point here is to show that the graph stays essentially regular during the execution of the algorithm, as long as the average degree is high enough. $\triangledown$

Problem 8.13 [39]. We are given a d-regular graph G of girth at least 5 where each vertex has a list of $c := d/\log_2 d$ colours. (The girth of a graph is the length of its smallest cycle.) Consider the following algorithm: Each vertex *wakes up* with probability $p := 1/\log_2 d$. Each awaken vertex picks a tentative colour at random from its own list and checks for possible colour conflicts with the neighbours. If none of the neighbours picks thesame tentative colour, the colour becomes final. If a colour c becomes the final colour of a neighbour of a vertex u, c is deleted from u's colour list.

- For a given vertex, let X be the number of its uncoloured neighbours. Prove that X is concentrated around its expectation.
- For a given vertex, let Y be the number of colours not chosen by its neighbours. Prove that Y is concentrated around its expectation.
- For given vertex u and colour c, let Z be the number of uncoloured neighbours of u that retain c in their list. Prove that Z is concentrated around its expectation.
- Can you show similar bounds on X, Y, Z for graphs of girth 3 and 4? $\triangledown$

Problem 8.14 (Bernstein inequality for martingales)**.** In this problem we outline how to strengthen Theorem 8.1 to derive the tighter bound in (8.5). In the proof of Theorem 8.1, we used the inequality $e^x \leq 1 + x + x^2$. Now we shall tighten the analysis. Set $e^x := 1 + x + x^2 g(x)$.

(a) Show that g is a non-decreasing function. Hence deduce that for $x \leq b$,
$$e^x \leq 1 + x + x^2 g(b).$$

(b) Use (a) to deduce that if X is a random variable with $X \leq b$ and $E[X] = 0$, then
$$E[e^X] \leq e^{g(b) var(X)}.$$

(c) Deduce that in place of (8.4) we can write
$$E[e^{\lambda D_i} | X_{i-1}] \leq e^{g(b)\lambda^2 v_i}.$$

(d) Use (c) to show that
$$E[e^{\lambda Z_n}] \leq e^{g(\lambda b)\lambda^2 V}.$$

(e) Use Markov's inequality and choose an optimal value of λ to get
$$P[Z_n > t] \leq e^{-(V/b^2)[(1+\epsilon)\ln(1+\epsilon)-\epsilon]},$$
where $\epsilon := bt/V$.

(f) Use the calculus fact that for all $x \geq 0$, $(1+x)\ln(1+x) - x \geq 3x^2/(6+2x)$ to finally deduce that
$$P[Z_n > t] \leq e^{-\frac{t^2}{2V(1+bt/3V)}}.$$ $\triangledown$

9

Interlude: The Infamous Upper Tail

9.1 Motivation: Non-Lipschitz Functions

Consider the random graph $G(n, p)$ with $p = p(n) = n^{-3/4}$. Let X be the number of triangles in this graph. We have $E[X] = \binom{n}{3} p^3 = \Theta(n^{3/4})$. The random variable X is a function of the $\binom{n}{2}$ independent variables corresponding to whether a particular edge is present or not. Changing any of these variables could change the value of X by as much as $n - 2$ in the worst case. Applying the method of bounded differences with these Lipschitz coefficients is useless to obtain a non-trivial concentration result for deviations of the order of $\epsilon E[X] = \Theta(n^{3/4})$ for a fixed $\epsilon > 0$.

Exercise 9.1. *Try to apply the method of average bounded differences or the method of bounded variances and see if you get any meaningful results.*

The essential problem here is that the function under consideration is not Lipschitz, with sufficiently small constants to apply the method of bounded differences. This initiated a renewed interest in methods to prove concentration for functions which are not "smooth" in the worst-case Lipschitz sense of the method of bounded differences but are nevertheless "smooth" in some "average" sense. We have already seen that the method of average bounded differences and method of bounded variances are such methods. Here we briefly describe two new methods that apply well to problems such as counting triangles in a random graph.

9.2 Concentration of Multivariate Polynomials

Let $X_{i,j}$ be the indicator random variable for whether the edge ij is included in the random graph $G(n, p)$. Then, the number of triangles X_{K_3} in $G(n, p)$ can be written as

$$X_{K_3} = \sum_{1 \le i < j < k \le n} X_{j,k} X_{k,i} X_{i,j}.$$

Formally, this can be seen as a multivariate polynomial in the $\binom{n}{2}$ variables $X_{i,j}$, and motivates the setting of the Kim–Vu inequality.

Let U be a base set and $\mathcal{H}$ be a family of subsets of U of size at most k for some $0 < k \le n$. Let $X_u, u \in U$, be independent 0/1 random variables with $\mathrm{E}[X_u] = p_u, u \in U$. Consider the function of $X_u, u \in U$, given by the following multivariate polynomial:

$$Z := \sum_{I \in \mathcal{H}} w_I \prod_{u \in I} X_u,$$

where $w_I, I \in \mathcal{H}$, are positive coefficients. In the aforementioned example the base set U is the set of all $\binom{n}{2}$ edges and the family $\mathcal{H}$ consists of the $\binom{n}{3}$ 3-element subsets of edges that form a triangle (so $k = 3$ and all coefficients $w_I = 1$).

For each subset A of size at most k, define a polynomial Z_A as follows:

$$Z_A := \sum_{A \subseteq I \in \mathcal{H}} w_I \prod_{u \in I \setminus A} X_u.$$

Formally, this is the partial derivative $\partial Z / \partial X_A$. Set

$$E_j(Z) := \max_{|A| \ge j} \mathrm{E}[Z_A], \quad 0 \le j \le k.$$

Heuristically, $E_j(Z)$ can be interpreted as the maximum *average* effect of a group of at least j underlying variables – this will play the role of "average" Lipschitz coefficients in place of the worst-case Lipschitz coefficients. The following result holds.

Theorem 9.1 (Kim–Vu multivariate polynomial inequality). *For any $k \le n$, there are positive numbers a_k, b_k such that for any $\lambda \ge 1$,*

$$\Pr\left[|Z - \mathrm{E}[Z]| \ge a_k \lambda^k \sqrt{E_0(Z) E_1(Z)}\right] \le b_k \exp\{-\lambda/4 + (k-1)\log n\}.$$

(For definiteness, we can take $a_k := 8^k \sqrt{k!}$ and $b_k := 2e^2$.)

To apply this to the number of triangles in the random graph $G(n, p)$, consider the base set $\binom{n}{2}$, take $\mathcal{H}$ to be the family of 3-element subsets forming a triangle and consider the multivariate polynomial:

$$Z := \sum_{1 \le i < j < \ell \le n} X_{j,\ell} X_{\ell,i} X_{i,j},$$

and $X_{i,j}$ is the indicator variable for whether the edge ij is included. As we saw, with $p = n^{-3/4}$, we have $E[Z] = \Theta(n^{3/4})$.

Let us compute the terms Z_A so that we can determine E_j, $j = 0, 1$. If $|A| = 1$, that is, it contains only one edge ij, then Z_A is the number of triangles that contain this edge:

$$Z_A = \sum_{\ell \neq i, j} X_{j,\ell} X_{i,\ell}.$$

If $|A| = 2$ then $Z_A > 0$ only if the two edges e, $f \in A$ touch, that is, $e \cap f \neq \emptyset$, and a third edge g forms a triangle. That is, $Z_A := X_{wz}$, where $e := uw$ and $f := vz$. Finally, if $|A| = 3$ then Z_A is either 1 or 0. Thus, $E_1(Z) = \max_{|A| \geq 1} E[Z_A] = 1$ and $E_0(Z) = \max_{|A| \geq 0} E[Z_A] = E[Z]$.

Setting $\lambda := cn^{1/8}$ for a constant c chosen to make $a_3 \lambda^3 \sqrt{E[Z]} = \epsilon E[Z]$ and applying Theorem 9.1 gives

$$\Pr\left[|Z - E[Z]| \geq \epsilon E[Z]\right] \leq b_3 \exp\left(-\lambda/4 + 2\log n\right) = e^{-\Theta(n^{1/8})}.$$

Stronger estimates can be obtained via refinements of this technique [50, 86], achieving a factor of $\Theta(n^{-3/8})$ in the exponent.

9.3 The Deletion Method

The setting here is similar to that in the Kim–Vu inequality: Let $\mathcal{H}$ be a family of subsets of a base set U and suppose each set in $\mathcal{H}$ is of size at most k for some $k \leq n$. Let $(X_I, I \in \mathcal{H})$ be a family of non-negative random variables. These do not necessarily have the monomial structure as in Kim–Vu. Rather, only a local-dependence property is postulated: each X_I is independent of $(X_J \mid I \cap J = \emptyset)$. Note that this is true of the monomials in the Kim–Vu inequality. The object of study is the sum $Z := \sum_I X_I$.

Theorem 9.2 (Janson–Rucinski). *Let $\mathcal{H}$ be a family of subsets of $[n]$ of size at most k for some $k \leq n$ and let $(X_I, I \in \mathcal{H})$ be a family of non-negative random variables such that each X_I is independent of $(X_J \mid I \cap J = \emptyset)$. Let $Z := \sum_I X_I$ and $\mu := E[Z] = \sum_I E[X_I]$. Further, for $I \subseteq [n]$, let $Z_I := \sum_{I \subseteq J} X_J$ and let $Z_1^* := \max_u Z_{\{u\}}$. If $t > 0$, then for every real $r > 0$,*

$$\Pr[Z \geq \mu + t] \leq (1 + t/\mu)^{-r/2} + \Pr\left[Z_1^* > \frac{t}{2kr}\right]$$

$$\leq (1 + t/\mu)^{-r/2} + \sum_u \Pr\left[Z_{\{u\}} > \frac{t}{2kr}\right].$$

The proof is surprisingly short and elementary (see [45, 46]).

To apply this to the problem of counting the number of triangles in $G(n, p)$ with $p = n^{-3/4}$, consider again the base set $\binom{[n]}{2}$ of all possible edges and the family $\mathcal{H}$ to be the family of 3-element subsets of edges forming a triangle. An element u is thus an edge and $Z_{\{u\}}$ is the number of triangles that contain the edge u. For $I \in \mathcal{H}$, the variable X_I is the indicator for whether the triangle formed by the three edges in I exists in $G(n, p)$.

To apply the deletion method of Janson–Rucinski, we need to estimate the term $\sum_u \Pr[Z_{\{u\}} > t/2kr]$. Note that the number of triangles containing a given edge u is binomially distributed, with each such triangle occurring with probability p^2. Thus, for a fixed edge u, the Chernoff–Hoeffding bound yields

$$\Pr[Z_{\{u\}} > \mu/2r] \le e^{-\mu/2r},$$

as long as $\mu/2r > 2n^{-1/2}$. And since there are n^2 potential edges u we have the bound $n^2 e^{-\mu/2r}$ for the sum in the second term in the Janson–Rucinski theorem. Thus,

$$\Pr[Z > 2\mu] \le 2^{-r/2} + n^2 e^{-\mu/2r} \le e^{-r/9} + n^2 e^{-\mu/2r}.$$

Choosing $r = c\sqrt{\mu}$ gives

$$\Pr[Z > 2\mu] \le n^2 e^{-cn^{3/8}},$$

which is stronger than the result obtained earlier using the multivariate polynomial inequality. To see a very revealing and exhaustive comparison of the use of various methods for the study of the "infamous upper tail" of problems such as counts of fixed subgraphs in the random graph, see [45]. We end by quoting [46],

> neither of these methods seems yet to be fully developed and in a final version, and it is likely that further versions will appear and turn out to be important for applications. It would be most interesting to find formal relations and implications between Kim and Vu's method and our new method, possibly by finding a third approach that encompasses both methods.

9.4 Problems

Problem 9.1. Consider the number X_H of copies of a fixed graph H in the random graph $G(n, p)$ for different ranges of the parameter p. Let $\mu := E[X_H]$ and apply the Kim–Vu multivariate polynomial bound.

(a) For $H := K_3$ (triangle), show that

$$\Pr[X_{K_3} \geq 2\mu] \leq n^4 \begin{cases} \exp\{-cn^{1/3}p^{1/6}\} & \text{if } p \geq n^{-1/2}, \\ \exp\{-cn^{1/2}p^{1/2}\} & \text{otherwise.} \end{cases}$$

(b) For $H := K_4$, show that

$$\Pr[X_{K_4} \geq 2\mu] \leq n^{10} \begin{cases} \exp\{-cn^{1/6}p^{1/12}\} & \text{if } p \geq n^{-2/5}, \\ \exp\{-cn^{1/3}p^{1/2}\} & \text{otherwise.} \end{cases}$$

(c) For $H := C_4$ (the cycle on four vertices), show that

$$\Pr[X_{C_4} \geq 2\mu] \leq n^6 \begin{cases} \exp\{-cn^{1/4}p^{1/8}\} & \text{if } p \geq n^{-2/3}, \\ \exp\{-cn^{1/2}p^{1/2}\} & \text{otherwise.} \end{cases} \qquad \triangledown$$

Problem 9.2. Consider the number X_H of copies of a fixed graph H in the random graph $G(n, p)$ for different ranges of the parameter p. Let $\mu := \mathbb{E}[X_H]$ and apply the Janson–Rucinski deletion method.

(a) For $H := K_3$ (triangle), show that

$$\Pr[X_{K_3} \geq 2\mu] \leq n^2 \exp\{-cn^{3/2}p^{3/2}\}.$$

(b) For $H := K_4$, show that

$$\Pr[X_{K_4} \geq 2\mu] \leq n^2 \begin{cases} \exp\{-cn^2p^3\} & \text{if } p \leq n^{-1/2}, \\ \exp\{-cn^{4/3}p^{5/3}\} & \text{otherwise.} \end{cases}$$

(c) For $H := C_4$ (the cycle on four vertices), show that

$$\Pr[X_{C_4} \geq 2\mu] \leq n^2 \begin{cases} \exp\{-cn^{4/3}p\} & \text{if } p \geq n^{-2/3}, \\ \exp\{-cn^2p^2\} & \text{otherwise.} \end{cases} \qquad \triangledown$$

10

Isoperimetric Inequalities and Concentration

In this chapter we introduce the notion of isoperimetric inequalities. These inequalities constitute another important approach to proving concentration inequalities. We start by explaining what an isoperimetric inequality means in an abstract form and then give a few classical examples. We explain how isoperimetric inequalities easily yield concentration inequalities. Finally we concentrate on an important isoperimetric inequality in discrete product spaces with a Hamming distance, showing how, in many situations, it is essentially equivalent to the method of bounded differences.

This chapter lays the groundwork for Chapters 12 and 13, where methods are developed to prove such isoperimetric inequalities which then yield powerful concentration inequalities.

10.1 Isoperimetric Inequalities

Everyone has heard about the mother of all isoperimetric inequalities:

$$\text{Of all planar geometric figures with a given perimeter,} \atop \text{the circle has the largest possible area.} \qquad (10.1)$$

An abstract form of isoperimetric inequalities is usually formulated in the setting of a space (Ω, P, d) that is simultaneously equipped with a probability measure P and a metric d. We will call such a space an *MM-space*. Since our applications usually involve finite sets Ω and discrete distributions on them, we will not specify any more conditions.

Given $A \subseteq \Omega$, the *t-neighbourhood* of A is the subset $A_t \subseteq \Omega$ defined by

$$A_t := \{x \in \Omega \mid d(x, A) \le t\}. \qquad (10.2)$$

Here, by definition,

$$d(x, A) := \min_{y \in A} d(x, y).$$

An abstract isoperimetric inequality in such an MM-space (Ω, P, d) asserts that

there is a "special" family of subsets $\mathcal{B}$ such that for any $A \subseteq \Omega$, for all $B \in \mathcal{B}$ with $P(B) = P(A)$, $P(A_t) \leq P(B_t)$. $\qquad$ (10.3)

To relate this to (10.1), take the underlying space to be the Euclidean plane with Lebesgue measure and Euclidean distance, and the family $\mathcal{B}$ to be balls in the plane. By letting $t \to 0$, an abstract isoperimetric inequality yields (10.1).

Often an abstract isoperimetric inequality is stated in the following form.

Assertion 10.1. *In a space* (Ω, P, d), *for any* $A \subseteq \Omega$,

$$P(A)P(\overline{A_t}) \leq g(t). \qquad (10.4)$$

Such a result is often proved in two steps:

1. Prove an abstract isoperimetric inequality in the form (10.3) for a suitable family $\mathcal{B}$.
2. Explicitly compute $P(B)$ for $B \in \mathcal{B}$ to determine g.

(In Section 10.4, there is an exception to this rule: the function g there is bounded from above directly.)

10.2 Isoperimetry and Concentration

An isoperimetric inequality such as (10.4) implies measure concentration if the function g decays sufficiently fast to zero as $t \to \infty$. Thus, if $A \subseteq \Omega$ satisfies $\Pr(A) \geq 1/2$, then (10.4) implies $\Pr(A_t) \geq 1 - 2g(t)$. If g goes sufficiently fast to 0, then $\Pr(A_t) \to 1$. We can conclude that

almost all the measure is concentrated around any subset of measure at least a half!

10.2.1 Concentration of Lipschitz Functions

The approach also yields concentration of Lipschitz functions on a space (Ω, d, P). Let f be a Lipschitz function on Ω with constant 1; that is,

$$|f(x) - f(y)| \leq d(x, y).$$

A *median* or *Lévy mean* of f is a real number $M[f]$ such that

$$P(f \geq M[f]) \geq 1/2 \quad \text{and} \quad P(f \leq M[f]) \geq 1/2.$$

Exercise 10.1. *Let (Ω, P) be a probability space and let f be a real-valued function on Ω. Define*

$$med(f) := \sup\{t \mid P[f \leq t] \leq 1/2\}.$$

Show that

$$P[f < med(f)], \qquad P[f > med(f)] \quad \leq \quad 1/2.$$

Set

$$A := \{x \in \Omega \mid f(x) \leq M[f]\}.$$

Then, by definition of a median, $\Pr(A) \geq 1/2$. Note that since f is Lipschitz,

$$\{x \mid f(x) > M[f] + t\} \subseteq \overline{A_t},$$

and hence,

$$\Pr[f(x) > M[f] + t] \leq \Pr(\overline{A_t}) \leq 2g(t) \to 0.$$

Exercise 10.2. *Show that (10.4) also implies a similar bound on*

$$\Pr[f(x) > M[f] - t].$$

Exercise 10.3. *Show that it suffices to impose a one-sided condition on f,*

$$f(x) \leq f(y) + d(x, y)$$

or

$$f(x) \geq f(y) - d(x, y)$$

to obtain two-sided concentration around a median.

In earlier chapters, we have seen concentration results around the expectation. Isoperimetric inequalities yield inequalities that are naturally centred around the median. However, this is usually not an issue, provided the concentration is strong enough. Intuitively, if there is strong concentration, then the mean and the median themselves are very close to each other, so concentrations around the mean or median are essentially equivalent. In Problems 10.1 and 10.2 you are asked to do the calculations to check this in a few specific cases. We will return to this in Chapter 11.

To get a quantitative bound on how good the concentration is, one needs to look at the behaviour of g in (10.4). Let (Ω, P, d) be an MM-space, and let

$$D := \max\{d(x, y) \mid x, y \in \Omega\}.$$

For $0 < \epsilon < 1$, let

$$\alpha(\Omega, \epsilon) := \max\{1 - P(A_{\epsilon D}) \mid P(A) \geq 1/2\}.$$

So a space with small $\alpha(\Omega, \epsilon)$ is one in which there is measure concentration around sets of measure at least $1/2$.

A family of spaces $(\Omega_n, d_n, P_n), n \geq 1$, is called

- a *Lévy family* if

$$\lim_{n \to \infty} \alpha(\Omega_n, \epsilon) = 0;$$

- a *concentrated Lévy family* if there are constants $C_1, C_2 > 0$ such that for all $n \geq 1$,

$$\alpha(\Omega_n, \epsilon) \leq C_1 \exp\left(-C_2 \epsilon \sqrt{n}\right);$$

- a *normal Lévy family* if there are constants $C_1, C_2 > 0$ such that, for all $n \geq 1$,

$$\alpha(\Omega_n, \epsilon) \leq C_1 \exp\left(-C_2 \epsilon^2 n\right).$$

10.2.2 A Classical Example: The Euclidean Sphere

We give a classical example for illustration. We omit the proof since this example is only for illustration and not used in the rest of this book. For the sphere S^{n-1} with the usual Euclidean metric inherited from R^n, an r-ball is a spherical cap, that is, an intersection of S^{n-1} with a half-space.

Theorem 10.1 (Isoperimetry for Euclidean sphere). *For any measurable $A \subseteq S^{n-1}$ and any $t \geq 0$,*

$$\Pr(A_t) \geq \Pr(C_t),$$

where C is a spherical cap with $\Pr(C) = \Pr(A)$.

A calculation for spherical caps then yields the following.

Theorem 10.2 (Measure concentration on the sphere). *Let $A \subseteq S^{n-1}$ be a measurable set with $\Pr(A) \geq 1/2$. Then,*

$$P(A_t) \geq 1 - 2e^{-t^2 n/2}.$$

Note that the sphere S^{n-1} has diameter 2 and so this inequality shows that the family of spheres $\{S^{n-1} \mid n \geq 1\}$ is a normal Lévy family.

10.3 The Hamming Cube

In this section we discuss an isoperimetric example that is of central importance to us. Consider the *Hamming cube* $Q_n := \{0, 1\}^n$ with uniform measure, or equivalently, the product measure with each coordinate equiprobably 0 or 1, and the *Hamming metric*:

$$d(x, y) := |\{i \in [n] \mid x_i \neq y_i\}.$$

That is, the space is just the familiar one of all outcomes of n fair coin tosses, and the distance between two outcome sequences is the number of trials with different results.

An r-ball in this space is $B^r := \{x \mid d(x, 0^n) \leq r\}$; that is, the set of all 0/1 sequences that has at most r 1s. Clearly,

$$\Pr(B^r) = \frac{1}{2^n} \sum_{0 \leq i \leq r} \binom{n}{i}.$$

Note that the t-neighbourhood of an r-ball is an $(r + t)$ ball: $B_t^r = B^{r+t}$.

A classical result from extremal set theory ([11], section 16) is as follows.

Theorem 10.3 (Harper's isoperimetric inequality). *If $A \subseteq Q_n$ satisfies $\Pr(A) \geq \Pr(B^r)$, then $\Pr(A_t) \geq \Pr(B^{r+t})$.*

This immediately yields the following.

Corollary 10.1 (Measure concentration for the Hamming cube). *Let $A \subseteq Q_n$ be such that $\Pr(A) \geq 1/2$. Then $\Pr(A_t) \geq 1 - e^{-2t^2/n}$.*

Since the diameter of Q_n is n, this shows that the family of cubes $\{Q^n \mid n \geq 1\}$ is a normal Lévy family.

Exercise 10.4. *Use the Chernoff–Hoeffding bound to deduce Corollary 10.1 from Harper's isoperimetric inequality.*

Exercise 10.5. *Deduce the Chernoff bound for independent, identically distributed (i.i.d.) variables corresponding to fair coin flips from Corollary 10.1.*

We will not prove Harper's inequality here, but in Chapter 12 we will develop information-theoretic methods to prove Corollary 10.1.

We can generalise this example in the natural way. Let (Ω, P, d) be a product space with

- $\Omega = \prod_{i \in [n]} \Omega_i$, where each Ω_i is an arbitrary finite set.
- $P = \prod_i P_i$, where each P_i is an arbitrary measure on the space Ω_i.
- $d(x, y) = \sum_{i \in [n]} \alpha_i$, where each α_i is a non-negative real.

In Chapter 12, we will prove the following.

Theorem 10.4. *In a general product space as given previously,*

$$P(A)P(\overline{A_t}) \leq \exp\left(-t^2 \Big/ 2 \sum_i \alpha_i^2\right).$$

10.4 Martingales and Isoperimetric Inequalities

In this section, we show that in many settings, Theorem 10.4 is essentially equivalent to the Method of Bounded Differences.

In Section 10.2 we saw that an isoperimetric inequality yields the method of bounded differences, that is, concentration for Lipschitz functions. Recall this argument again to show the following.

Exercise 10.6 (Method of bounded differences from isoperimetry). *Deduce a result essentially equivalent to the simple method of bounded differences from Theorem 10.4.* (HINT: *Use Problem 10.2.*)

In this section we see that, conversely, isoperimetric inequalities in product spaces with a Hamming metric can be derived via the method of bounded differences. Consider first the space $\{0, 1\}^n$ with the uniform measure (which is also the product measure with $p = 1/2$ in each coordinate) and the Hamming metric d_H. Let A be a subset of size at least 2^{n-1} so that $\mu(A) \geq 1/2$. Consider the function $f(x) := d_H(x, A)$, the Hamming distance of x to A. Surely, f is 1-Lipschitz. Let $X_1, \ldots, X_n$ be independent and uniformly distributed in $\{0, 1\}$. Then, by applying the method of bounded differences,

$$\mu[f > \mathrm{E}[f] + t], \qquad \mu[f < \mathrm{E}[f] - t] \leq e^{-2t^2/n}.$$

In particular,

$$1/2 \leq \mu(A)$$
$$= \mu(f = 0)$$
$$\leq \mu(f \leq E[f] - E[f])$$
$$\leq e^{-2E[f]^2/n}.$$

Thus, $E[f] \leq t_0 := \sqrt{\frac{\ln 2}{2} n}$.

Applying the method of bounded differences once again,

$$\Pr[f \geq t + t_0] \leq \Pr[f \geq E[f] + t] \leq e^{-2t^2/n}.$$

Thus, for $t \geq t_0$, we have,

$$\Pr[f \geq t] \leq e^{-2(t-t_0)^2/n}.$$

Now, $(t - a)^2 \geq t^2/4$ for $t \geq 2a$, so if $t \geq t_0$, then

$$\Pr[f \geq t] \leq e^{-t^2/2n}.$$

Moreover, for $0 \leq t \leq t_0$, $e^{-t^2/2n} \geq 1/2$, hence taken together, for all $t \geq 0$,

$$\Pr[f \geq t] \leq e^{-t^2/2n},$$

which is the isoperimetric inequality for the discrete cube.

Exercise 10.7. *Show that for any $A \subseteq \{0, 1\}^n$,*

$$\min\left(\Pr(A), \Pr(\overline{A_t})\right) \leq e^{-t^2/2n}.$$

Rework the preceding argument to deduce Theorem 10.4.

Exercise 10.8. *Show that in a general product space (Ω, P, d), for any $A \subseteq \Omega$,*

$$\min\left(\Pr(A), \Pr(\overline{A_t})\right) \leq e^{-t^2/2\sum_i \alpha_i^2};$$

hence, if $\Pr(A) \geq 1/2$, then

$$\mu(A_t) \geq 1 - \exp\left(\frac{-t^2}{2\sum_i \alpha_i^2}\right).$$

In the next chapter we will see a powerful extension of this inequality.

10.5 Pointers to the Literature

Ledoux ([56], chap. 1) has a thorough discussion of isoperimetric inequalities and concentration. The issue of concentration around the mean or the median is addressed in Problem 1.7 and the following discussion there (see also [67]). Examples of isoperimetric inequalities in different spaces are discussed in Ledoux ([56], section 2.1). Matoušek ([63], chap. 14) has a nice discussion and many examples.

10.6 Problems

Problem 10.1 (Expectation versus median). In this problem, we check that concentrations around the expectation or the median are essentially equivalent.

(a) Let (Ω_n, P_n, d_n), $n \geq 1$, be a normal Lévy family. Let Ω_n have diameter D_n. Show that if f is a 1-Lipschitz function on Ω_n, then for some constant $c > 0$,

$$|M[f] - E[f]| \leq c\frac{D_n}{\sqrt{n}}.$$

(b) Deduce that if $f : S^{n-1} \to R$ is 1-Lipschitz, then for some constant $c > 0$,

$$|M[f] - E[f]| \leq c\frac{1}{\sqrt{n}}.$$

(c) Deduce that if $f : Q^n \to R$ is 1-Lipschitz, then for some constant $c > 0$,

$$|M[f] - E[f]| \leq c\sqrt{n}. \qquad \triangledown$$

Problem 10.2 (Mean vs. median in product spaces). Show that in a product space,

$$|M[f] - E[f]| \leq (\sqrt{\pi}/2)\sqrt[2]{2\sum_i \alpha_i^2}.$$

(HINT: Note that

$$E[f] - M[f] = E[f - M[f]] \leq E[f - M[f]]^+.$$

Now use the concentration around the median from Theorem 10.4 to estimate this (see [67], lemma 4.6). $\qquad \triangledown$

Problem 10.3 (Brunn–Minkowski). Recall the famous *Brunn–Minkowski* inequality: for any non-empty compact subsets $A, B \subseteq R^n$,

$$\mathrm{vol}^{1/n}(A) + \mathrm{vol}^{1/n}(B) \leq \mathrm{vol}^{1/n}(A + B).$$

Deduce the isoperimetric inequality for R^n with Lebesgue measure and Euclidean distance form this: for any compact subset $A \subseteq R^n$ and any $t \geq 0$,

$$\mu(A_t) \geq \mu(B_t),$$

where B is a ball with $\mu(B) = \mu(A)$. (HINT: Note that $A_t = A + tB$, where B is a ball of unit radius.)   ▽

Problem 10.4 (Measure concentration in expander graphs). The *edge expansion* $\Phi(G)$ of a graph $G = (V, E)$ is defined by

$$\Phi(G) := \min \left\{ \frac{e(A, V \setminus A)}{|A|} \mid \emptyset \neq A \subseteq V, |A| \leq |V|/2 \right\},$$

where $e(A, B)$ denotes the number of edges with one endpoint in A and the other in B. Regard G as an MM-space by G with the usual graph distance metric and equipped with the uniform measure P on V. Suppose $\Phi := \Phi(G) > 0$ and that the maximum degree of a vertex in G is Δ. Prove the following measure concentration inequality: if $A \subseteq V$ satisfies $P(A) \geq 1/2$, then $P(A_t) \geq 1 - \frac{1}{2}e^{-t\Phi/\Delta}$. (A constant-degree *expander graph* G satisfies $\Phi(G) \geq c_1$ and $\Delta \leq c_2$ for constants $c_1, c_2 > 0$.)   ▽

Problem 10.5 (Concentration for permutations). Apply the average method of bounded differences to establish an isoperimetric inequality for the space of all permutations with the uniform measure and transposition distance.   ▽

Problem 10.6 (Measure concentration and length). Schectmann, generalising Maurey, introduced the notion of *length* in a finite metric space (Ω, d). Say that (Ω, d) has length at most ℓ if there are constants $c_1, \ldots, c_n > 0$ with $\sqrt{\sum_i c_i^2} = \ell$ and a sequence of partitions $P_0 \preceq \cdots \preceq P_n$ of Ω with P_0 trivial, P_n discrete and such that whenever we have sets $A, B \in P_k$ with $A \cup B \subseteq C \in P_{k-1}$, then $|A| = |B|$ and there is a bijection $\phi : A \rightarrow B$ with $d(x, \phi(x)) \leq c_k$ for all $x \in A$.

(a) Show that the discrete Hamming cube Q_n with the Hamming metric has length at most $\sqrt{n}$ by considering the partitions induced by the equivalence relations $x \equiv_k y$ if and only if $x_i = y_i$, $i \leq k$, for $0 \leq k \leq n$.
(b) Let $\alpha := (\alpha_1, \ldots, \alpha_n) \geq 0$. Show that the discrete Hamming Cube Q_n with the weighted Hamming metric $d_\alpha(x, y) := \sum_{x_i \neq y_i} \alpha_i$ has length at most $\|\alpha\|_2$.
(c) Show that the group of permutations S_n equipped with the usual transposition metric has small length.
(d) Show that Lipschitz functions on a finite metric space of small length with uniform measure are strongly concentrated around their mean, that is, establish the following.

Theorem 10.5. *Let (Ω, d) be a finite metric space of length at most ℓ, and let f be a Lipschitz function; that is, $|f(x) - f(y)| \leq d(x, y)$ for all* *x, y* $\in \Omega$. *Then, if P is the uniform measure on* Ω,

$$P(f \geq E[f] + a), \qquad P(f \leq E[f] - a) \leq e^{-a^2/2\ell^2}.$$

(e) Generalise to the case when *P* is not the uniform distribution by requiring that the aforementioned map $\phi : A \to B$ is measure preserving. Show that a similar result holds for the concentration of Lipschitz functions with this condition. ▽

Problem 10.7 (Diameter, Laplace functional and concentration). Let (Ω, P, d) be an MM-space. The *Laplace functional*, $E = E_{\Omega, P, d}$, is defined by

$$E(\lambda); = \sup\{E[e^{\lambda f}] \mid f : \Omega \to R \text{ is 1-Lipschitz and } E[f] = 0\}.$$

(a) Show that if $E(\lambda) \leq e^{a\lambda^2/2}$ for some $a > 0$, then $\Pr[|f - Ef| > t] \leq e^{-t^2/2a}$. (HINT: Recall the basic Chernoff bound argument.)

(b) Show that the Laplace functional is sub-additive under products: let $(\Omega_i, P_i, d_i), i = 1, 2$, be two spaces, and let (Ω, P, d) be the product space with $\Omega := \Omega_1 \times \Omega_2$, $P := P_1 \times P_2$ and $d := d_1 + d_2$. Then

$$E_{\Omega, P, d} \leq E_{\Omega_1, P_1, d_1} \cdot E_{\Omega_2, P_2, d_2}.$$

(c) If (Ω, d) has diameter at most 1, show that $E(\lambda) \leq e^{-\lambda^2/2}$. (HINT: First note that by Jensen's inequality, $e^{E[f]} \leq E[e^f]$; hence if $E[f] = 0$, then $E[e^{-f}] \geq 1$.) Now, let f be 1-Lipschitz, and let X and Y be two independent variables distributed according to P. Then,

$$E[e^{\lambda f(X)}] \leq E[e^{\lambda f(X)}]E[e^{-\lambda f(Y)}]$$

$$= E[e^{\lambda(f(X) - f(Y))}]$$

$$= E\left[\sum_{i \geq 0} \frac{\lambda^i (f(X) - f(Y))^i}{i!}\right]$$

$$= \sum_{i \geq 0} E\left[\frac{\lambda^i (f(X) - f(Y))^i}{i!}\right].$$

Argue that the terms for odd *i* vanish and bound the terms for even *i* by using the Lipschitz condition on *f*.

(d) Deduce the Chernoff–Hoeffding bound from (b) and (c). ▽

11

Talagrand's Isoperimetric Inequality

In this chapter we introduce a powerful and versatile inequality due to Talagrand [85]. Our aim here is to state the inequality without proof, derive nicely packaged versions of it, as we did in the case of martingales and the method of bounded differences, and illustrate them with applications to several examples. We defer the proof to later chapters: in Chapters 13 and 14 we give two different proofs after developing the necessary machinery. Expositions of direct proofs appear in [2, 67, 84] in addition to the original [85].

11.1 Statement of the Inequality

Talagrand's inequality is an isoperimetric inequality where the familiar notion of a Hamming metric is replaced by a more general notion of Talagrand's (pseudo)-distance. In this section we state a simplified version of the inequality which is sufficient for all the applications in this book, leaving the more involved general statement and its proof for later chapters.

Recall from last chapter that the setting for an isoperimetric inequality is a space Ω equipped with a probability measure P and a metric d. An isoperimetric inequality in this scenario states that if $A \subseteq \Omega$ is such that $P(A) \geq 1/2$, then $P(A_t) \geq 1 - q(t)$ for some rapidly decreasing function q. Recall also the definition of t-neighbourhood set:

$$A_t := \{x \in \Omega \mid d(x, A) \leq t\}.$$

Talagrand's inequality applies in the setting where $\Omega = \prod_{i \in I} \Omega_i$ is a product space indexed by some finite index set I with the product measure $\prod_{i \in I} P_i$, where P_i is an arbitrary measure on the Ω_i, for $i \in I$. In other words, it applies to functions $f(X_1, \ldots, X_n)$, where the X_i's are independent. We will always assume this setting in the following.

Let us now introduce the notion of Talagrand's pseudo-distance. Recall the normalised *weighted Hamming distance*, d_α, specified by a given set of non-negative reals α_i, $i \in [n]$, with $\sum_i \alpha_i^2 = 1$:

$$d_\alpha(x, y) := \sum_{x_i \neq y_i} \alpha_i. \tag{11.1}$$

The new notion is a non-uniform version of this, where we have a set of (potentially) different weights $\alpha_i = \alpha_i(x)$ associated with each point $x \in \Omega$.

Definition 11.1 (A Talagrand-type pseudo-distance). *Let $\alpha(x)_i$, $i \in [n]$, be non-negative reals for each $x \in \Omega$ such that*

$$\sum_i \alpha_i^2(x) = 1.$$

Talagrand's pseudo-distance *on Ω is given by*

$$d_\alpha(x, y) := \sum_{x_i \neq y_i} \alpha(x)_i. \tag{11.2}$$

This is the same as the normalised weighted Hamming distance (11.1), except that it involves a set of non-uniform weights $\alpha(x)_i$, $i \in [n]$. As usual, for $A \subseteq \Omega$,

$$d_\alpha(x, A) := \min_{y \in A} d_\alpha(x, y).$$

We will also extend the definition of t-neighbourhood set A_t in the obvious way to Talagrand's pseudo-distance: $A_t := \{x \mid d_\alpha(x, A) \leq t\}$.

Theorem 11.1 (Talagrand's inequality). *Let A be a subset in a product space with a Talagrand pseudo-distance (11.2). Then for any $t > 0$,*

$$\Pr[A]\Pr[\overline{A_t}] \leq e^{-t^2/4}. \tag{11.3}$$

This inequality will be stated in a seemingly stronger but equivalent form in a later chapter and will be proved using two different methods in Chapters 13 and Chapter 14. However, for all the applications we consider, the aforementioned form suffices and is most convenient.

The inequality should be compared with the statement of Harper's isoperimetric inequality for product spaces and weighted Hamming distance (Theorem 10.3 and Corollary 10.1). The main difference here is that Talagrand's pseudo-distance is non-uniform and asymmetric, which is the source of its strength.

To gain some intuition about Talagrand's distance, let us set $\alpha(x)_i := 1/\sqrt{n}$ for each $i \in [n]$ and each $x \in \Omega$; then we get

$$d_\alpha(x, A) = \min_{y \in A} \sum_{x_i \neq y_i} \frac{1}{\sqrt{n}}$$

$$= d^H(x, A)/\sqrt{n}, \tag{11.4}$$

where d^H is the familiar Hamming distance. This implies that for any $t > 0$,

$$A_{t/\sqrt{n}}^{d_\alpha} = A_t^H. \tag{11.5}$$

These two simple observations give us some notable consequences. They relate the Hamming distance with the Talagrand pseudo-distance, and therefore, intuitively, this should allow us to derive the isoperimetric inequalities of the last chapter from Talagrand's inequality.

As a first consequence, let us derive the Chernoff–Hoeffding bounds. Consider the product space $\{0, 1\}^n$ equipped with the product measure, where $\Pr[0] = 1/2 = \Pr[1]$ in each coordinate. Take

$$A := \{x \in \{0, 1\}^n \mid \sum_i x_i \geq n/2\}.$$

Note that

$$A_t^H = \{x \in \{0, 1\}^n \mid \sum_i x_i \geq n/2 - t\},$$

and by (11.5) and Talagrand's inequality (11.3), we get

$$\Pr[\overline{A_t^H}] = \Pr[\overline{A_{t/\sqrt{n}}^{d_\alpha}}]$$

$$\leq \frac{1}{\Pr[A]} e^{-t^2/4n}$$

$$\leq 2e^{-t^2/4n}, \quad \text{since } \Pr[A] \geq 1/2.$$

This is a disguised form of the Chernoff bound (except for small constant factors) for deviations below the mean.

Exercise 11.1. *By considering $A' := \{x \in \{0, 1\}^n \mid \sum_i x_i \leq n/2\}$, derive similarly the Chernoff bound for deviations above the mean.*

Exercise 11.2. *Show that one can extend this to the heterogeneous case as well (once again upto constant factors).*

Now let $A \subseteq \{0, 1\}^n$ be an arbitrary set with $\Pr[A] \geq 1/2$. By the same reasoning as before, we get

$$\Pr[\overline{A_t^H}] \leq 2e^{-t^2/4n},$$

a cleaner form of the isoperimetric inequality we derived using martingales and the method of bounded differences.

11.2 The Method of Non-Uniformly Bounded Differences

One can extract out from Talagrand's inequality a nicely packaged lemma that generalises the method of bounded differences and that is well suited for the applications.[1]

Theorem 11.2 (The method of non-uniformly bounded differences). *Let f be a real-valued function on a product space $\Omega = \prod_{i \in [n]} \Omega_i$ such that for each $x \in \Omega$, there exist non-negative reals $\alpha_i(x)$, $i \in [n]$, with*

$$f(x) \leq f(y) + \sum_{x_i \neq y_i} \alpha_i(x), \quad \text{for all } y \in \Omega, \tag{11.6}$$

or

$$f(x) \geq f(y) - \sum_{x_i \neq y_i} \alpha_i(x), \quad \text{for all } y \in \Omega. \tag{11.7}$$

Furthermore, suppose that there exists a constant $c > 0$ such that uniformly for all $x \in \Omega$,

$$\sum_i \alpha_i^2(x) \leq c \tag{11.8}$$

(even though the $\alpha_i(x)$ may be different individually). Then

$$\Pr[|f - \mathsf{M}[f]| > t] \leq 2e^{-t^2/4c}, \tag{11.9}$$

where $\mathsf{M}[f]$ is the median of f.

Proof. Set $A = A(a) := \{y \mid f(y) \leq a\}$, where a is a parameter to be fixed later. If (11.6) holds, we have

$$f(x) \leq f(y) + \sum_{x_i \neq y_i} \alpha_i(x),$$

---

[1] In Steele ([84], lemma 6.2.1), this is stated with some additional superfluous conditions.

for any y. Hence minimising over $y \in A$, we have

$$f(x) \leq \min_{y \in A} f(y) + \sum_{x_i \neq y_i} \alpha_i(x)$$

$$\leq a + \sum_{x_i \neq y_i} \alpha_i(x)$$

$$= a + ||\alpha(x)|| \sum_{x_i \neq y_i} \hat{\alpha}_i(x)$$

$$\leq a + \sqrt{c} d_{\hat{\alpha}}(x, A),$$

where $\hat{\alpha}$ is the normalised version of α and the last line uses (11.8). Hence, applying Talagrand's inequality for $\hat{\alpha}$,

$$\Pr[f(X) \geq a + t] \leq \Pr[d_{\hat{\alpha}}(X, A) \geq t/\sqrt{c}]$$

$$\leq \frac{1}{\Pr[A]} e^{-t^2/4c},$$

by applying Talagrand's inequality in the last step. Hence,

$$\Pr[f(X) \geq a + t]\Pr[A] \leq \exp\left(\frac{-t^2}{4c}\right).$$

Recalling that $A := \{y \mid f(y) \leq a\}$, write this as

$$\Pr[f(X) \geq a + t]\Pr[f(X) \leq a] \leq \exp\left(\frac{-t^2}{4c}\right).$$

Setting $a := \mathsf{M}[f]$ and $a := \mathsf{M}[f] - t$ successively gives the result. ∎

Remark: Concentration around Mean or Median? The preceding inequality gives concentration around the median which is often hard to compute compared with the expectation. How do we convert this into a concentration around the expectation as in previous chapters? We discussed this issue in Chapter 10, where we observed that provided the concentration is strong enough, whether it is around the mean or median is essentially equivalent in many situations. Problem 11.4 (items (a) and (b)) asks you to check that this is the case generically here, and you are asked to check this in many specific examples given next.

Remark: Method of bounded differences vs method of non-uniformly bounded differences. Note that condition (11.6) or (11.7) is just like the Lipschitz condition in the method of bounded differences except that the bounding parameters can be non-uniform, that is, a different set of parameters for each x. This is the crucial feature that makes this version substantially more powerful than the usual method of bounded differences, as we later illustrate with some examples. Note also that we need only that *either* of the two conditions to hold.

Let us now apply Theorem 11.2 to several examples, some of which we have already analysed with the other methods developed in this book.

11.2.1 Chernoff–Hoeffding Bounds

Let $f(x_1, \ldots, x_n) := \sum_i x_i$ with $x_1, \ldots, x_n \in [0, 1]$. Take $\alpha_i(x) := x_i$; then clearly (11.6) is satisfied. Moreover, $\sum_i \alpha_i^2 \leq n$. Hence,

$$\Pr[|f - M[f]| > t] \leq 2e^{-t^2/n},$$

which is just the Chernoff–Hoeffding bound upto constant factors.

11.2.2 Balls and Bins

Consider again the situation of Section 7.2, the number of non-empty bins when m balls are thrown independently and uniformly at random into n bins. If $m \geq n$ it is of interest to obtain a bound of the form $e^{-\Theta(t^2/n)}$ rather than $e^{-\Theta(t^2/m)}$.

Let $x_i = k$ denote the fact that ball i landed in bin k. For a given configuration $x = (x_1, \ldots, x_n)$ of balls in the bins, let $\alpha_i(x) := 1$ if ball i is the lowest-numbered ball in its bin and 0 otherwise. Then if f is the number of non-empty bins,

$$f(x) \leq f(y) + \sum_{x_i \neq y_i} \alpha_i(x).$$

Since $\sum_i \alpha_i^2(x) \leq n$, we get the bound

$$\Pr[|f - M[f]| > t] \leq 2e^{-t^2/n}.$$

The ease of this derivation should be compared with the somewhat cumbersome case analysis of Section 7.2.

Exercise 11.3. *Check that in this case, concentration around* $M[f]$ *can be used to deduce similar concentration around* $E[f]$.

11.2.3 Random Minimum Spanning Tree

Consider the complete graph K_n with random independent edge lengths X_e, each uniformly distributed in $(0, 1)$. Let L_n denote the corresponding length of a minimum spanning tree. Frieze [33] showed that

$$E[L_n] \to \zeta(3) := \sum_{j \geq 1} \frac{1}{j^3} \approx 1.202,$$

as $n \to \infty$.

We shall show that L_n is sharply concentrated around $\zeta(3)$. We start with an auxiliary fact, namely, that long edges are not important. For $0 < b < 1$, let $L_n^{(b)}$ denote the length of the minimum spanning tree when the edge lengths X_e are replaced by $\min(b, X_e)$.

Lemma 11.1 (Frieze–McDiarmid [34]). *For any $t > 0$, there exist constants $c > 0$ and $v > 0$ such that if we set $b := c/n$, then*

$$\Pr[L_n - L_n^{(b)} > t] \leq e^{-vn}, \quad \text{for all } n.$$

Let us therefore concentrate on $L_n^{(b)} = mst(Y)$, the minimum spanning tree length with edge weights $Y_e := \min(b, X_e)$. Set $\alpha_e(y) := y_e$ if $e \in mst(y)$ and 0 otherwise. Clearly

$$mst(y) \leq mst(z) + \sum_{y_e \neq z_e} y_e, \quad \text{for all } z,$$

and $\sum_e \alpha_e^2(y) \leq (n-1)b^2 \leq c^2/n$ for $b := c/n$. Thus applying Proposition 11.2,

$$\Pr[|L_n^{(b)} - m| > t] \leq 2e^{-2nt^2/c},$$

where $m := m(b)_n$ is a median of $L_n^{(b)}$. Combining this with Lemma 11.1,

$$\Pr[|L_n - m| > t] \leq \Pr[L - L_n^{(b)} > t] + \Pr[|L_n^{(b)} - m| > t]$$
$$\leq e^{-vn} + 2e^{-2nt^2/c}.$$

It follows that for any $t > 0$, there exists a $\delta = \delta(t) > 0$ such that

$$\Pr[|L_n - m| > t] \leq e^{-\delta n}, \quad \text{for all } n.$$

In Problem 11.7, you are asked to work out how to replace m here by $\zeta(3)$.

11.2.4 Stochastic Travelling Salesman Problem

Consider again the problem of Section 7.3. Let $X_1, \ldots, X_n$ be points selected uniformly and independently at random in the unit square and let T_n denote the length of the minimum travelling salesman problem (TSP) tour through these

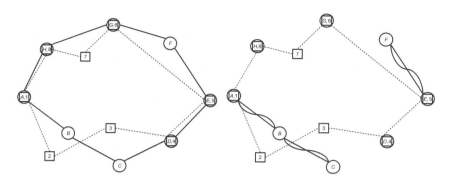

Figure 11.1. Left: the tours $x = A, B, \ldots, H$ and $y = 1, 2, \ldots, 8$. Right: the tour $y \cup U'$.

points. Recall that $\mu := E[T_n] = \Theta(\sqrt{n})$. In Section 7.3 we derived a bound of the form

$$\Pr[|T_n - \mu| > t] \leq 2e^{-\Theta(t^2/\log n)}.$$

Our aim now is to derive a stronger bound of the form

$$\Pr[|T_n - M[T_n]| > t] \leq 2e^{-\Theta(t^2)}.$$

This was a notable success of Talagrand's inequality over the previous approaches using Martingales.

In order to apply Proposition 11.2, we need to find suitable $\alpha(x)_i$, $i \in [n]$. That is, we need them to satisfy

$$T_n(x) \leq T_n(y) + \sum_{x_i \neq y_i} \alpha(x)_i. \tag{11.10}$$

Many proofs in the literature [67, 84] use the existence of *space-filling curves* to do this. Actually, all one needs is the following simple but surprising fact.

Proposition 11.1. *There is a constant $c > 0$ such that for any set of n points $x_1, \ldots, x_n \in [0, 1]^2$, there is a permutation $\sigma : [n] \to [n]$ satisfying $\sum_{i \in [n]} |x_{\sigma(i)} - x_{\sigma(i+1)}|^2 \leq c$ (where the final index $n + 1$ is taken modulo n). That is, there is a tour through all points such that the sum of the squares of the lengths of all edges in the tour is bounded by an absolute constant c.*

In Problem 11.6 we outline a completely elementary proof of this fact. Assuming this, let $C(x)$ be the tour whose existence is ensured by Proposition 11.1 for the points $x_1, \ldots, x_n$. We will use this tour to "stitch" in the points x into the optimal tour for the points $y_1, \ldots, y_n$ and satisfy (11.10). Please refer to Figure 11.1. Take $\alpha(x)_i$ to be twice the lengths of the two edges incident to x_i

in $C(x)$. Now, we verify that with this choice, (11.10) is satisfied. First, we note that the inequality is trivially true if $x \cap y = \emptyset$; that is, x and y have no points in common. Otherwise, consider the cycle $C(x)$ and mark the points common to x and y on this tour. Double each edge in $C(x)$. Starting at a point in $x \cap y$ follow $C(x)$ until the last point before hitting another vertex of $x \cap y$. At this point, follow the cycle backwards (using the doubled edges) to the starting point. In this way, all the points in x have been attached by small cycles to a point in $x \cap y$. Let U' be the union of these cycles. Note that the sum of the lengths of the edges in U' is at most $\sum_{x_i \neq y_i} \alpha_i$. Finally, consider the graph consisting of vertex set $x \cup y$ and edge set $TSP(y) \cup U'$. By "short-circuiting", we can extract a tour of $x \cup y$ of length at most that of the edges in $TSP(y) \cup U'$. Since the length of a tour through x is at most that of a tour through $x \cup y$ and $TSP(x)$ is an optimal tour through x, this verifies (11.10).

Since $\sum_i \alpha_i^2(x) \leq 4c$, where c is the constant given by Proposition 11.1, applying Theorem 11.2, we arrive at the truly Gaussian tail bound:

$$\Pr[|T_n - \mathrm{M}[T_n]| > t] \leq e^{-t^2/4c}.$$

11.3 Certifiable Functions

Another simple but very versatile packaged form of Talagrand's inequality rests on the definition of certifiable functions.

Definition 11.2 (Certifiable functions). *Let $f(x_1, \ldots, x_n)$ be a real-valued function on a product space $\Omega = \prod_i \in [n] \Omega_i$. f is r-certifiable if for every $x = (x_1, \ldots, x_n) \in \Omega$, there exists a set of indices $J(x) \subseteq [n]$ such that*

- $|J(x)| \leq r \times f(x)$; *and,*
- *if y agrees with x on the coordinates in $J(x)$, then $f(y) \geq f(x)$.*

The set $J(x)$ is said to be a certificate *for $f(x)$.*

Let us see a few examples of certifiable functions.

Let f be the number of heads when a coin is tossed n times. This function is 1-certifiable. Indeed, denoting with $x = (x_1, \ldots, x_n)$, $x_i \in \{0.1\}$, a given outcome of the coin tosses, we define $J(x) := \{i : x_i = 1\}$. Then, if y agrees with x on $J(x)$, clearly $f(y) \geq f(x)$.

For another example, let $f(x_1, \ldots, x_m)$ denote the number of non-empty bins when m balls are thrown uniformly at random into n bins, with the usual convention that $x_i = k$ means that ball i landed in bin k. This function too is 1-certifiable. Let $i \in J(x)$ if and only if, in configuration x, ball i is the lowest-numbered ball in its bin. Then, if y and x agree on $J(x)$, $f(y) \geq f(x)$.

Theorem 11.3. *Let* $f : \Omega \to \mathbb{R}$ *be* r-*certifiable and suppose it is Lipschitz with constant* c *(i.e. changing any coordinate in the argument changes the value of* f *by at most* c*). Then for all* $t > 0$,

$$\Pr[f > M[f] + t] \leq 2 \exp\left(-\frac{t^2}{4c^2 r(M[f] + t)}\right)$$

and

$$\Pr[f < M[f] - t] \leq 2 \exp\left(-\frac{t^2}{4c^2 r M[f]}\right),$$

where $M[f]$ *is the median of* f.

Proof. For each $x \in \Omega$, let $J(x)$ be the certifying subset for $f(x)$. Set $\alpha(x)_i := 1/\sqrt{|J(x)|}$ if $i \in J(x)$ and 0 otherwise. Note that $||\alpha|| = 1$.

Set $A := \{x \mid f(x) \leq a\}$ (for some a be determined later), and let $\hat{y} := \operatorname{argmin}\{d_\alpha(x, y) \mid y \in A\}$. Define y' by setting

$$y'_i := \begin{cases} x_i, & \text{if } i \in J(x), \\ \hat{y}_i, & \text{otherwise.} \end{cases} \tag{11.11}$$

Note that $f(y') \geq f(x)$ since $J(x)$ is the set of certifying indices for $f(x)$.
Then,

$a \geq f(y)$ by definition of $\hat{y}$

$\displaystyle \geq f(y') - \sum_{y'_i \neq y_i} c$ since f is Lipschitz with constant c

$\displaystyle = f(y') - \sum_{x_i \neq y_i} c$ by (11.11)

$\displaystyle \geq f(x) - \sum_{x_i \neq y_i} c$ since $J(x)$ is a lower bound certificate for x.   (11.12)

Now consider the weighted distance with the normalised weights α:

$$d_\alpha(x, A) = \sum_{x_i \neq y_i} 1/\sqrt{|J(x)|}$$

$$= \frac{1}{c\sqrt{|J(x)|}} \sum_{x_i \neq y_i} c$$

$$\geq \frac{1}{c\sqrt{|J(x)|}}(f(x) - a) \quad \text{using (11.12)}$$

$$\geq \frac{1}{c\sqrt{r}} \frac{f(x) - a}{\sqrt{f(x)}}. \tag{11.13}$$

In the last line, we used the certificate condition that $|J(x)| \leq r f(x)$.

The function $u \mapsto (u - a)/\sqrt{u}$ is monotone increasing for $u \geq a$, so for any $a \geq 0$, if $f(x) \geq a + t$, then $\frac{f(X)-a}{\sqrt{f(X)}} \geq \frac{t}{\sqrt{a+t}}$.

Thus,

$$\Pr[f(X) \geq a + t] \leq \Pr\left[\frac{f(X) - a}{\sqrt{f(X)}} \geq \frac{t}{\sqrt{a + t}}\right]$$

$$\leq \Pr\left[d_\alpha(x, A) \geq \frac{1}{c\sqrt{r}} \frac{t}{\sqrt{a + t}}\right] \quad \text{using (11.13)}$$

$$\leq \frac{1}{P(A)} \exp\left(-\frac{1}{4c^2 r} \frac{t^2}{a + t}\right).$$

In the last step we applied Talagrand's inequality (11.3). That is, recalling the definition of A,

$$\Pr[f(X) \leq a] \Pr[f(X) \geq a + t] \leq \exp\left(-\frac{1}{4c^2 r} \frac{t^2}{a + t}\right).$$

Putting $a := M[f]$ and $a := M[f] - t$, we get the result. ∎

Remark: Concentration around Mean or Median? Once again, the preceding inequality gives concentration around the median and we want to convert this into concentration around the mean, which is easier to compute. Remember again from Chapter 10 that provided the concentration is strong enough, whether it is around the mean or median is essentially equivalent in many situations. Problem 11.4 (items (c) and (d)) asks you to check that this is generically the case here, and you are asked to check this in many specific examples given next.

For instance, if we apply Theorem 11.3 to the balls-and-bins example, since $f = (\# \text{non-empty bins})$ is 1-certifiable and 1-Lipschitz, we immediately see that

$$\Pr[f > M[f] + t] \leq 2e^{-t^2/4(M[f]+t)}, \quad \Pr[f < M[f] - t] \leq 2e^{-t^2/4M[f]}.$$

Exercise 11.4. *Convert this bound into a concentration around the mean, plug in the value for the mean and deduce an exponential concentration result in an interval of size $\epsilon E[f]$ for any $\epsilon > 0$.*

Let us now see a couple of more sophisticated examples.

11.3.1 Increasing Subsequences

Given a sequence of reals $x := (x_1, \ldots, x_n)$, an *increasing subsequence* in x is a set of indices $1 \leq i_1 < i_2 < \cdots < i_k \leq n$ such that $x_{i_1} \leq x_{i_2} \leq \cdots \leq x_{i_k}$. Let $I(x)$ denote the maximum length of an increasing subsequence in x.

Let $J = J(x)$ denote the set of indices in such a maximum length-increasing subsequence in x. Clearly, $I(x) = |J|$ and J is a certificate for $I(x)$. Observing that I is clearly 1-Lipschitz, we get that if $X_1, \ldots, X_n$ are independently and uniformly distributed in $[0, 1]$, then for $I = I(X_1, \ldots, X_n)$,

$$\Pr[I > M[I] + t] \leq 2e^{-t^2/4(M[I]+t)}, \quad \Pr[I < M[I] - t] \leq 2e^{-t^2/4M[I]}.$$

It is known that $I \to 2\sqrt{n}$ as $n \to \infty$, so this result shows that with high probability, I is confined to an interval of size $O(n^{\frac{1}{4}})$ which is the best known bound and significantly better than what one could obtain from the simple method of bounded differences.

Exercise 11.5. *Apply the simple method of bounded differences and compare with the preceding bounds.*

11.3.2 Edge Colouring: Take 5

Recall the edge-colouring algorithm that was analysed in Section 7.4.2 via the method of bounded differences in averaged form and in Section 8.2.2 with the method of bounded variances. Every edge e of a Δ-regular graph G picks a tentative colour uniformly and independently at random from its own list $L_e := [\Delta(G)]$ of available colours. The tentative colour becomes final if none of the adjacent edges picks it. As before, we focus on a vertex u to prove a concentration bound of the form

$$\Pr(|Z - EZ| > t) \leq 2e^{-\Theta(t^2/\Delta)}, \tag{11.14}$$

where Z is the number of edges incident on u that successfully colour. Alternatively, we can give a sharp concentration result on the number of edges around u that are *not* successfully coloured.

The underlying product space is $[\Delta]^{E(u)}$, where $E(u)$ is the set of edges that are incident on u or on a neighbour of u. The function f we consider is the number of edges around u that are *not* coloured successfully. Clearly, f is Lipschitz with all constants 2. Moreover, it is 2-certifiable. To see this, observe that for each edge e that is unsuccessful, there is at least another edge that gets the same tentative colour – fix one such edge arbitrarily as a witness to this fact. For a given tentative colouring T, the index set $J = J(T) \subseteq E(u)$ consists of all unsuccessful edges together with their witnesses. The edge set J includes each unsuccessful edge e and its witness, so it has at most twice as many edges as unsuccessful ones (when is it less than twice as many?). Clearly, if another tentative colour assignment T' agrees with T on these coordinates, it has at least the same number of unsuccessful edges.

Therefore, applying Theorem 11.3, we get the result

$$\Pr[f > \text{M}[f] + t] \leq 2e^{-t^2/32(\text{M}[f]+t)}$$

and

$$\Pr[f < \text{M}[f] - t] \leq 2e^{-t^2/32\text{M}[f]}.$$

Exercise 11.6. *Convert this concentration result around* $\text{M}[f]$ *into one around* $\text{E}[f]$, *compute the latter and derive an exponential concentration result of type* *(11.14).*

11.4 Pointers to the Literature

Other expositions of Talagrand's isoperimetric inequality are [2, 67, 84]. The original paper is the monumental tour de force [85]. Other applications in graph-colouring problems can be found in [73]. McDiarmid [68] gives an extension of Talagrand's inequality to permutation distributions, which is particularly useful in graph-colouring applications. A further extension is given in [59].

11.5 Problems

Problem 11.1 (Concentration for hereditary functions of index sets). For $x, y \in \Omega$ and $J \subseteq I$, we use the notation $x_J = y_J$ to mean $x_j = y_j$, $j \in J$. Let $\phi(x, J)$ be a Boolean property such that it is

- a *property of index sets*; that is, if $x_J = y_J$, then $\phi(x, J) = \phi(y, J)$, and
- *non-increasing on the index sets*; that is, if $J \subseteq J'$, then $\phi(x, J') \leq \phi(x, J)$.

We shall say that ϕ is a *hereditary property of index sets*.

Given a hereditary property of index sets ϕ, let f_ϕ be the function given by

$$f_\phi(x) := \max_{J:\phi(x,J)} |J|. \tag{11.15}$$

A function f such that $f = f_\phi$ for some hereditary property ϕ of index sets will be called a *hereditary function of index sets*.

(a) Show that the length of a longest increasing subsequence in a sequence of reals $x_1, \ldots, x_n$ is a hereditary function of index sets.
(b) Show that the number of non-empty bins when m balls are assigned to n bins is a hereditary function of the index set $[m]$.
(c) By showing that a hereditary function of index sets is certifiable, establish the following.

Theorem 11.4. *Let f be a hereditary function of index sets. Then for all $t > 0$,*

$$\Pr[f > M[f] + t] \leq 2\exp\left(\frac{-t^2}{4(M[f] + t)}\right)$$

and

$$\Pr[f < M[f] - t] \leq 2\exp\left(\frac{-t^2}{4M[f]}\right),$$

where $M[f]$ is a median of f.

Hence deduce sharp concentration results for the examples in (a) and (b).

▽

Problem 11.2 (Cliques in random graphs). Let G be a graph on the vertex set $[n]$ and let $\omega(G)$ denote the size of the largest clique in G.

(a) Show that $\omega(G)$ is a hereditary property of index sets. (HINT: You need to define the appropriate base index set properly.)
(b) The Erdös–Renyi random graph $G(n, p)$ is the (undirected) graph on vertex set $[n]$ and edge set E defined by picking each possible edge $(i, j) \in [n] \times [n]$ independently with probability p. Deduce a sharp concentration result on $\omega(G(n, p))$. ▽

Problem 11.3 (Vapnik–Chervonenkis Dimension). One of the central notions in statistical learning theory is the *Vapnik–Chervonenkis* (VC) dimension. Let $\mathcal{A}$ be a collection of subsets of a base set X and let $x := (x_1, \ldots, x_n) \in X^n$. The *trace* of $\mathcal{A}$ on x is defined by

$$\mathrm{tr}(x) = \mathrm{tr}_\mathcal{A}(x) := \{A \cap \{x_1, \ldots, x_n\} \mid A \in \mathcal{A}\}.$$

That is, it is the collection of subsets that can be obtained by intersecting sets in $\mathcal{A}$ with $\{x_1, \ldots, x_n\}$. The number of such subsets, $T(x) := |\mathrm{tr}(x)|$, is called the *shatter coefficient* of $\mathcal{A}$ for x. A subset $\{x_{i_1}, \ldots, x_{i_k}\} \subseteq \{x_1, \ldots, x_n\}$ is said to be *shattered* if $T(x_{i_1}, \ldots, x_{i_k}) = 2^k$. Finally, the *VC dimension* $D(x) = D_\mathcal{A}(x)$ is defined to be the largest cardinality of a subset of $\{x_1, \ldots, x_n\}$ shattered by $\mathcal{A}$. Show that the VC dimension is a hereditary function of index sets and hence deduce a sharp concentration result for the VC dimension of a subset of points chosen independently at random. ▽

Problem 11.4 (Mean versus median). Let Y be a random variable with mean μ and median m. Show

(a) If $\Pr[|Y - m| > t] \leq ae^{-t^2/b}$ for some $a, b > 0$, then show that $|\mu - m| \leq (\sqrt{\pi}/2)a\sqrt{b}$ (see [67]).
(b) In the other direction, if $\Pr[|Y - \mu| > t] \leq ae^{-t^2/b}$ for some $a, b > 0$, then $|\mu - m| \leq \sqrt{b\ln(2a)}$.

(c) If $\Pr[|Y - m| > t] \le a \exp\left(-t^2/b(m + t)\right)$, for some $a, b > 0$, then
   $|\mu - m| \le \sqrt{\pi/2}a\sqrt{bm} + 2abe^{-m/2b} = O(\sqrt{m})$ (if a and b are
   constants; see [67]).

(d) In the other direction, If $\Pr[|Y - \mu| > t] \le a \exp\left(-t^2/b(\mu + t)\right)$, for
   some $a, b > 0$, then $|\mu - m| \le \max\left(\sqrt{2\mu b \ln(2a)}, 2b \ln(2a)\right) = O(\sqrt{\mu})$
   (if a and b are constants). $\qquad\qquad\triangledown$

Problem 11.5 (Longest common subsequence). Given two sequences $x = (x_1, \ldots, x_n)$ and $y = (y_1, \ldots, y_n)$, let $C(x, y)$ denote the maximum length of a longest common subsequence of x and y. Let $X = (X_1, \ldots, X_n)$ and $Y = (Y_1, \ldots, Y_n)$ be two independent families of independent random variables. Deduce sharp concentration results for $C(X, Y)$ using the simple method of bounded differences as well as via Talagrand's inequality and compare the bounds. $\qquad\qquad\triangledown$

Problem 11.6 (An amazing fact). In this problem, we outline an elementary proof due to D. J. Newman of the following amazing fact: for any set of points in the unit square, there is a tour going through all the points such that the sum of the squares of the lengths of the edges in the tour is bounded by an absolute constant.

(a) Show that for any set of points in a right-angled triangle, there is a tour that starts at one endpoint of the hypotenuse, ends at the other endpoint and goes through all the points such that the sum of the lengths of the edges is bounded by the square of the hypotenuse. (HINT: Drop a perpendicular to the hypotenuse from the opposite vertex and use induction.)

(b) Use (a) to deduce the amazing fact with the constant 4. $\qquad\triangledown$

Problem 11.7. Show that $|m - \zeta(3)| \le 2t/3$ for sufficiently large n in our analysis of the random minimum spanning tree and hence convert the concentration result there into a concentration around $\zeta(3)$. $\qquad\qquad\triangledown$

Problem 11.8 (Steiner tree). Obtain a Gaussian concentration result for the length of a minimum *Steiner tree* containing a set of n points independently and uniformly distributed in the unit square. (A Steiner tree of a set of points is a tree containing the given subset among its vertices; i.e. it could contain additional vertices.) (HINT: Use the same tour as we used in the analysis of the TSP.) $\qquad\qquad\triangledown$

Problem 11.9. Can you work out the edge- and vertex-colouring examples of Sections 7.4.3 and 8.2.3 using Talagrand's inequality? And Problem 7.5? $\quad\triangledown$

12

Isoperimetric Inequalities and Concentration via Transportation Cost Inequalities

In this chapter, we give an introduction to the first of two recent approaches to concentration via powerful information-theoretic inequalities: the so-called transportation cost inequalities. These inequalities relate two different notions of "distance" between probability distributions and lead easily to concentration results. In this chapter, we prove such inequalities in the familiar and simple setting of the Hamming cube with the product measure, leading to an isoperimetric inequality that is essentially equivalent to the simple methods of bounded differences in many situations. Besides the intrinsic interest of this inequality, perhaps the main reason to follow this approach is that the methodology employed in this chapter applies more generally to other settings, and in particular it will be used in the next chapter to derive Talagrand's isoperimetric inequality. The proof of the latter introduces a few complications and it is therefore useful to see first the general methodology applied to a simpler, and yet meaningful, case.

12.1 Distance between Probability Distributions

Perhaps the best-known notion of "distance" between probability distributions is the L_1 or *total variation* distance:

$$d_1(Q, R) := \frac{1}{2} \sum_x |Q(x) - R(x)|. \tag{12.1}$$

This is a special case of a more general way of defining a distance between two distributions Q and R on a metric space (Ω, d), the so-called *coupling distance*:

$$d_1(Q, R) := \inf_{\pi(Y,Z)} E_\pi [d(Y, Z)], \tag{12.2}$$

where the inf ranges over all couplings π of Q and R, that is, joint distributions $\pi(Y, Z)$ with the marginals $\pi(Y) \sim Q$ and $\pi(Z) \sim R$. (The symbol $\sim$ denotes that two random variables have the same distribution.) The intuitive idea is as follows: pick random variables Y and Z according to Q and R respectively and compute the expected distance between them. The added crucial qualification is that Y and Z are not picked independently, but via the best coupling.

Exercise 12.1 (Metric properties). *Show that (12.2) defines a bonafide metric on the space of probability distributions on Ω^n.*

In Problem 12.2, you are asked to show that when the distance on the space is the Dirac distance, $d(x, y) = 1[x \neq y]$, then (12.2) reduces to the total variation distance.

A transportation cost inequality in an MM-space (Ω, P, d) is an inequality of the form

$$d_1(Q, P) \leq c\sqrt{D(Q\|P)}, \quad \text{for any distribution } Q \text{ on } \Omega. \tag{12.3}$$

Here D is the information-theoretic measure called *Kullback–Liebler divergence* or *relative entropy* [23], [chap. 2]:

$$D(Q\|R) := \sum_x Q(x) \log \frac{Q(x)}{R(x)}.$$

Our aim in the next few sections is to establish an inequality like (12.3) in a specific setting, namely, product spaces. But first, in the next section, we shall see that a transportation cost inequality of this kind readily translates into a concentration of measure inequality.

Exercise 12.2. *Let $\Omega^n := [n]^n$ with the discrete Dirac metric in each component and consider the following distributions:*

- *The product distribution P^n,*

$$P^n(i_1, \ldots, i_n) := \prod_i \frac{1}{n} = \frac{1}{n^n}.$$

- *The* permutation *distribution Q^n, which is concentrated and uniformly distributed on permutations σ of $[n]$,*

$$Q^n(\sigma(1), \ldots, \sigma(n)) = \frac{1}{n!}.$$

Compute $\|P^n - Q^n\|_1, d_1(P^n, Q^n), D(Q^n\|P^n)$. (Note that $D(P^n\|Q^n)$ is undefined.)

12.2 Transportation Cost Inequalities Imply Isoperimetric Inequalities and Concentration

A transportation cost inequality in an MM-space (Ω, P, d) immediately yields an isoperimetric inequality. First, some notation: for a point $x \in \Omega$ and a subset $A \subseteq \Omega$, define[1]

$$d_1(x, A) := \min_{y \in A} d_1(x, y),$$

and for subsets $A, B \subseteq \Omega$, define

$$
\begin{aligned}
d_1(A, B) &:= \min_{x \in A} d(x, B) \\
&= \min_{x \in A, y \in B} d(x, y).
\end{aligned}
$$

Proposition 12.1 (Transportation cost implies isoperimetry). *Let (Ω, P, d) be an MM-space satisfying the Transportation cost inequality (12.3). Then, for $A, B \subseteq \Omega$,*

$$d_1(A, B) \leq c \left(\sqrt{\log \frac{1}{P(A)}} + \sqrt{\log \frac{1}{P(B)}} \right).$$

Proof. Take Q and R to be the measure P conditioned on A and B respectively:

$$
Q(x) := \begin{cases} P(x)/P(A) & \text{if } x \in A, \\ 0 & \text{otherwise} \end{cases}
$$

and

$$
R(x) := \begin{cases} P(x)/P(B) & \text{if } x \in B, \\ 0 & \text{otherwise} \end{cases}
$$

Note that

$$
\begin{aligned}
D(Q\|P) &= \sum_{Q(x)>0} Q(x) \log \frac{Q(x)}{P(x)} \\
&= \sum_{x \in A} \frac{P(x)}{P(A)} \log \frac{1}{P(A)} \\
&= \log \frac{1}{P(A)}.
\end{aligned}
$$

(12.4)

---

[1] Note that we overload the notation d_1 here, but in this case the arguments are points and subsets, as opposed to distributions, so there should be no confusion in any given context.

Similarly,

$$D(R||P) = \log \frac{1}{P(B)}. \tag{12.5}$$

Then,

$d_1(A, B) \le d_1(Q, R),$ since the min is at most an average

$\qquad \le d_1(Q, P) + d_1(R, P),$ by the triangle inequality

$\qquad \le c\sqrt{D(Q||P)} + c\sqrt{D(R||P)},$ by the transportation cost inequality

$\qquad = c \left(\sqrt{\log \frac{1}{P(A)}} + \sqrt{\log \frac{1}{P(B)}} \right),$ by (12.4) and (12.5).   ∎

To obtain the familiar product form of the isoperimetric inequality, take $B := \overline{A_t}$. Then

$t \le d_1(A, \overline{A_t})$

$\qquad \le c \left(\sqrt{\log \frac{1}{P(A)}} + \sqrt{\log \frac{1}{P(\overline{A_t})}} \right).$

$\qquad \le \sqrt{2}c \left(\sqrt{\log \frac{1}{P(A)} + \log \frac{1}{P(\overline{A_t})}} \right),$ (concavity of $\sqrt{\cdot}$)

$\qquad = \sqrt{2}c \; \sqrt{\log \frac{1}{P(A)P(\overline{A_t})}}.$

Hence,

$$P(A)P(\overline{A_t}) \le e^{-t^2/2c^2}.$$

As we have seen before in Chapter 10, such an isoperimetric inequality implies concentrations of Lipschitz functions. One can also deduce concentration results for Lipschitz functions directly from the transportation cost inequality as outlined in Problem 12.3.

12.3 Transportation Cost Inequality in Product Spaces with the Hamming Distance

In this section, we state and prove a transportation cost inequality for product measures with the Hamming distance (with the discrete Dirac distance in each coordinate). Given MM-spaces $(\Omega_i, P_i, d_i), i \in [n]$, the product space (Ω, P, d) is defined by setting

- $\Omega := \Omega_1 \times \cdots \times \Omega_n$ and
- $P := P_1 \times \cdots \times P_n$,

and the distance $d = d_H$ is given by the Hamming metric,

$$d_H(x^n, y^n) := \sum_i d_i(x_i, y_i).$$

Exercise 12.3. *Recall the coupling distance (12.2). In the setting of a product space, verify that this becomes*

$$d_1(Q^n, R^n) := \min_{\pi(Y^n, Z^n)} \sum_{i \in [n]} \mathrm{E}_\pi d_i(Y_i, Z_i),$$

where the minimum is over all couplings π of Q^n and R^n; that is, $\pi(Y^n, Z^n)$ is a joint distribution of random variables $Y^n := (Y_1, \ldots, Y_n)$ and $Z^n := (Z_1, \ldots, Z_n)$ with $\pi(Y^n) \sim Q^n$ and $\pi(Z^n) \sim R^n$.

Theorem 12.1 (Transportation cost inequality for product measures and Hamming distance)**.** *Let (Ω, P, d) be a product space; that is, for arbitrary MM-spaces $(\Omega_i, P_i, d_i), i \in [n]$,*

- $\Omega := \Omega_1 \times \cdots \times \Omega_n$,
- $P := P_1 \times \cdots \times P_n$ *and*
- $d(x^n, y^n) := \sum_i 1[x_i \neq y_i]$.

Then for any measure Q on Ω,

$$d_1(Q, P) \leq \sqrt{\frac{n}{2}D(Q||P)}.$$

Exercise 12.4. *Deduce a familiar isoperimetric inequality for product spaces from this transportation cost inequality. (*HINT*: Use Proposition 12.2.)*

The proof of Theorem 12.1 is by induction on the dimension and will be carried out in the next two sections. *All the action takes place in the base case, that is, dimension one.* The extension to higher dimensions is by "abstract nonsense".

12.3.1 One Dimension

In one dimension, the basic result is as follows:

Theorem 12.2 (Pinsker's inequality)**.**

$$d_1(Q, R) \leq \sqrt{\frac{1}{2}D(Q||R)}.$$

Proof. First, we prove the inequality in the special case when $\Omega = \{0, 1\}$. Let $q := Q(1)$ and $r := R(1)$, and assume without loss of generality that $q \geq r$. Then, we need to prove that

$$q \log \frac{q}{r} + (1 - q) \log \frac{1 - q}{1 - r} \geq 2(q - r)^2. \tag{12.6}$$

This is an exercise in elementary calculus, left to the reader.

For the general case, let $A^* := \{x \in \Omega \mid Q(x) \geq R(x)\}$ and define measures Q^* and R^* on $\{0, 1\}$ by

$$Q^*(1) := Q(A^*), \qquad R^*(1) := R(A^*).$$

Then,

$$\begin{aligned} D(Q\|R) &\geq D(Q^*\|R^*), \quad \text{by Jensen's inequality} \\ &\geq 2 \left(Q^*(1) - R^*(1)\right)^2 \\ &= 2d_1^2(Q, R). \end{aligned}$$ ∎

Exercise 12.5. *Establish (12.6) by calculus.*

12.3.2 Higher Dimensions

As remarked, the "tensorisation" step to higher dimensions in the proof of Theorem 12.1 is by "abstract nonsense". We will do it in an abstract general setting because, besides being natural, it is also useful in this form for other applications (other than the one given earlier for simple product measures).

Recall that given MM-spaces $(\Omega_i, P_i, d_i), i \in [n]$, the product space (Ω, P, d) is defined by setting the following:

- $\Omega := \Omega_1 \times \cdots \times \Omega_n$.
- $P := P_1 \times \cdots \times P_n$.
- The distance $d = d_H$ is given by the Hamming metric

$$d_H(x^n, y^n) := \sum_i d_i(x_i, y_i).$$

The coupling distance (12.2) in this setting equals

$$d_1(Q^n, R^n) := \inf_{\pi(Y^n, Z^n)} \sum_{i \in [n]} E_\pi d_i(Y_i, Z_i), \tag{12.7}$$

where the inf is over all couplings π of Q^n and R^n; that is, $\pi(Y^n, Z^n)$ is a joint distribution of random variables $Y^n := (Y_1, \ldots, Y_n)$ and $Z^n := (Z_1, \ldots, Z_n)$ with $\pi(Y^n) \sim Q^n$ and $\pi(Z^n) \sim R^n$.

Proposition 12.2 (Tensorisation of transportation cost). *Let* $(\Omega_i, P_i, d_i), i \in [n]$*, be MM-spaces that each satisfies the transportation cost inequality:*

$$d_i(Q_i, P_i) \leq c\sqrt{D(Q_i||P_i)}, \quad \text{for any distribution } Q_i \text{ on } \Omega_i,$$

for some constant $c > 0$*. Let* (Ω, P, d) *be the product space as defined earlier. Then* (Ω, P, d) *satisfies the transportation cost inequality:*

$$d(Q, P) \leq c\sqrt{n \, D(Q||P)}, \quad \text{for any distribution } Q \text{ on } \Omega.$$

Proof. It suffices to construct a coupling $\pi(Y^n, X^n)$ with $\pi(Y^n) \sim Q$ and $\pi(X^n) \sim P$ such that

$$E_\pi\left[d(Y^n, X^n)\right] = \sum_i E_\pi\left[d_i(Y_i, X_i)\right] \leq c\sqrt{n \, D(Q||P)}.$$

Introduce the notational abbreviations

$$Q(y^i) := \pi(Y^i = y^i), \qquad Q_i(y_i \mid y^{i-1}) := \pi(Y_i = y_i \mid Y^{i-1} = y^{i-1}).$$

Define

$$\Delta_i(y^{i-1}) := D(Q_i(\cdot \mid y^{i-1})||P_i(\cdot \mid y^{i-1})) = D(Q_i(\cdot \mid y^{i-1})||P_i),$$

where the second equality is because P is a product measure. By the *chain rule for divergence*,

$$D(Q||P) = \sum_{i=1}^{n} \sum_{y^{i-1} \in \Omega^{i-1}} \Delta_i(y^{i-1})Q(y^{i-1}).$$

We construct the coupling π inductively. Assume that the joint distribution on (Y^{i-1}, X^{i-1}) has already been defined. To extend the distribution, we define the joint distribution of (Y_i, X_i) conditioned on $(Y^{i-1} = y^{i-1}, X^{i-1} = x^{i-1})$ for any y^{i-1}, x^{i-1}. First, define the marginals by

$$\pi(Y_i = z \mid Y^{i-1} = y^{i-1}, X^{i-1} = x^{i-1}) := Q_i(z \mid y^{i-1})$$

and

$$\pi(X_i = z \mid Y^{i-1} = y^{i-1}, X^{i-1} = x^{i-1}) := P_i(z).$$

That is, both Y_i and X_i are conditionally independent of X^{i-1} given $Y^{i-1} = y^{i-1}$.

Now, we use the transportation cost inequality satisfied by the component space Ω_i to construct a coupling of (Y_i, X_i) with these marginals so that for all y^{i-1},

$$E_\pi\left[d_i(Y_i, X_i) \mid Y^{i-1} = y^{i-1}\right] \leq c\sqrt{\Delta_i(y^{i-1})}.$$

Finally, we verify that this inductively constructed coupling satisfies the desired inequality:

$$\sum_i \mathrm{E}_\pi\left[d_i(Y_i, X_i)\right] = \sum_i \sum_{y^{i-1}} \mathrm{E}_\pi\left[d_i(Y_i, X_i) \mid Y^{i-1} = y^{i-1}\right] Q(y^{i-1})$$

$$\leq \sum_i \sum_{y^{i-1}} c\sqrt{\Delta_i(y^{i-1})}Q(y^{i-1})$$

$$= cn \sum_i \sum_{y^{i-1}} \sqrt{\Delta_i(y^{i-1})}\frac{Q(y^{i-1})}{n}$$

$$\leq cn \sqrt{\sum_i \sum_{y^{i-1}} \Delta_i(y^{i-1})\frac{Q(y^{i-1})}{n}}, \quad \text{by concavity of } \sqrt{\cdot}$$

$$= c\sqrt{nD(Q\|P)}, \quad \text{by the chain rule for divergence.} \quad \blacksquare$$

We can now complete the proof of the transportation cost inequality in product spaces with the Hamming distance.

Proof Theorem 12.1). Combine Pinsker's inequality with the abstract tensorisation of Proposition 12.2. ∎

12.4 An Extension to Non-Product Measures

In this section we state, without proof, a theorem due to Marton which extends the transportation cost inequality from independent distributions to certain dependent distributions where one has some handle to control the dependence. This extension is quite useful as shown by the application in Problem 12.5.

Theorem 12.3 (Transportation cost inequality with controlled dependence). *Let (Ω, Q, d) be MM-space with the following:*

- $\Omega := \Omega_1 \times \cdots \times \Omega_n$.
- $d(x^n, y^n) := \sum_i d_i(x_i, y_i)$, *for arbitrary metrics d_i on Ω_i for each $i \in [n]$.*
- Q *a measure on Ω such that for each $k \geq 0$ and each $x^k, \hat{x}^k$ differing only in the last coordinate (i.e. $x_i = \hat{x}_i, i < k$ and $x_i \neq \hat{x}_i$), there is a coupling $\pi(Y_k^n, Z_k^n)$ of the distributions $Q(\cdot \mid x^k)$ and $Q(\cdot \mid \hat{x}^k)$ such that*

$$\mathrm{E}_\pi\left[\sum_{i>k} d_i(Y_i, Z_i) \mid x^k, \hat{x}^k\right] \leq u.$$

Then for any other measure R,

$$d(R, Q) \leq (u + 1)\sqrt{\frac{n}{2}D(R||Q)}.$$

Exercise 12.6. *Check that the transportation cost inequality for product measures is a special case of Theorem 12.3.*

12.5 Pointers to the Literature

The approach to measure concentration via transportation cost was introduced by Marton [61]. The extension to dependent measures is from Marton [62]. Ledoux ([56], chap. 6) covers the transportation cost approach in more detail.

12.6 Problems

Problem 12.1. Prove the following alternative characterisations of the total variation distance:

$$d_1(Q, R) = \frac{1}{2}E_Q\left[\left|1 - \frac{R(Y)}{Q(Y)}\right|\right] \tag{12.8}$$

$$= E_Q\left[\left(1 - \frac{R(Y)}{Q(Y)}\right)_+\right] \tag{12.9}$$

$$= \sum_y \left(1 - \frac{R(y)}{Q(y)}\right)_+ Q(y)$$

$$= \sum_y \left(1 - \frac{Q(y)}{R(y)}\right)_+ R(y)$$

$$= E_R\left[\left(1 - \frac{Q(Y)}{R(Y)}\right)_+\right] \tag{12.10}$$

$$= \max_{A \subseteq \Omega} |Q(A) - R(A)| \tag{12.11}$$

$\triangledown$

Problem 12.2. Show that the total variation distance is also given by

$$d_1(Q, R) = \min_{\pi(Y,Z)} E_\pi[Y \neq Z], \tag{12.12}$$

where the minimum ranges over all couplings $\pi(Y, Z)$ of Q and R: $\pi(Y) \sim Q$ and $\pi(Z) \sim R$.

Problem 12.3. Use the transportation cost inequality to directly deduce a measure concentration result for Lipschitz functions. Let (Ω, P, d) be an MM-space satisfying a transportation cost inequality

$$d_1(Q, P) \le c\sqrt{D(Q\|P)},$$

and let f be a Lipschitz function on Ω. Let

$$A := \{x \in \Omega \mid f(x) > \mathrm{E}_P[f] + t\}.$$

Let Q be the measure P conditioned on A.

(a) Argue that

$$d_1(Q, P) \ge \mathrm{E}_Q[f] - \mathrm{E}_P[f] \ge t.$$

(b) Deduce that

$$P[f > \mathrm{E}_P[f] + t] \le e^{-2t^2/c^2 n}.$$

(c) Similarly deduce the other tail inequality. $\triangledown$

Problem 12.4 (A weighted transportation cost inequality in product spaces). Let $\alpha := (\alpha_1, \ldots, \alpha_n) \ge 0$ and let (Ω, P_i, d_i) be arbitrary MM-spaces. Consider the product space (Ω, P, d_α) with Ω and P as usual, but with the *weighted Hamming metric*

$$d_\alpha(x^n, y^n) := \sum_i \alpha_i d_i(x_i, y_i). \tag{12.13}$$

Prove a version of the transportation cost inequality in this setting which reduces to the unweighted version proved in this chapter. $\triangledown$

Problem 12.5 (Transportation cost and concentration for permutations). Consider the group of permutations S_n as an MM-space by endowing it with the uniform distribution P and the transposition distance d between permutations. Show that this space satisfies the transportation cost inequality

$$d(Q, P) \le \sqrt{2n D(Q\|P)}.$$

Deduce an isoperimetric inequality and a measure concentration result for Lipschitz functions on permutations. (HINT: Apply Marton's theorem 12.3.)

$\triangledown$

Problem 12.6. Prove Theorem 12.3 and give a weighted analogue. $\triangledown$

13

Quadratic Transportation Cost and Talagrand's Inequality

13.1 Introduction

In this chapter, we prove Talagrand's convex distance inequality via the transportation cost method, an approach pioneered by Kati Marton [62] and further developed by Amir Dembo [25]. This approach is particularly interesting because:

- It places both the theorem and its proof in its natural place within the context of isoperimetric inequalities.
- It places a standard structure on the proof as opposed to the somewhat ad hoc nature of the original inductive proof of Talagrand.
- It isolates very clearly the essential content of the proof in one dimension and shows that the extension to higher dimensions is routine.
- It also allows a stronger version of the method of bounded differences that leads to concrete improvements in applications.
- It allows generalisation to dependent measures.

13.2 Review and Road Map

Recall the set-up for the isoperimetric inequality for product measures and a weighted Hamming distance: (Ω, P, d_α), where $\Omega := \prod_{i \in [n]} \Omega_i$ and $P := \prod_i P_i$ for arbitrary spaces (Ω_i, P_i), $i \in [n]$, and the weighted Hamming distance defined by

$$d_\alpha(x, y) := \sum_{i \in [n]} \alpha_i [x_i \neq y_i], \tag{13.1}$$

for a fixed $\alpha := (\alpha_1, \ldots, \alpha_n) \geq 0$ with norm 1; that is, $\sum_i \alpha_i^2 = 1$.

161

To prove the isoperimetric inequality in the preceding setting via the transportation cost method, we introduced a distance between probability measures on Ω that reflected (13.1): namely, if Q and R are distributions on Ω, define

$$d_{1,\alpha}(Q, R) := \inf_{\pi(Y,Z)} \sum_{i \in [n]} \alpha_i [Y_i \neq Z_i], \qquad (13.2)$$

where the inf is over couplings $\pi(YZ)$ of Q and R (with Y distributed according to Q and Z according to R).

We then proved the *transportation cost inequality* for this distance in product spaces: for any other distribution Q on Ω,

$$d_{1,\alpha}(Q, P) \leq \sqrt{\frac{D(Q||P)}{2}}. \qquad (13.3)$$

From this information-theoretic inequality, the isoperimetric inequality for product spaces and the weighted Hamming distance followed readily: for any two subsets $A, B \subseteq \Omega$,

$$P(X \in A) \cdot P(d_{1,\alpha}(X, A) > t) \leq e^{-2t^2}. \qquad (13.4)$$

In the non-uniform setting, we have for every point $x \in \Omega$, a non-negative unit norm vector $\alpha(x) := (\alpha_1(x), \ldots, \alpha_n(x))$, that is, a function $\alpha : x \rightarrow \alpha(x)$ with $||\alpha(x)||_2 = 1$, and one defines an asymmetric notion of "distance" by

$$d_{2,\alpha}(x, y) := \sum_{i \in [n]} \alpha_i(x)[x_i \neq y_i], \qquad (13.5)$$

(The reason for the subscript "2" will emerge shortly.)

As usual, for $A \subseteq \Omega$,

$$d_{2,\alpha}(x, A) := \min_{y \in A} d_{2,\alpha}(x, y).$$

The goal is to prove the following isoperimetric inequality which is analogous to (13.4), which was used in the applications in the previous chapter:

Theorem 13.1. *For any $A \subseteq \Omega$,*

$$P(X \in A)P(d_{2,\alpha}(X, A) > t) \leq e^{-t^2/4}.$$

Some thought shows that proving such an inequality is tantamount to proving the inequality for all possible α simultaneously in the following sense: Define, for $x \in \Omega$ and $A \subseteq \Omega$,

$$d_2(x, A) := \sup_{||\alpha||=1} d_{2,\alpha}(x, A). \qquad (13.6)$$

This is just Talagrand's convex distance between a point and a subset. Then we will prove the following.

Theorem 13.2 (Talagrand's convex distance inequality). *For any $A \subseteq \Omega$,*

$$P(X \in A)P(d_2(X, A) > t) \leq e^{-t^2/4}.$$

To prove this via the transportation cost method, we need to introduce a distance between probability measures in Ω that reflects (13.5) and (13.6). For probability measures Q and R on Ω, define

$$d_2(Q, R) = \inf_{\pi(Y,Z)} \sup_{E_Q[||\alpha||_2] \leq 1} E_\pi \left[\sum_{i \in [n]} \alpha(Y_i)[Y_i \neq Z_i] \right]. \tag{13.7}$$

(The sup is over all functions $\alpha : \Omega \to R^n$ such that $E_Q[||\alpha(X)||] \leq 1$.) In Problem 13.1 you are asked to show that this notion of "distance" satisfies a triangle inequality. We will show that this "distance" satisfies a transportation cost inequality and as a consequence yields Talagrand's convex distance inequality.

13.3 An L_2 (Pseudo)-Metric on Distributions

13.3.1 One Dimension

An L_2 notion of "distance" between two distributions Q and R on a space is given by the following definition:

$$d_2(Q, R) := \left(E_Q \left(1 - \frac{R(Y)}{Q(Y)} \right)^2 \right)^{1/2}$$

$$= \left(\sum_y \left(1 - \frac{R(y)}{Q(y)} \right)^2 Q(y) \right)^{1/2} \tag{13.8}$$

$$= \left(\sum_y \frac{R^2(y)}{Q(y)} - 1 \right)^{1/2}. \tag{13.9}$$

Note that this definition is *asymmetric*.

Compare this with the variational distance $d_1(Q, R)$:

$$d_1(Q, R) := \frac{1}{2} E_Q \left[\left| 1 - \frac{R(Y)}{Q(Y)} \right| \right]$$

$$= E_Q \left[\left(1 - \frac{R(Y)}{Q(Y)} \right)_+ \right]$$

$$= \sum_y \left(1 - \frac{R(y)}{Q(y)} \right)_+ Q(y).$$

An alternate characterisation of d_2 is via couplings.

Proposition 13.1.

$$d_2(Q, R) = \inf_{\pi(Y,Z)} \sup_{E_Q[\alpha] \le 1} E_\pi\left[\alpha(Y)[Y \ne Z]\right] \tag{13.10}$$

$$= \inf_{\pi(Y,Z)} \sum_y (\pi(Z \ne y \mid Y = y))^2 Q(Y = y). \tag{13.11}$$

Here,

- *The* inf *is over all joint distributions* π *with marginals Q and R.*
- *The* sup *is over all* $\alpha : \Omega \to \mathbb{R}$.

Proof. We will show that for *any* joint distribution π,

$$\sup_{\|\alpha\| \le 1} E_\pi[\alpha(Y)[Y \ne Z]] = \sum_y (\pi(Z \ne y \mid Y = y))^2 Q(Y = y).$$

To show that the left-hand side is at most the right-hand side, we use the Cauchy–Schwartz inequality

$$E_\pi[\alpha(Y)[Y \ne Z]] = \sum_y \alpha(y)\pi(Z \ne y) \mid Y = y]Q(Y = y)$$

$$\le \left(\sum_y (\alpha(y))^2 Q(Y = y)\right)^{1/2}$$

$$\times \left(\sum_y (\pi(Z \ne y \mid Y = y))^2 Q(Y = y)\right)^{1/2}$$

$$\le \left(\sum_y (\pi(Z \ne y \mid Y = y))^2 Q(Y = y)\right)^{1/2}.$$

The verification of other direction is left as an exercise.   ∎

Exercise 13.1. *Choose α suitably to prove the other direction.*

13.3.2 Tensorisation to Higher Dimensions

For probability measures Q and R on Ω^n, (13.7) reduces to

$$d_2(Q, R) = \inf_{\pi(Y^n, Z^n)} \sup_{E_q[\|\alpha\|_2] \le 1} E_\pi\left[\sum_{i \in [n]} \alpha(Y_i)[Y_i \ne Z_i]\right].$$

(The sup is over all functions $\alpha_i : \Omega_i \to \mathbb{R}$ such that $E_Q[\|\alpha(X)\|_2] \leq 1$.) In Problem 13.1 you are asked to show that this notion of "distance" satisfies a triangle inequality.

An alternate characterisation is

$$d_2(Q, R) = \inf_{\pi(Y^n, Z^n)} \sum_i \sum_{y^n} \left(\pi(Z_i \neq y_i \mid Y^n = y^n) \right)^2 Q(Y^n = y^n).$$

13.4 Quadratic Transportation Cost

Theorem 13.3 (Quadratic transportation cost inequality in product spaces). *Let (Ω, P) be a product space with $\Omega := \prod_{i \in [n]} \Omega_i$ and $P := \prod_{i \in [n]} P_i$, where (Ω_i, P_i) are arbitrary spaces. Then, for any other measure Q on Ω,*

$$d_2(Q, P) \leq \sqrt{2D(Q \| P)}.$$

The proof is by induction on dimension where all the action once again is in dimension one.

13.4.1 Base Case: One Dimension

In one dimension, for the L_1 distance d_1, the standard inequality is *Pinsker's inequality*:

$$d_1(Q, R) \leq \sqrt{\frac{1}{2}D(Q \| R)}. \tag{13.12}$$

We need an analogous inequality for d_2. Note that because the distance d_2 is not symmetric (unlike d_1), we actually need two inequalities. However there is an elegant symmetric version due to Samson [82] from which the two asymmetric inequalities we need follow.

Theorem 13.4. *For any two distributions Q and R,*

$$d_2^2(Q, R) + d_2^2(R, Q) \leq 2D(R \| Q). \tag{13.13}$$

Hence,

$$d_2(Q, R), d_2(R, Q) \leq \sqrt{2D(R \| Q)}. \tag{13.14}$$

Exercise 13.2. *Consider two distributions Q and R on the two-point space $\Omega := \{0, 1\}$. Compute $d_1(Q, R), d_2(Q, R)$ and $D(Q \| R)$. Verify that*

- $d_1(Q, R), d_2(Q, R) \leq D(Q \| R)$.
- $d_1(Q, R) \leq d_2(Q, R)$.

Exercise 13.3. *Write down the inequality in the case of a two-point space and compare with Pinsker's inequality.*

Proof (Theorem 13.4). Consider the function

$$\Psi(u) := u \log u - u + 1,$$

and

$$\Phi(u) := \Psi(u)/u.$$

By elementary calculus, it is easy to check that for $0 \leq u \leq 1$,

$$\Psi(u) \geq \frac{1}{2}(1-u)^2,$$

whereas for $u \geq 1$,

$$\Phi(u) \geq \frac{1}{2}(1 - \frac{1}{u})^2.$$

Since

$$u \log u - u + 1 = \Psi(u)[u \leq 1] + u\Phi(u)[u > 1],$$

we have,

$$u \log u - u + 1 \geq \frac{1}{2}(1-u)_+^2 + \frac{u}{2}\left(1 - \frac{1}{u}\right)_+^2.$$

Putting $u := Q(X)/R(X)$ and taking expectations with respect to the measure $R(X)$ gives the lemma. ∎

13.4.2 Tensorisation to Higher Dimensions

Once we have the inequality in one dimension, it is routine (but tedious) to extend the inequality to higher dimensions. We phrase the tensorisation lemma in a general abstract fashion to emphasise its generality (which is useful in other applications).

Proposition 13.2 (Tensorisation of quadratic cost). *Let $(\Omega_i, P_i, d_i), i = 1, 2$, be spaces that separately satisfy a quadratic transportation cost inequality: for any measures Q_i on Ω_i,*

$$d_2(Q_i, P_i) \leq \sqrt{2D(Q_i \| P_i)}, \quad i = 1, 2.$$

Let $\Omega := \Omega_1 \times \Omega_2$ be the product space with product measure $P := P_1 \times P_2$ and distance $d(x, y) := d(x_1, y_1) + d(x_2, y_2)$. Then, the measure P also *satisfies a quadratic transportation cost inequality: for any measure Q on* Ω,

$$d_2(Q, P) \le \sqrt{2D(Q\|P)}.$$

Proof. Coordinate by coordinate extension of the coupling, as in the previous chapter (see also Ledoux [56], theorem 6.9, pages 130–131). ∎

Now we can complete the proof of the quadratic transportation cost inequality in product spaces.

Proof (Theorem 13.3). Induction using Proposition 13.2 with Theorem 13.4 as the base case. ∎

13.5 Talagrand's Inequality via Quadratic Transportation Cost

Exercise 13.4. *Verify that if* $d_2(A, B) := \min_{x \in A} d_2(x, B)$, *where* $d_2(x, B)$ *is Talagrand's convex distance and* $d_2(Q, R)$ *is the distance as defined earlier for any probability distributions* Q *and* R *concentrated on* A *and* B *respectively, then* $d_2(A, B) \le d_2(Q, R)$,

Corollary 13.1 (Talagrand's convex distance inequality in product spaces).

$$d_2(A, B) \le \sqrt{2 \log \frac{1}{P(A)}} + \sqrt{2 \log \frac{1}{P(B)}}.$$

Proof. Take $Q(C) := P(C \mid A)$, $R(C) := P(C \mid B)$. Then,

$$d_2(A, B) \le d_2(Q, R), \quad \text{since the min is at most an average}$$

$$\le d_2(Q, P) + d_2(R, P), \quad \text{triangle inequality}$$

$$\le \sqrt{2D(Q\|P)} + \sqrt{2D(R\|P)}, \quad \text{transportation cost inequality}$$

$$= \sqrt{2 \log \frac{1}{P(A)}} + \sqrt{2 \log \frac{1}{P(B)}}. \qquad \blacksquare$$

To obtain the familiar product form of Talagrand's inequality, take $B := \overline{A_t}$. Then

$$
\begin{aligned}
t &\leq d(A, \overline{A_t}) \\
&\leq \sqrt{2\log \frac{1}{P(A)}} + \sqrt{2\log \frac{1}{P(\overline{A_t})}}. \\
&\leq 2\sqrt{\log \frac{1}{P(A)} + \log \frac{1}{P(\overline{A_t})}}, \quad \text{concavity of } \sqrt{\cdot} \\
&= 2\sqrt{\log \frac{1}{P(A)P(\overline{A_t})}}.
\end{aligned}
$$

Hence,

$$
P(A)P(\overline{A_t}) \leq e^{-t^2/4}.
$$

13.6 Extension to Dependent Processes

In this section, we state (without proof) an extension of the quadratic transportation cost inequality for certain classes of dependent measures. The result is due independently to Kati Marton and P.-M. Samson. In the formulation given next, we follow Samson [82].

Let Q be a measure on Ω and let $X_1, \ldots, X_n$ be distributed according to Q. To quantify the amount of dependence between these variables, introduce an upper triangular matrix $\Gamma = \Gamma(Q)$ with ones on the diagonal.

For $1 \leq i < j \leq n$, denote the vector $(X_i, \ldots, X_j)$ by X_i^j. For every $1 \leq i \leq n$, every $x_1, \ldots, x_{i-1}$ with $x_k \in \Omega_k$ and $x_k, x_k' \in \Omega_k$, set

$$
\begin{aligned}
a_j(x_1^{i-1}, x, x_i') := d_1 \big(&Q(\cdot \mid X_1^{i-1} = x_1^{i-1}, X_i = x_i), \\
&Q(\cdot \mid X_1^{i-1} = x_1^{i-1}, X_i = x_i') \big).
\end{aligned}
$$

That is, take the total variation distance between the two conditional distributions of Q where the two conditionings differ only at one point. Set

$$
\Gamma_{i,j}^2 := \sup_{x_i, x_i'} \sup_{x_1, \ldots, x_{i-1}} a_j(x_1^{i-1}, x, x_i').
$$

Theorem 13.5 (Transportation cost inequality for dependent measures). *For any probability measure R on Ω,*

$$
d_2(R, Q), \; d_2(Q, R) \leq \|\Gamma(Q)\| \sqrt{2D(R\|Q)}. \tag{13.15}
$$

Exercise 13.5. *Recover the inequality for independent measures from this one.*

13.7 Pointers to the Literature

The transportation cost approach to proving Talagrand's inequality was pioneered by Kati Marton. Dembo [25] contains systematic generalisations to several other geometric inequalities. The proof of the inequality in one dimension and the extension to dependent measures are from Samson [82]. Ledoux ([56], section 6.3) contains a complete exposition.

13.8 Problems

Problem 13.1. Show that the asymmetric and non-uniform notion of distance in (13.5) satisfies a triangle inequality. ▽

Problem 13.2 (Transportation cost and concentration for permutations). Establish a quadratic transportation cost inequality for the group of permutations S_n by applying Theorem 13.5. ▽

Problem 13.3 (Method of bounded differences revisited). The quadratic transportation cost inequality, Theorem 13.3, can be used to give a direct proof of a somewhat stronger version of the method of bounded differences.

(a) Prove the following.

Theorem 13.6 (Method of average non-uniform bounded differences).
Let Q be a measure in a product space $\Omega = \prod_{i \in [n]} \Omega_i$, satisfying a quadratic transportation cost inequality: there is a constant $c_1 > 0$ such that for any other measure R,

$$d_2(Q, R) \le c_1 \sqrt{D(R \| Q)}.$$

Let f be a function such that there is a function $\beta : \Omega \to R^n$ with

$$E_Q \left[\sum_i \beta_i^2(X) \right] \le c_2^2,$$

and such that

$$f(x^{(n)}) \le f(y^{(n)}) + \sum_{i \in [n]} \beta_i(x) d_i(x_i, y_i),$$

for any $x^{(n)}, y^{(n)} \in \Omega$. Then

$$\Pr[f < Ef - t] \leq \exp\left(\frac{-t^2}{c_1^2 \cdot c_2^2}\right).$$

(b) Show that if we assume

$$f(x^{(n)}) \geq f(y^{(n)}) - \sum_{i \in [n]} \beta_i(x) d_i(x_i, y_i),$$

then one obtains a similar concentration on $\Pr[f > Ef + t]$.

(c) **Subgraph counts.** Consider the random graph $G(n, p)$ with vertex set $[n]$ and where each possible edge ij is present with probability p independently.

Let H be a fixed graph and let Y_H denote the number of copies of H in $G(n, p)$. The study of Y_H is a classical topic in the theory of random graphs with a vast literature. We are interested in concentration results obtained by estimating the probability $P[Y_H > (1 + \epsilon)E[Y_H]]$ for a fixed small constant $\epsilon > 0$.

Consider for illustration the case $H := K_3$. Clearly, $E[Y_{K_3}] = \binom{n}{3} p^3 = \Theta(p^3 n^3)$. Vu obtained the first exponential bound:

$$P[Y_{K_3} > (1 + \epsilon)E[Y_{K_3}]] \leq \exp(-\Theta(p^{3/2} n^{3/2})).$$

Subsequently, Kim and Vu by using a "divide-and-conquer" martingale argument improved this to the near optimal

$$P[Y_{K_3} > (1 + \epsilon)E[Y_{K_3}]] \leq \exp(-\Theta(p^2 n^2)).$$

Show how to obtain this easily from the average version of the method of bounded differences given in part (a). ▽

14

Log-Sobolev Inequalities and Concentration

14.1 Introduction

In this chapter, we give an introduction to log-Sobolev inequalities and their use in deriving concentration of measure results. This is a third important methodology for concentration of measure (the other two being martingales and transportation cost) and it appears to be the most powerful of the three.

Given a probability space (Ω, P) and a function $f : \Omega \to R$, define the *entropy* of f by

$$\text{Ent}_P(f) := E_P[f \log f] - E_P[f] \log E_P[f]. \qquad (14.1)$$

By Jensen's inequality applied to the convex function $\psi(x) := x \log x$, $\text{Ent}_P(f) \geq 0$ for any f.

A *logarithmic Sobolev inequality* or just log-Sobolev inequality bounds $\text{Ent}_P[f]$, for a "smooth" function f, by an expression involving its gradient. In R^n, which is the original context in which log-Sobolev inequalities were introduced, a measure P satisfies a log-Sobolev inequality if for some $C > 0$ and all "smooth enough" functions f,

$$\text{Ent}_P(f) \leq 2C E_P[|\nabla f|^2]. \qquad (14.2)$$

We will first introduce a discrete version of this inequality and prove it using tools from information theory. The methods developed will then be applied to derive a modified version of these inequalities, which will yield, as a consequence, another proof of Talagrand's inequality and other concentration inequalities that are useful in applications of randomized algorithms.

14.2 A Discrete Log-Sobolev Inequality on the Hamming Cube

We are interested here in discrete settings: what is the analogue of ∇f in a discrete setting in order to formulate a version of (14.2)?

Consider the familiar Hamming cube $\{0, 1\}^n$. Here a natural analogue of ∇f would be

$$\nabla f := (D_1 f, \ldots, D_n f),$$

where, for each $i \in [n]$,

$$D_i f(x) := f(x) - f(\sigma_i x),$$

and $\sigma_i(x)$ is the result of flipping the bit in the ith position in x.

Theorem 14.1 (Log-Sobolev inequality in the hamming cube). *For any function* $f : \{0, 1\}^n \to R$ *and a product distribution* P,

$$\text{Ent}_P(f^2) \le \frac{1}{2} \sum_{1 \le i \le n} E_P[|D_i f|^2]. \tag{14.3}$$

The log-Sobolev inequality (14.3) yields the familiar measure concentration results for Lipschitz functions on the Hamming cube. Before proving Theorem 14.1, let us see how this application can be derived. We will follow an argument that Ledoux [56] attributes to Herbst.

14.2.1 Concentration: The Herbst Argument

Let F be 1-Lipschitz (with respect to the Hamming metric in the cube) and apply (14.3) to the function $f^2 := e^{sF}$ for some $s \in R$ to be chosen later.

To bound the right-hand side in (14.3), we use the Lipschitz property of F and elementary calculus to get, for $|s| \le 1$,

$$|D_i(e^{sF/2})| := |e^{sF(x)/2} - e^{sF(\sigma_k(x))/2}|$$
$$\le |s|e^{sF(x)/2}.$$

Putting this into (14.3),

$$\text{Ent}_P(e^{sF}) \le \frac{ns^2}{2} E_P[e^{sF}]. \tag{14.4}$$

Now, we introduce some *generatingfunctionology*: let

$$G(s) := E_P[e^{sF}]$$

be the (exponential moment) generating function of F. Then, the left-hand side is (with $E = E_P$)

$$sE[Fe^{sF}] - E[e^{sF}]\log E[e^{sF}] = sG'(s) - G(s)\log G(s),$$

and the right-hand side is

$$\frac{ns^2}{2}G(s).$$

Hence we arrive at the following differential inequality for $G(s)$:

$$sG'(s) - G(s)\log G(s) \leq \frac{ns^2}{2}G(s). \tag{14.5}$$

Let $\Psi(s) := \log G(s)/s$; then from (14.5), we get

$$\Psi'(s) \leq \frac{ns}{2}$$

$$\leq \frac{n}{2}, \quad \text{since } s \leq 1.$$

Thus,

$$\Psi(s) \leq \frac{ns}{2} + a$$

for some constant a. The constant is determined by noting that

$$\lim_{s\to 0} \Psi(s) = \lim_{s\to 0} \frac{G'(0)}{G(0)} = E[f].$$

Hence,

$$\Psi(s) \leq E[f] + \frac{ns}{2};$$

that is,

$$E[e^{sF}] =: G(s) \leq \exp\left(sE[F] + \frac{ns^2}{2}\right). \tag{14.6}$$

Thus we have arrived at a bound on the moment-generating function of F and this yields as usual, via Markov's inequality applied to e^{sF}, the concentration bound

$$\Pr\left(F > E[F] + t\right) \leq \exp\left(\frac{-t^2}{2n}\right).$$

14.3 Tensorisation

We will now develop a methodology for proving log-Sobolev inequalities that ultimately reduces to proving a simple one-dimensional inequality. This will be used to prove Theorem 14.1 and also modified versions which, in turn, will be used to derive Talagrand's inequality and other concentration inequalities.

The following proposition enables one to reduce the proof of a log-Sobolev inequality in product spaces to a single dimension.

Proposition 14.1 (Tensorisation of entropy). *Let $X_1, \ldots, X_n$ be independent random variables, with X_i taking values in (Ω_i, μ_i), $i \in [n]$. Let f be a non-negative function on $\prod_i \Omega_i$. Then with $P := \prod_i P_i$ and $P_{-i} := \prod_{j \neq i} P_j$,*

$$\mathrm{Ent}_P(f) \leq \sum_{i \in [n]} \mathrm{E}_{P_{-i}}[\mathrm{Ent}_{P_i}[f \mid X_j, j \neq i]]. \tag{14.7}$$

As a first application of Proposition 14.1, we prove Theorem 14.1.

Proof (Theorem 14.1). By Proposition 14.1, it suffices to prove the inequality in one dimension, where it amounts to

$$u^2 \log u^2 + v^2 \log v^2 - (u^2 + v^2) \log \frac{u^2 + v^2}{2} \leq (u - v)^2 \tag{14.8}$$

for any real u, v. This is easily checked by elementary calculus. Thus,

$$\mathrm{Ent}_P(f^2) \leq \sum_{i \in [n]} \mathrm{E}_{P_{-i}}[\mathrm{E}_{P_i}[f^2 \mid X_j, j \neq i]]$$

$$\leq \sum_{i \in [n]} \mathrm{E}_{P_{-i}}[\frac{1}{2} \mathrm{E}_{P_i}[D_i f^2 \mid X_j, j \neq i]]$$

$$= \frac{1}{2} \sum_{1 \leq i \leq n} \mathrm{E}_P[|D_i f|^2].$$
■

Exercise 14.1. *Verify (14.8).*

Proposition 14.1 itself follows fairly easily from a basic inequality in information theory known as Han's inequality [23]. In fact, we need a generalisation of this inequality to relative entropy, which we state without proof.

Given a distribution Q on a product space $\Omega := \prod_i \Omega_i$, let Q_{-i} denote the distribution on the product space $\Omega_{-i} := \prod_{j \neq i} \Omega_j$, and is given by

$$Q_{-i}(x_{-i}) := \sum_{x_i \in \Omega_i} Q(x),$$

where $x := (x_1, \ldots, x_n)$ and $x_{-i} := (x_1, \ldots, x_{i-1}, x_{i+1}, \ldots, x_n)$.

Lemma 14.1 (Han's inequality for relative entropy). *Let P be the product measure on Ω and let Q be any other measure on Ω. Then*

$$D(Q\|P) \geq \frac{1}{n-1} \sum_{i \in [n]} D(Q_{-i}\|P_{-i})$$

or

$$D(Q\|P) \leq \sum_{i \in [n]} (D(Q\|P) - D(Q_{-i}\|P_{-i})).$$

Proof (Theorem 14.1). First note that if the inequality is true for a random variable f, it is also true for cf for any constant $c > 0$, so we may rescale to assume $E[f] = 1$. Define

$$Q(x) := f(x)P(x),$$

so that

$$D(Q\|P) = \mathrm{Ent}_P[f].$$

Thus,

$$
\begin{aligned}
\mathrm{Ent}_P[f] &= D(Q\|P) \\
&\leq \sum_{i \in [n]} (D(Q\|P) - D(Q_{-i}\|P_{-i})) \\
&= \sum_{i \in [n]} \mathrm{E}_{P_{-i}}[\mathrm{Ent}_{P_i}[f \mid X_j, j \neq i]].
\end{aligned}
$$

■

14.4 Modified Log-Sobolev Inequalities in Product Spaces

In this section, we use the methods developed so far to derive a modified version of the log-Sobolev inequalities which will be used to attain our final goal: namely, Talagrand's inequality and other concentration inequalities.

Let $X_1, \ldots, X_n$ be independent random variables and let $X_1', \ldots, X_n'$ be independent identical copies of the variables $X_1, \ldots, X_n$. Let $Z := f(X_1, \ldots, X_n)$ be a positive-valued random variable, and for each $i \in [n]$, set

$$Z_i' := f(X_1, \ldots, X_{i-1}, X_i', X_{i+1}, \ldots, X_n).$$

Theorem 14.2 (Symmetric log-Sobolev inequality in product spaces). *Let $X_i, X_i', i \in [n]$, and $Z, Z_i', i \in [n]$, be as given previously. Then*

$$\mathrm{Ent}[e^{sZ}] \leq \sum_{i \in [n]} \mathrm{E}[e^{sZ} \psi(-s(Z - Z_i'))], \tag{14.9}$$

where $\psi(x) := e^x - x - 1$. Moreover,

$$\text{Ent}[e^{sZ}] \leq \sum_{i \in [n]} \text{E}\left[e^{sZ}\tau(-s(Z - Z_i'))[Z > Z_i']\right] \qquad (14.10)$$

and

$$\text{Ent}[e^{sZ}] \leq \sum_{i \in [n]} \text{E}\left[e^{sZ}\tau(-s(Z_i' - Z))[Z < Z_i']\right], \qquad (14.11)$$

where $\tau(x) := x(e^x - 1)$.

Proof. We use Proposition 14.1 applied to the function e^{sZ} and bound each term in the sum on the right-hand side. Lemma 14.2 implies that if Y' is any positive function of $X_1, \ldots, X_{i-1}, X_i', X_{i+1}, \ldots, X_N$, then

$$\text{E}_i[Y \log Y] - \text{E}_i[Y] \log \text{E}_i[Y] \leq \text{E}_i[Y(\log Y - \log Y') - (Y - Y')].$$

(E_i is the expectation over X_i with all other variables fixed).

Applying this to $Y := e^{sZ}$ and $Y' := e^{Z_i'}$, we get

$$\text{E}_i[Y \log Y] - \text{E}_i[Y] \log \text{E}_i[Y] \leq \text{E}_i\left[e^{sZ}\psi\left(-s(Z - Z_i')\right)\right].$$

This yields (14.9).

To prove the other two inequalities, write

$$e^{sZ}\psi\left(-s(Z - Z_i')\right) = e^{sZ}\psi\left(-s(Z - Z_i')\right)[Z > Z_i']$$
$$+ e^{sZ}\psi\left(s(Z_i' - Z)\right)[Z < Z_i'].$$

By symmetry, the conditional expectation of the second term may be written as

$$\text{E}_i\left[e^{sZ}\psi\left(s(Z_i' - Z)\right)[Z < Z_i']\right] = \text{E}_i\left[e^{sZ_i'}\psi\left(s(Z - Z_i')\right)[Z > Z_i']\right]$$
$$= \text{E}_i\left[e^{sZ}e^{-s(Z-Z_i')}\psi\left(s(Z - Z_i')\right)[Z > Z_i']\right].$$

Thus,

$$\text{E}_i\left[e^{sZ}\psi\left(-s(Z - Z_i')\right)\right] = \text{E}_i\left[e^{sZ}\psi\left(-s(Z - Z_i')\right)\right.$$
$$\left. + e^{-s(Z-Z_i')}\psi\left(s(Z - Z_i')\right)[Z > Z_i']\right].$$

Now (14.10) follows by noting that $\psi(x) + e^x\psi(-x) = x(e^x - 1) =: \tau(x)$. The proof of (14.11) is symmetric to that of (14.10). ∎

Lemma 14.2. *Let Y be a positive random variable. Then, for any $u > 0$,*

$$\text{E}[Y \log Y] - (\text{E}[Y]) \log(\text{E}[Y]) \leq \text{E}[Y \log Y - Y \log u - (Y - u)].$$

Proof. For any $x > 0$, $\log x \leq x - 1$; hence,

$$\log \frac{u}{\mathrm{E}[Y]} \leq \frac{u}{\mathrm{E}[Y]} - 1,$$

and so

$$\mathrm{E}[Y] \log \frac{u}{\mathrm{E}[Y]} \leq u - \mathrm{E}[Y],$$

which is equivalent to the statement in the lemma. ∎

14.5 The Method of Bounded Differences Revisited

As a first application of the modified log-Sobolev inequalities, we derive a version of the method of bounded differences. As in the last section, we have a set of independent random variables $X_1, \ldots, X_n$ and an independent identical copy $X_1', \ldots, X_n'$. We are interested in a function $Z = Z(X_1, \ldots, X_n)$ and denote $Z_i' := Z(X_1, \ldots, X_{i-1}, X_i', X_{i+1}, \ldots, X_n)$. That is, Z' is the same as Z except that in the ith coordinate we use an independent identical copy X_i' in place of X_i. Compare the condition of the following result to the simple method of bounded differences.

Theorem 14.3 (Method of bounded differences). *If*

$$\sum_{i \in [n]} (Z - Z_i')^2 \leq C,$$

for some constant $C > 0$, then

$$\Pr[Z > \mathrm{E}[Z] + t], \Pr[Z < \mathrm{E}[Z] - t] \leq \exp(-t^2/4C).$$

Proof. Observe that for $x < 0$, $\tau(-x) \leq x^2$ and hence for any $s > 0$, we have, by (14.10),

$$\mathrm{Ent}[e^{sZ}] \leq \mathrm{E}\left[e^{sZ} \sum_{i \in [n]} s^2 (Z - Z_i')^2 [Z > Z_i'] \right]$$

$$\leq \mathrm{E}\left[e^{sZ} \sum_{i \in [n]} s^2 (Z - Z_i')^2 \right]$$

$$\leq s^2 C \mathrm{E}[e^{sZ}],$$

where in the last step, we used the hypothesis.

Now we complete the Herbst argument via *generatingfunctionology*. Introduce the generating function $G(s) : -E[e^{sZ}]$ and observe that the left-hand side is

$$\text{Ent}[e^{sZ}] = sG'(s) - G(s)\log G(s),$$

so

$$\text{Ent}[e^{sZ}] = sG'(s) - G(s)\log G(s) \le s^2 C G(s).$$

Divide both sides by $s^2 F(s)$ and observe that the left-hand side is then the derivative of

$$\Psi(s) := \frac{\log G(s)}{s}.$$

Hence, we have

$$\Psi'(s) \le C,$$

which integrates to

$$\Psi(s) \le sC + a$$

for some constant a. The constant is determined by noting that

$$\lim_{s \to 0} \Psi(s) = \lim_{s \to 0} \frac{G'(s)}{G(s)} = \frac{G'(0)}{G(0)} = E[Z],$$

so

$$\Psi(s) \le E[Z] + Cs,$$

which gives a bound on the moment-generating function

$$G(s) \le \exp\left(E[Z]s + s^2 C\right).$$

This bound yields the desired concentration via the usual argument of applying Markov's inequality to e^{sZ}. ∎

Exercise 14.2. *Check that it is sufficient to assume*

$$\sum_{i \in [n]} (Z - Z_i')^2 [Z > Z_i'] \le C,$$

for the preceding proof.

14.6 Self-Bounding Functions

In this section, we give an application of the methods developed to deduce concentration for a wide class of functions called *self-bounding* functions. This class covers, for instance, the class of certifiable functions we discussed in Chapter 11.

Let g be a function from a product space $\Omega := \prod_{i=1}^n \Omega_i$ to the non-negative reals. For each $i \in [n]$, define g_i from Ω to the reals by setting $g_i(x)$ to be the infimum of $g(x')$ over all $x' \in \Omega$ that differ from x in only the ith coordinate. (Thus note that $g(x) - g_i(x) \geq 0$.) Given reals $a \geq 0$ and b, we say that g is (a, b)-*self-bounding* if for each $x \in \Omega$, $g(x) - g_i(x) \leq 1$ and

$$\sum_i (g(x) - g_i(x)) \leq ag(x) + b.$$

The following concentration result for self-bounding functions can be derived from the log-Sobolev inequalities in product spaces.

Theorem 14.4 (Concentration for self-bounding functions [13, 69]). *Let g be a (a, b)-self-bounding function, and let $X := (X_1, \ldots, X_n)$ be independent variables. Then for each $t > 0$,*

$$\Pr[g(X) > \mathrm{E}[g] + t] \leq \exp\left(-t^2/2(a\mathrm{E}[g] + b + at)\right)$$

and

$$\Pr[g(X) < \mathrm{E}[g] - t] \leq \exp\left(-t^2/2(a\mathrm{E}[g] + b + t/3)\right).$$

Exercise 14.3. *Check that $\sum_i x_i$ is $(1, 0)$-self-bounding and deduce a Chernoff–Hoeffding–like bound.*

Certifiable (or configuration) functions are an important class of self-bounding functions (see Problem 14.5).

14.7 Talagrand's Inequality Revisited

In this section we show how Talagrand's inequality follows easily via log-Sobolev inequalities. Recall the setting of Talagrand's inequality: we have a product distribution in a product space and Talagrand's convex distance between a point x and a subset A in the space:

$$d_T(x, A) := \sup_{\|\alpha\| = 1} d_\alpha(x, A), \tag{14.12}$$

where

$$d_\alpha(x, A) : = \min_{y \in A} d_\alpha(x, y)$$

$$= \min_{y \in A} \sum_{i \in [n]} \alpha_i [x_i \neq y_i].$$

Recall that Talagrand's inequality states that for any subset A,

$$P(A)P(\overline{A_t}) \leq e^{-t^2/4},$$

where $A_t := \{x \mid d_T(x, A) \leq t\}$.

To deduce Talagrand's inequality from the modified log-Sobolev inequalities, we start by writing Talagrand's distance in an equivalent form:

$$d_T(x, A) = \inf_{\nu \in D(A)} \sup_{\|\alpha\|=1} \sum_i \alpha_i E_\nu[x_i \neq Y_i], \qquad (14.13)$$

where $D(A)$ is the set of probability distributions concentrated on A.

Exercise 14.4. *Check that (14.13) is equivalent to Definition (14.12).*

Now we apply Sion's minimax theorem: if $f : X \times Y$ is convex and lower semicontinuous with respect to the first argument, concave and upper semicontinuous with respect to the second argument and X is convex and compact, then

$$\inf_x \sup_y f(x, y) = \sup_y \inf_x f(x, y) = \min_x \sup_y f(x, y).$$

Applying this to the characterisation (14.13), we have

$$d_T(x, A) = \inf_{\nu \in D(A)} \sup_{\|\alpha\|=1} \sum_i \alpha_i E_\nu[x_i \neq Y_i]$$

$$= \sup_{\|\alpha\|=1} \inf_{\nu \in D(A)} \sum_i \alpha_i E_\nu[x_i \neq Y_i]$$

and the saddle point is achieved by some pair (ν, α).

Let Z denote the random variable $d_T(X, A)$. Given $X = (X_1, \ldots, X_n)$, let $(\hat{\nu}, \hat{\alpha})$ denote the saddle point corresponding to X. Then,

$$Z_i' := \inf_\nu \sup_\alpha \sum_j \alpha_j E_\nu \left[X_j^{(i)} \neq Y_j \right]$$

$$\geq \inf_\nu \sum_j \hat{\alpha}_j E_\nu \left[X_j^{(i)} \neq Y_j \right],$$

where $X_j^{(i)} = X_j$ if $j \neq i$ and $X_i^{(i)} = X_i'$. Let $\tilde{\nu}$ denote the distribution achieving the infimum in the last line. Then

$$Z = \inf_{\nu} \sum_j \hat{\alpha}_j E_\nu \left[X_j \neq Y_j \right]$$

$$\leq \sum_j \hat{\alpha}_j E_{\tilde{\nu}} \left[X_j \neq Y_j \right].$$

Hence,

$$Z - Z_i' \leq \sum_j \hat{\alpha}_j E_{\tilde{\nu}} \left([X_j \neq Y_j] - [X_j^{(i)} \neq Y_i] \right)$$

$$= \hat{\alpha}_i E_{\tilde{\nu}} \left([X_i \neq Y_j] - [X_i' \neq Y_i] \right)$$

$$\leq \hat{\alpha}_i.$$

Hence,

$$\sum_i (Z - Z_i')^2 [Z > Z_i'] \leq \sum_i \hat{\alpha}_i^2 = 1.$$

Now from the observation of the proof in Theorem 14.3 needed in Exercise 14.2, we get the result.

14.8 Pointers to the Literature

Our exposition is based on a combination of Ledoux ([56], sections 5.1 and 5.4) and the notes of Lugosi [60]. A nice survey of the entropy method in the context of other techniques is in [81]. The original article developing the modified log-Sobolev inequalities with many other variations is in [14]. Bobkov and Götze [6] compare the relative strengths of the transportation cost and log-Sobolev inequalities.

14.9 Problems

Problem 14.1. Consider the Hamming cube with non-homogeneous product measure.

(a) Derive a log-Sobolev inequality analogous to (14.3).
(b) Use the log-Sobolev inequality to derive a concentration result for Lipschitz functions on the cube. $\qquad \triangledown$

Problem 14.2. Consider the convex cube $[0, 1]^n$ with non-homogeneous product measure where the expected value on coordinate $i \in [n]$ is p_i.

(a) Derive a log-Sobolev inequality analogous to (14.3). (HINT: Use a convexity argument to reduce this to the previous problem.)
(b) Use the log-Sobolev inequality to derive a concentration result for Lipschitz functions on the convex cube. $\triangledown$

Problem 14.3. Relax the condition of Theorem 14.3 as follows to get a average version of the method of bounded differences. Show that if

$$\mathrm{E}\left[\sum_i (Z - Z_i')^2 [Z > Z_i'] \mid X_1, \ldots, X_n\right] \leq C,$$

then for all $t > 0$,

$$\Pr[Z > \mathrm{E}[Z] + t] \leq e^{-t^2/4C},$$

while if

$$\mathrm{E}\left[\sum_i (Z - Z_i')^2 [Z < Z_i'] \mid X_1, \ldots, X_n\right] \leq C,$$

then for all $t > 0$,

$$\Pr[Z < \mathrm{E}[Z] - t] \leq e^{-t^2/4C}.$$ $\triangledown$

Problem 14.4. (Minimum spanning tree [30]). Recall the minimum spanning tree problem with random weights: we have a complete graph on n vertices, with each edge e carrying a weight X_e uniformly and independently distributed in $[0, 1]$. Let Z denote the cost of the minimum spanning tree with edge costs $\min(X_e, c/n)$ for some constant $c > 0$. Apply Problem 14.3 to deduce a sharp concentration result. Let Z_i' be the same as Z except that the variable X_e is replaced by an independent copy X_e'.

(a) Let I denote the edges that contribute to Z, that is, are part of the minimum spanning tree. Argue that

$$\sum_e (Z - Z_e')^2 [Z > Z_i'] \leq \sum_{e \in I} (c/n)^2 + \sum_{e \notin I} (c/n)^2 [X_i' < b/n].$$

(b) Hence show that

$$E\left[\sum_i (Z - Z_i')^2 [Z > Z_i'] \mid X_1, \dots, X_n\right],$$

$$E\left[\sum_i (Z - Z_i')^2 [Z < Z_i'] \mid X_1, \dots, X_n\right] \le 2c^3/n.$$

(c) Deduce that

$$\Pr[|Z - E[Z]| > \epsilon] \le 2\exp(-\epsilon^5 n/64). \qquad \triangledown$$

Problem 14.5 (Configuration functions and self-bounding functions). Recall the notion of a *certifiable function*: let g be a real-valued function on a product space such that

certifiable There are reals $r \ge 0$ and d such that if $g(x) = s$, then there is a set of at most $rs + d$ coordinates that certify $g(x) \ge s$. (That is, if x' agrees with x on these $rs + d$ coordinates, then $g(x') \ge s$.)

(This is slightly more general than the definition in Section 11.3.) Show that g is (r, d)-self-bounding and hence deduce a sharp concentration result for configuration functions. $\qquad \triangledown$

Problem 14.6. By exhibiting appropriate self-bounding functions, rework the concentration results for (a) balls and bins and (b) edge colouring. $\qquad \triangledown$

Appendix A
Summary of the Most Useful Bounds

A.1 Chernoff–Hoeffding Bounds

$X_1, \ldots, X_n$ are independent random variables with values in $[0, 1]$ (unless otherwise stated) and $X := \sum_i X_i$.

Absolute deviations For any $t > 0$,

$$\Pr[X > \mathrm{E}[X] + t], \Pr[X < \mathrm{E}[X] - t] \le e^{-2t^2/n}.$$

Deviations around the mean For any $\epsilon > 0$,

$$\Pr[X > (1 + \epsilon)\mathrm{E}[X]] < \exp\left(-\epsilon^2 \mathrm{E}[X]/3\right),$$
$$\Pr[X < (1 - \epsilon)\mathrm{E}[X]] < \exp\left(-\epsilon^2 \mathrm{E}[X]/2\right).$$

When $\mathrm{E}[X]$ is not known exactly, it can be replaced by an upper bound in the right-hand side of the first inequality and by a lower bound in the second.

Large t If $t \ge 6\mathrm{E}[X]$, then

$$\Pr[X > t] \le 2^{-t}.$$

These bounds can also be used when the variables are negatively dependent.

A.2 Bounds for Well-Behaved Functions

Again, $X_1, \ldots, X_n$ denote independent random variables (unless otherwise stated) and f is a function of n real arguments.

Method of bounded differences If changing the value of the ith variable changes the value of f by at most c_i, then

$$\Pr[f > \mathrm{E}[f] + t], \Pr[f < \mathrm{E}[f] - t] \le \exp\left(-2t^2 \Big/ \sum_i c_i^2\right).$$

(This can also be used when the $X_1, \ldots, X_n$ are negatively dependent.)

Method of non-uniformly bounded differences If there are numbers $c_i(x)$ such that

$$f(x) \ge f(y) - \sum_{x_i \neq y_i} c_i(x)$$

or

$$f(x) \le f(y) + \sum_{x_i \neq y_i} c_i(x),$$

and $\sum_i c_i(x)^2 \le C$ for all x, then

$$\Pr[f > \mathrm{M}[f] + t], \Pr[f < \mathrm{M}[f] - t] \le \exp\left(-t^2/2C\right).$$

(This can be converted into essentially equivalent concentration about the mean in many situations using Problems 11.4.)

Method of bounded differences, take 2 Let $X_1', \ldots, X_n'$ be an independent identical copy of $X_1, \ldots, X_n$ and let $f_i' := f(X_1, \ldots, X_{i-1}, X_i', X_{i+1}, \ldots, X_n)$. If

$$\mathrm{E}\left[\sum_i (f - f_i')^2 [f > f_i'] \mid X_1, \ldots, X_n\right] \le C,$$

then for all $t > 0$,

$$\Pr[f > \mathrm{E}[f] + t] \le e^{-t^2/4C},$$

while if

$$\mathrm{E}\left[\sum_i (f - f_i')^2 [f < f_i'] \mid X_1, \ldots, X_n\right] \le C,$$

then for all $t > 0$,

$$\Pr[Z < \mathrm{E}[Z] - t] \le e^{-t^2/4C},$$

Certifiable f If

(a) changing the value of any argument changes the value of f by at most c, and

(b) for every x, there is a subset $J(x) \subseteq [n]$ of size at most $rf(x)$
such that if y agrees with x on $J(x)$, then $f(y) \geq f(x)$,
then

$$\Pr[f > \mathrm{M}[f] + t] \leq 2\exp\left(-\frac{t^2}{4c^2 r(\mathrm{M}[f] + t)}\right)$$

and

$$\Pr[f < \mathrm{M}[f] - t] \leq 2\exp\left(-\frac{t^2}{4c^2 r\mathrm{M}[f]}\right).$$

(This can be converted into essentially equivalent concentration about the mean in many situations using Problem 11.4.)

Method of average bounded differences If

$$|\mathrm{E}[f \,|\, X_{i-1}, X_i = a_i] - \mathrm{E}[f \,|\, X_{i-1}, X_i = a_i']| \leq c_i$$

or

$$|\mathrm{E}[f \,|\, X_{i-1}, X_i = a_i] - \mathrm{E}[f \,|\, X_{i-1}]| \leq c_i,$$

then

$$\Pr[f > \mathrm{E}[f] + t], \Pr[f < \mathrm{E}[f] - t] \leq \exp\left(-2t^2 \Big/ \sum_i c_i^2\right).$$

The variables $X_1, \ldots, X_n$ are arbitrary and need not be independent. Coupling is often useful to compute the required bound on the conditional distributions.

Method of bounded variances If (a) each X_i takes on two values, a "good" value with probability p_i and a "bad" value with probability $1 - p_i$, and (b) the function f is Lipschitz with coefficients c_i, then

$$\Pr[f > \mathrm{E}f + t] \leq \exp\left(-t^2 \Big/ \sum_i p_i(1 - p_i)c_i^2\right)$$

and

$$\Pr[f < \mathrm{E}f - t] \leq \exp\left(-t^2 \Big/ \sum_i p_i(1 - p_i)c_i^2\right).$$

This holds, for instance, when each X_i takes values in a finite set A_i that can be partitioned into a good set G_i and a bad set B_i, such that $\Pr[X_i \in G_i] = p_i$. The p_i's "weaken" the effect of the c_i's.

Bibliography

[1] W. Aiello, F. Chung, and L. Lu. Random evolution in massive graphs. In *Proceedings of the 42nd IEEE Symposium on Foundations of Computer Science*, 2001, pages 510–519.

[2] N. Alon and J. Spencer. *The Probabilistic Method*, third edition. John Wiley, Hoboken, NJ, 2008.

[3] N. Alon, J.-H. Kim, and J. Spencer. Nearly perfect matchings in regular simple hypergraphs. *Isr. J. Math.*, 100:171–187, 1997.

[4] M. Bellare and J. Rompel. Randomness-efficient oblivious sampling. In *Proceedings of the 35th Annual Symposium on the Foundations of Computer Science, FOCS*. IEEE, Santa Fe, NM, 1994, pages 276–287.

[5] D. Blackwell. An analog of the minimax theorem for vector payoffs. *Pac. J. Math.*, 6:1–8, 1956.

[6] S. G. Bobkov and F. Götze. Exponential integrability and transportation cost related to logarithmic sobolev inequalities. *J. Funct. Anal.*, 163:1–28, 1999.

[7] P. Boldi and S. Vigna. The webgraph framework I: Compression techniques. In *Proceedings of the 13th International World Wide Web Conference*, 2004, pages 595–601.

[8] P. Boldi and S. Vigna. Codes for the World Wide Web. *Internet Math.*, 2(4):407–429, 2005.

[9] B. Bollobás, O. Riordan, J. Spencer, and G. E. Tusnády. The degree sequence of a scale-free random graph process. *Random Struct. Algorithms*, 18(3):279–290, 2001.

[10] B. Bollobás. Chromatic number, girth and maximal degree. *Discrete Math.*, 24(3):311–314, 1978.

[11] B. Bollobás. *Combinatorics: Set Systems, Hypergraphs, Families of Vectors and Combinatorial Probability*. Cambridge University Press, Cambridge, 1986.

[12] C. Borgs, J. T. Chayes, C. Daskalakis, and S. Roch. First to market is not everything: An analysis of preferential attachment with fitness. In *Proceedings of the 39th Annual ACM Symposium on Theory of Computing*, 2007, pages 135–144.

[13] G. Lugosi, S. Boucheron, and P. Massart. A sharp concentration inequality with applications. *Random Struct. Algorithms*, 16:277–292, 2000.

[14] S. Boucheron, G. Lugosi, and P. Massart. Concentration inequalities using the entropy method. *Ann. Probab.*, 31(3):1583–1614, 2003.

[15] G. Buehrer and K. Chellapilla. A scalable pattern mining approach to web graph compression with communities. In *WSDM '08: Proceedings of the International Conference on Web Search and Web Data Mining*. ACM, New York, USA, 2008, pages 95–106.

[16] J. W. Byers, J. Considine, and M. Mitzenmacher. Geometric generalizations of the power of two choices. In *SPAA '04: Proceedings of the Sixteenth Annual ACM Symposium on Parallelism in Algorithms and Architectures*. ACM, New York, USA, 2004, pages 54–63.

[17] N. Cesa-Bianchi and G. Lugosi. *Prediction, Learning, and Games*. Cambridge University Press, Cambridge, 2006.

[18] S. Chaudhuri and D. Dubhashi. Probabilistic recurrence relations revisited. *Theor. Comput. Sci.*, 181(1):45–56, 1997.

[19] H. Chernoff. A measure of asymptotic efficiency for tests of hypothesis based on the sum of observations. *Ann. Math. Stat.*, 23:493–509, 1952.

[20] F. Chierichetti, R. Kumar, S. Lattanzi, A. Panconesi, and P. Raghavan. Is the web a social graph? Manuscript.

[21] F. Chierichetti, A. Panconesi, P. Raghavan, M. Sozio, A. Tiberi, and E. Upfal. Finding near neighbors through cluster pruning. In *PODS '07: Proceedings of the Twenty-Sixth ACM SIGMOD-SIGACT-SIGART Symposium on Principles of Database Systems*. ACM, New York, USA, 2007, pages 103–112.

[22] V. Chvátal. The tail of the hypergeometric distribution. *Discrete Math.*, 25(3):285–287, 1979.

[23] T. M. Cover and J. A. Thomas. *Elements of Information Theory*, second edition. Wiley-Interscience, Hoboken, NJ, 2006.

[24] S. Dasgupta and A. Gupta. An elementary proof of a theorem of Johnson and Lindenstrauss. *Random Struct. Algorithms*, 22(1):60–65, 2003.

[25] A. Dembo. Information inequalities and concentration of measure. *Ann. Probab.*, 25(2):927–939, 1997.

[26] F. den Hollander. *Large Deviations*, volume 14. Fields Institute Monographs. American Mathematical Society, Providence, RI, 2000.

[27] D. P. Dubhashi and D. Ranjan. Balls and bins: A study in negative dependence. *Random Struct. Algorithms*, 13(2):99–124, 1998.

[28] D. Dubhashi, D. A. Grable, and A. Panconesi. Near-optimal, distributed edge colouring via the nibble method. *Theor. Comput. Sci.*, 203(2):225–251, 1998.

[29] D. P. Dubhashi. Martingales and locality in distributed computing. In *Foundations of Software Technology and Theoretical Computer Science (Chennai, 1998)*, volume 1530. Lecture Notes in Computer Science. Springer, Berlin, 1998, pages 174–185.

[30] A. D. Flaxman, A. Frieze, and M. Krivelevich. On the random 2-stage minimum spanning tree. *Random Struct. Algorithms*, 28(1):24–36, 2006.

[31] D. P. Foster and R. Vohra. Regret in the on-line decision problem. *Games Econ. Behav.*, 29(1–2):7–35, 1999.

[32] Yoav Freund and Robert E. Schapire. Adaptive game playing using multiplicative weights. *Games Econ. Behav.*, 29(1–2):79–103, 1999.

[33] A. M. Frieze. On the value of a random minimum spanning tree problem. *Discrete Appl. Math.*, 10(1):47–56, 1985.

[34] A. M. Frieze and C. J. H. McDiarmid. On random minimum length spanning trees. *Combinatorica*, 9(4):363–374, 1989.

[35] N. Garg, G. Konjevod, and R. Ravi. A polylogarithmic approximation algorithm for the group Steiner tree problem. In *Proceedings of the Ninth Annual ACM-SIAM Symposium on Discrete Algorithms (San Francisco, CA, 1998)*. ACM, New York, USA, 1998, pages 253–259.

[36] D. Gillman. A Chernoff bound for random walks on expander graphs. *Siam J. Comput.*, 27(4):1203–1220, 1998.

[37] D. Grable. A large deviation inequality for functions of independent, multi-way choices. *Comb. Probab. Comput.*, 7(1):57–63, 1998.

[38] D. Grable and A. Panconesi. Nearly-optimal, distributed edge-colouring in $O(\log \log n)$ rounds. *Random Struct. Algorithms*, 10(3):385–405, 1997.

[39] D. A. Grable and A. Panconesi. Fast distributed algorithms for Brooks–Vizing colorings. *J. Algorithms*, 37(1):85–120, 2000. Special issue for the best papers of the *Ninth Annual ACM-SIAM Symposium on Discrete Algorithms*, San Francisco, CA, 1998.

[40] G. Grimmett and Stirzaker D. *Probability and Random Processes*, second edition. Clarendon Press, Oxford, 1993.

[41] O. Häggström. *Finite Markov Chains and Algorithmic Applications*. Cambridge University Press, Cambridge, 2002.

[42] T. P. Hayes. Randomly coloring graphs of girth at least five. In *STOC '03: Proceedings of the Thirty-Fifth Annual ACM Symposium on Theory of Computing*. ACM, New York, USA, 2003, pages 269–278.

[43] W. Hoeffding. Probability inequalities for the sum of bounded random variables. *J. Am. Stat. Assoc.*, 58:13–30, 1963.

[44] S. Janson. Large deviations for sums of partly dependent random variables. *Random Struct. Algorithms*, 24(3):234–248, 2004.

[45] S. Janson and A. Ruciński. The infamous upper tail. *Random Struct. Algorithms*, 20(3):317–342, 2002.

[46] S. Janson and A. Ruciński. The deletion method for upper tail estimates. *Combinatorica*, 24(4):615–640, 2004.

[47] W. B. Johnson and J. Lindenstrauss. Extensions of Lipschitz mappings into a Hilbert space. In *Conference in Modern Analysis and Probability (New Haven, Connecticut, 1982)*, volume 26. Contemporary Mathematics. American Mathematical Society, Providence, RI, 1984, pages 189–206.

[48] N. Kahale. Large deviation bounds for markov chains. *Comb. Probab. Comput.*, 6:465–474, 1997.

[49] R. M. Karp. Probabilistic recurrence relations. *J. Assoc. Comput. Mach.*, 41(6): 1136–1150, 1994.

[50] J. H. Kim and V. H. Vu. Divide and conquer martingales and the number of triangles in a random graph. *Random Struct. Algorithms*, 24(2):166–174, 2004.

[51] J. H. Kim. On Brooks' theorem for sparse graphs. *Comb. Probab. Comput.*, 4(2):97–132, 1995.

[52] J. Kleinberg and E. Tardos. *Algorithm Design*. Pearson–Addison Wesley, Boston, 2005.

[53] G. Konjevod, R. Ravi, and A. Srinivasan. Approximation algorithms for the covering Steiner problem. *Random Struct. Algorithms*, 20(3):465–482, 2002.

[54] D. C. Kozen. *The Design and Analysis of Algorithms*. Texts and Monographs in Computer Science. Springer-Verlag, New York, 1992.

[55] R. Kumar, P. Raghavan, S. Rajagopalan, D. Sivakumar, A. Tomkins, and E. Upfal. Stochastic models for the web graph. In *Proceedings of the 41st IEEE Symposium on Foundations of Computer Science*, 2000, pages 57–65.

[56] M. Ledoux. *The Concentration of Measure Phenomenon*. American Mathematical Society, Providence, RI, 2001.

[57] M. Luby. A simple parallel algorithm for the maximal independent set problem. *SIAM J. Comput.*, 15(4):1036–1053, 1986.

[58] M. Luby. Removing randomness in parallel computation without a processor penalty. *J. Comput. Syst. Sci.*, 47(2):250–286, 1993.

[59] M. J. Luczak and C. McDiarmid. Concentration for locally acting permutations. *Discrete Math.*, 265(1–3):159–171, 2003.

[60] G. Lugosi. Concentration of Measure Inequalities. Lecture Notes, unpublished, 2005.

[61] K. Marton. Bounding $\overline{d}$-distance by information divergence: A method to prove measure concentration. *Ann. Probab.*, 24(2):857–866, 1996.

[62] K. Marton. Measure concentration for a class of random processes. *Probab. Theory Relat. Fields*, 110(2):427–439, 1998.

[63] J. Matoušek. *Graduate Texts in Mathematics*, volume 212. Lectures on Discrete Geometry. Springer, New York, 2002.

[64] C. J. H. McDiarmid and R. B. Hayward. Large deviations for quicksort. *J. Algorithms*, 21(3):476–507, 1996.

[65] C. J. H. McDiarmid. On the method of bounded differences. In J. Siemons, editor, *Surveys in Combinatorics: Invited Papers at the 12th British Combinatorial Conference*, volume 141. London Mathematical Society Lecture Notes Series. Cambridge University Press, Cambridge, 1989, pages 148–188.

[66] C. McDiarmid. Centering sequences with bounded differences. *Comb. Probab. Comput.*, 6(1):79–86, 1997.

[67] C. McDiarmid. Concentration. In *Probabilistic Methods for Algorithmic Discrete Mathematics*, volume 16. Algorithms and Combinatorics. Springer, Berlin, 1998, pages 195–248.

[68] C. McDiarmid. Concentration for independent permutations. *Comb. Probab. Comput.*, 11(2):163–178, 2002.

[69] C. McDiarmid and B. Reed. Concentration for self-bounding functions and an inequality of Talagrand. *Random Struct. Algorithms*, 29(4):549–557, 2006.

[70] A. Mei and R. Rizzi. Online permutation routing in partitioned optical passive star networks. *IEEE Trans. Comput.*, 55(12):1557–1571, 2006.

[71] G. L. Miller and J. H. Reif. Parallel tree contraction and its applications. *Random. Comput.*, 5:47–72, 1989.

[72] M. Mitzenmacher and E. Upfal. *Probability and Computing*. Cambridge University Press, Cambridge, 2005.

[73] M. Molloy and B. Reed. *Graph Colouring and the Probabilistic method*, volume 23. Algorithms and Combinatorics. Springer-Verlag, Berlin, 2002.

[74] R. Motwani and P. Raghavan. *Randomized Algorithms*. Cambridge University Press, Cambridge, 1995.

[75] N. Nisan and A. Wigderson. Hardness vs. randomness. *J. Comput. Syst. Sci.*, 49(2):149–167, 1994.

[76] A. Panconesi and A. Srinivasan. Randomized distributed edge coloring via an extension of the Chernoff–Hoeffding bounds. *SIAM J. Comput.*, 26(2):350–368, 1997.

[77] A. Panconesi and J. Radhakrishnan. Expansion properties of (secure) wireless networks. In *SPAA '04: Proceedings of the Sixteenth Annual ACM Symposium on Parallelism in Algorithms and Architectures*. ACM, New York, USA, 2004, pages 281–285.

[78] R. Di Pietro, L. V. Mancini, A. Mei, A. Panconesi, and J. Radhakrishnan. Connectivity properties of secure wireless sensor networks. In *SASN '04: Proceedings of the 2nd ACM Workshop on Security of Ad Hoc and Sensor Networks*. ACM, New York, USA, 2004, pages 53–58.

[79] R. Di Pietro, L. V. Mancini, A. Mei, A. Panconesi, and J. Radhakrishnan. Redoubtable sensor networks. *ACM Trans. Inf. Syst. Secur.*, 11(3):1–22, 2008.

[80] W. Pugh. Skip lists: A probabilistic alternative to balanced trees. *Commun. ACM*, 33(6):668–676, 1990.

[81] O. Bosquet, S. Boucheron, and G. Lugosi. Concentration inequalities. In O. Bosquet, U. von Luxburg and G. Rätsh editors, *Advanced Lectures in Machine Learning*. Springer, Berlin, 2004, pages 208–240.

[82] P.-M. Samson. Concentration of measure inequalities for Markov chains and Φ-mixing processes. *Ann. Probab.*, 28(1):416–461, 2000.

[83] J. P. Schmidt, A. Siegel, and A. Srinivasan. Chernoff–Hoeffding bounds for applications with limited independence. *SIAM J. Discrete Math.*, 8(2):255–280, 1995.

[84] J. M. Steele. *Probability Theory and Combinatorial Optimization*. SIAM, Philadelphia, PA, 1997.

[85] M. Talagrand. Concentration of measure and isoperimetric inequalities in product spaces. *Publ. Math. IHES*, 81:73–205, 1995.

[86] V. H. Vu. Concentration of non-Lipschitz functions and applications. *Random Struct. Algorithms*, 20(3):262–316, 2002. Probabilistic methods in combinatorial optimization.

[87] T. Bohman. The triangle-free process. Manuscript. http://arxiv.org/0806.4375.

[88] S. Janson. Large deviations for sums of partly dependent random variables. *Random Struct. Algorithms*, 24(3):234–248, 2004.

Index

Printed in the United States
By Bookmasters